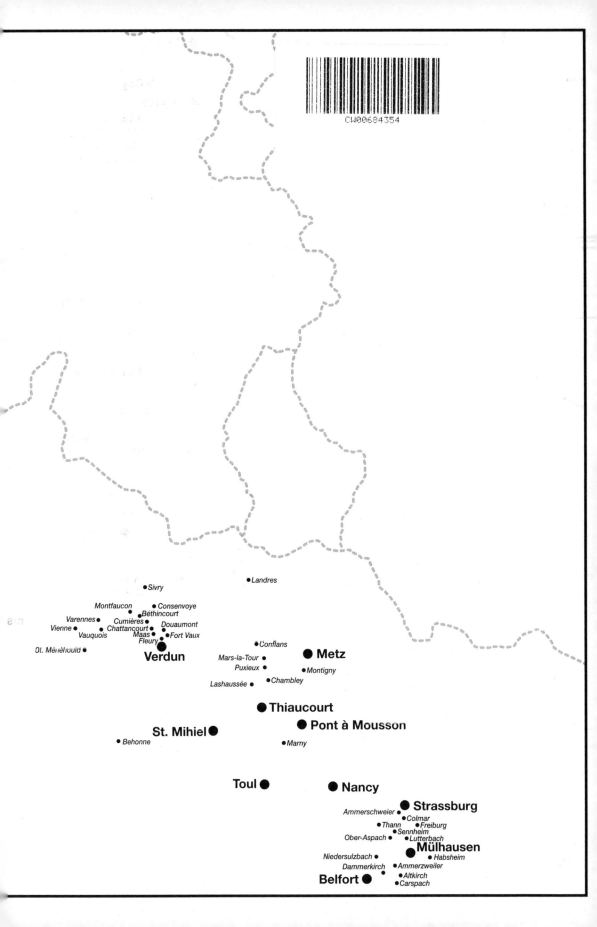

• Sivry

• Landres

Montfaucon • • Consenvoye
• Béthincourt
Varennes • Cumières • Douaumont
Vienne • Chattancourt •
Vauquois • Maas • Fort Vaux
Fleury
St. Ménehould • • Conflans

Verdun

Mars-la-Tour • **Metz**

Puxieux • • Montigny

Lashaussée • • Chambley

Thiaucourt

St. Mihiel
• Behonne

Pont à Mousson
• Marny

Toul **Nancy**

Ammerschweier • **Strassburg**
• Colmar
• Thann • Freiburg
• Sennheim
Ober-Aspach • • Lutterbach

Mülhausen
Niedersulzbach • • Habsheim
Dammerkirch • • Ammerzweiler
• Altkirch
Belfort • • Carspach

HERMANN GÖRING –
FIGHTER ACE

This book is dedicated to my longtime friend and colleague Stewart K. Taylor, one of the masters of World War I aviation history from whom I have learned much – and remain grateful

Other books by Peter Kilduff

The Red Baron

That's My Bloody Plane

Germany's Last Knight of the Air

U.S. Carriers at War

A-4 Skyhawk

Germany's First Air Force 1914-1918

Richthofen – Beyond the Legend of the Red Baron

Over the Battlefronts

The Red Baron Combat Wing

The Illustrated Red Baron

Talking With the Red Baron

Red Baron – The Life and Death of an Ace

Black Fokker Leader

HERMANN GÖRING – FIGHTER ACE

THE WORLD WAR I CAREER OF GERMANY'S MOST INFAMOUS AIRMAN

Peter Kilduff

Grub Street • London

Published by
Grub Street
4 Rainham Close
London
SW11 6SS

British Library Cataloguing in Publication Data
  Kilduff, Peter.
  Herman Göring: fighter ace.
  1. Göring, Herman, 1893-1946. 2. Fighter pilots –
  Germany – Biography. 3. World War, 1914-1918 –
  Ariel operations, German.
  I. Title
  940.4'4'943'092–dc22

ISBN-13: 9781906502669

Cover design by Sarah Driver

Book design and artwork by:
Roy Platten, Eclipse – roy.eclipse@btopenworld.com

Printed and bound by MPG Ltd, Bodmin, Cornwall

Grub Street Publishing only uses
FSC (Forest Stewardship Council) paper for its books.

Contents

Oberleutnant Hermann Göring, wearing his Pour le Mérite, in a sombre mood and standing by a Fokker D.VII, possibly 324/18, with which he scored his twentieth aerial victory.

FOREWORD

Hermann Göring lived for fifty-three years, ten months and nine days. For more than half that time his name became draped by infamy due to actions and crimes he committed during the Third Reich period of 1933-1945. After World War II ended, Göring was tried and sentenced to be executed for crimes against humanity, but cheated the hangman and died ignominiously by his own hand. All of that history is recounted in other books, many of which are listed in this book's bibliography.

But Göring's military activities in World War I have received very little coverage and have been overshadowed by his more horrific deeds during the Nazi régime. I became interested in his 1914-1918 military career in 1975, when I located and obtained copies of substantial research material on him from the U.S. Library of Congress and, later, from the U.S. Army Military History Institute. In more recent times, German archives – chiefly the Bundesarchiv Militärarchiv, the Landesarchiv Baden-Württemberg and the Militärgeschichtliches Forschungsamt – have been extremely helpful in providing copies of documentation that provide insight into Göring's early military service.

The thought of writing a book about what Göring did in World War I occurred while I was researching my previous book, *Black Fokker Leader: The First World War's Last Airfighter Knight* (London, 2009). The subject of that biography, the late Carl Degelow, related some of his unpleasant experiences with Göring to me and those comments gave rise to the questions: What events formed Göring's early life and led him to a military career? What motivated him to behave in ways that were (or should have been) out of keeping with a man who once showed such promise as a professionally trained member of the German officer corps? And what drove him to the levels he achieved during World War I?

There were no simple answers and certainly none with the brevity needed for a book that focused on Carl Degelow's experiences in World War I – without having it overshadowed by Göring's larger-than-life personality and his varied exploits. With those and other lingering questions in mind, I felt that a study of Göring's World War I activities – and some understanding of them – had to be my next project. This book is the result.

I am neither a psychologist nor a psychiatrist and I recognise the hazards of trying to delve into the mind of a person who died almost sixty-five years ago. Fortunately, during Göring's post-World War II examination and interrogation by members of the U.S. Army, he and his actions were analysed by both a qualified psychologist and a psychiatrist. Their observations appear at appropriate points in the book.

Those analyses took place in 1945-1946 and, since then, behavioural science advancements have led to new diagnostic criteria to help quantify behaviour such as that evidenced by Hermann Göring. In no way does such quantification relieve Göring of responsibility for his actions; rather, it may offer insight into why he did what he did. Worth considering is what Dr. Elsa Ronningstam wrote in *Identifying and Understanding the Narcissistic Personality* (pp. 8-9) about a "Nobel Prize complex", in which someone like Göring is 'intellectually and artistically gifted …and guided either by an active fantasy of being the powerful one (destined) or by passive fantasy of being the special one (chosen). However, [these] achievements become overshadowed by [a] preoccupation with acclaim, an attitude of "all or nothing," or "dreams of glory", of attaining a position of extraordinary power or worldwide recognition …'

As you read this book, I invite you to consider Göring as exhibiting those signs, as well as what is now identified as Narcissistic Personality Disorder (NPD). A person affected by NPD, Ronningstam notes (Ibid., p. 72), would have 'heightened self-confidence and self-worth, sense of invulnerability. Capacity for unusual risk taking and decision making, and to integrate unusual ideas, ideals and goals into real achievements or creative accomplishments.'

Also worthy of note, examples in the bibliography show two ways to spell his family name. This book uses 'Göring', with the umlauted 'o', which is the preferred family spelling. In English and other languages, the name is commonly transliterated as 'Goering', using 'oe' as the standard representation of 'ö'. The meaning of the name and its evolution to the current form are covered in Chapter One.

The reader will also note throughout the text and in Appendix I that, as another part of the research process, I postulate which air units and even individual airmen *most likely* fought against each other. This educated inference is made possible due to the availability of many archival sources that provide evidence of such encounters. In recent years, this form of research has become more conclusive with the help of books such as *The French Air Service War Chronology 1914-1918*, *The Jasta Pilots*, *The Sky Their Battlefield*, and other valued standard reference texts published by Grub Street, which are included in this book's bibliography. I am grateful to the authors of those books for their labours in compiling such works.

While researching and writing this book, I received help from many people and note with gratitude the kind efforts, encouragement and information provided by: Richard L. Baker, U.S. Army Military History Institute (PSD); Joachim Brauss, Kreisarchiv Neuwied; Tina Buttenberg, Stadtarchiv Rosenheim; Bonnie B. Coles, U.S. Library of Congress; Elke Conrads-Wirth, Landesarchiv Nordrhein-Westfalen; Jochen Dollwet, Stadtarchiv Wiesbaden; Achim Koch, Bundesarchiv Militärarchiv; Stephan Kühmayer, Deutsche Dienststelle (WASt); Oberstleutnant Harald Potempa, Militärgeschichtliches Forschungsamt; Jessy Randall, Colorado College Special Collections; and Dr. Wolfgang Mährle, Judith Bolsinger and Manfred Hennhöfer of the Landesarchiv Baden-

Württemberg. Kimberly Farrington of the Elihu Burritt Library of Central Connecticut State University exemplifies the valued help I received from my alma mater.

Valued colleagues and friends who have helped in so many ways include: Trudy Baumann, Jan Bodenbender, Dr. Lance J. Bronnenkant, Russell Folsom, Ted Hamady, Friedrich-Johann von Krusenstiern, Paul S. Leaman, James F. Miller, Julian Putkowski, and James Streckfuss.

My sincere thanks also go to this cadre of friends : Ronny Bar for his excellent colour artwork portraying various aircraft flown by Hermann Göring, Judy and Karl Kilduff and my long-time friend and mentor David E. Smith for their helpful review of and comments on the manuscript, my cultural mentor Klaus Littwin for helping me understand German linguistic nuances and providing valuable assistance in locating important research sources, Dr. M. Geoffrey Miller for strengthening my research with his medical expertise, long-time friends Oberbürgermeister i.R. Prof.Dr.(h c) Franz J. Rothenbiller and his wife Christa for their valued help in deciphering significant documentary material, and Stewart K. Taylor for sharing his encyclopaedic knowledge of British Commonwealth flight operations. I also extend profound gratitude to my colleague and friend of many years Greg Van Wyngarden for offering many useful suggestions and for sharing his artistic and historical resources.

I am grateful for the friendship, interest and support of all of these very helpful people.

Peter Kilduff

CHAPTER ONE
A SHINING IMAGE

'Nobody knows the real Göring. I am a man of many parts …
And those books put out by the [Nazi] party press, they are less than useless.'[1]

HERMANN GÖRING

Many books and articles have been written about Hermann Göring, but a lingering doubt hangs over most of them due to his expansive characterisation of events. Such behaviour seems to have been ingrained in his nature. Outwardly, he was a gregarious public figure, but, behind the scenes, Göring was secretive and tried to manipulate information about himself. He was much more concerned about how he and his actions appeared to others than with the actual facts.

Moving beyond the personal mythology that Hermann Göring cultivated during his lifetime, official German sources and many of his comrades credited him with being a skilled, tenacious and bold pilot in World War I. An example of his combat prowess – and how the story was distorted – is seen in reports of a harrowing encounter he survived over Combles, France on the late afternoon of Thursday, 2 November 1916.

Leutnant Hermann Göring in the cockpit of the Halberstadt D.II in which he fought off a patrol of British Nieuport fighters on 2 November 1916.

Göring was assigned to shoot down enemy aeroplanes trying to cross German lines in the waning days of the disastrous Anglo-French assault in the Battle of the Somme.[2] He flew near the frontlines in a Halberstadt D.II biplane fighter which, despite its delicate appearance, was considered to be exceptionally 'manoeuvrable and very strong'[3] for its time. The Halberstadt's fine points no doubt helped to save his life in the air battle about to take place. Some fifteen years later, a recounting of the incident helped to burnish Göring's public image when his rise to prominence in German politics made him want to have a formal published biography in circulation.

In the story published in 1932, Göring and two other fighter pilots were flying in hazy weather, looking for 'a big British aeroplane, with a crew of several men'.[4] It had been seen over their sector a few days earlier and Göring said he spotted the aircraft when it was still over British lines. Impulsively, he headed right toward it.

According to Göring's hand-picked author Martin H. Sommerfeldt:

'… [Just then] both accompanying German aeroplanes turn away and head back. Göring fails to ascertain … that about 1,000 metres above him there is a formation of at least twenty enemy fighter planes. But Göring … [draws] closer to the big aeroplane and attacks it in a dive … He fires at the rear machine-gun station and hits the gunner, but shortly thereafter a second man comes out and … opens fire. This one also falls, and a third man attempts to crawl to the rear area. Göring has likewise silenced the side machine-gun and now fires at the enemy craft and sets fire to its left engine. The aeroplane is forced homewards in a quiet gliding flight.

'At this moment Göring is attacked by a dozen British single-seaters. Deadly bursts of machine-gun fire rain down on him, several shots rupture his fuel tank; the well-known white streams of gasoline spurt out. Göring switches on his reserve tank. A new cone of fire shreds his wings, several hits strike the engine, a shot grazes his leg and a few seconds later he receives a dreadful blow to the right hip … He has scarcely any ammunition left and tries to escape by turning tightly. During one especially tight turn, which is almost a loop, the few bullets that he still has fall out of the ammunition box; any further armed opposition is pointless.

'In a last attempt at salvation, Göring goes into the most frantic power dive of his life down to the absolute lowest altitude. That move is a stroke of luck for him. The opponents … mutually break off the pursuit; as a result of the heavy ground mist the German flyer disappears from sight … But at the same time enemy ground machine-gun fire opens up. [Göring] "pushes on" … over the lines, always worried that the reserve fuel tank will not last or that the spilling gasoline could catch fire.

'When he has passed over enemy lines, he goes to shut off the engine, but at that moment everything goes black, [and] just then the engine quits and the rattling of it brings him back to consciousness … With his last bit of energy he lands near a cemetery, in the middle of which stands a church, bearing the Red Cross emblem on its roof. Thus he lands, so to speak, right on the operating table. A few minutes later he is already under the anaesthesia and being operated on.

'[His] machine shows over sixty hits. Göring has a grazing wound and a severe hip injury due to a ricochet, which … is evidenced by a scar of twenty-four centimetres'

A captured French Nieuport 17 of the type used by the Royal Flying Corps patrol that shot down Göring's aeroplane during the Battle of the Somme.

length. The backrest of [his] seat was knocked loose and jammed into the torn open hip. Accordingly, the loss of blood was extraordinarily heavy and it was inconceivable to the physician that Göring could ever return to flying with this severe wound.'[5]

History Revised

Not content with Sommerfeldt's seventy-eight-page 1932 biography, five years later Göring commissioned his long-time aide Dr. Erich Gritzbach to write a larger work. It offered a briefer version of the 2 November 1916 aerial combat, and noted that Göring was a seasoned air fighter, credited with shooting down two enemy aeroplanes,[6] a significant accomplishment for a wartime flyer. Gritzbach added:

'At the Somme Sector, the enemy's air force … [was] numerically superior to the Germans. In Göring's area the crewmen of a British large aeroplane especially distinguished themselves by frequent flying and well-executed bomb dropping. For weeks [Göring] was on the look-out for the "fat crate". On a hazy November day, he finally had the opponent before him.'[7]

Gritzbach described the remainder of the fight much as Sommerfeldt had, but eliminated the melodramatic landing in a cemetery, right near a field hospital. Indeed, the circumstances of Göring's incredibly lucky return to within German lines were noted in the weekly report of the Kommandeur der Flieger der 1. Armee [Officer in Charge of Aviation for the 1st Army], abbreviated as 'Kofl': 'On 2.11.16, Leutnant Göring of Jagdstaffel 5 attacked an enemy tractor biplane at 17.00 [hours, with] the enemy aircraft immediately going down in a steep dive. Before Ltn Göring could follow, he was attacked from the rear by six Nieuports. He was hit in the right hip, but managed to land safely at his own airfield [at Gonnelieu].'[8]

The Kofl report and other sources offer a more accurate – albeit less colourful – account of the event. For example, there is no mention of a two-engined British bomber, Göring's allusion to the Handley Page 0/100 bomber, which, with its 100-ft top wing span,[9] was one of the largest aircraft in World War I. The two-engined Handley Page came into service in late 1916, but at Dunkerque,[10] far west of Jasta 5. While flying over the Somme Sector, Göring could not have encountered the distinctive-looking British warplane, which did not have side-mounted machine guns, as Sommerfeldt stated.

It is more likely that Göring fought with a much smaller opponent, a Royal Aircraft Factory B.E.2d of 7 Squadron, Royal Flying Corps. With a top wing span of thirty-six feet and ten inches,[11] this single-engine machine would have been the 'tractor biplane' noted in the Kofl report. British records show that 7 Squadron's aerodrome at Warloy[12] was just over twenty-five kilometres due west of Combles, easily within range of where Göring pursued an enemy aircraft and was, in turn, attacked by six British Nieuport fighters.

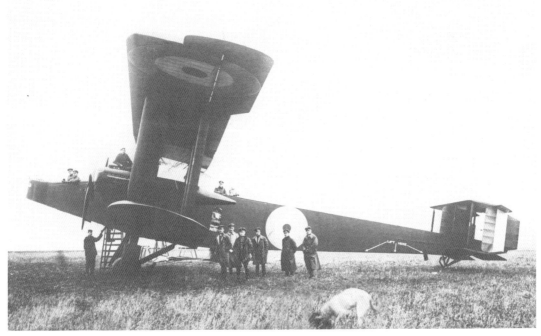

A captured Handley Page 0/100 bomber of the type that Göring claimed to have engaged in air combat over Combles on 2 November 1916.

Much smaller than the HP O/100, this downed Royal Aircraft Factory B.E.2 is an example of the aircraft that Göring most likely fought against on the day he was shot down.

According to the RFC casualty listing, the 7 Squadron crew of Sergeant Cecil P.J. Bromley (pilot) and Second-Lieutenant Geoffrey H. Wood (observer)[13] were helping artillery units range their guns when they were reported to have been 'shot down … at 4.45 p.m. Pilot died of wounds. Other pilots reported seeing the machine land, apparently under control, and then turn over on its nose.'[14]

In addition to the physical proximity of the two aerial combats, both took place at the same time of day, according to German and British records: The RFC aeroplane was seen to be hit at '4:45 p.m'. (1645 hours military time) and Göring reported being attacked fifteen minutes later at 1700 hours. Had another German pilot or a forward observer seen the British aircraft crash, Göring might have received credit for his third aerial victory. Likewise, had a British airman witnessed Göring's aeroplane crash land at Gonnelieu airfield, some twenty-five kilometres east of Combles, one of the Nieuport pilots could have claimed it as an aerial victory. But, as a survey of military records shows, many pilots on both sides of the lines were not recognised for such combat achievements; conversely, many aircraft that were seen spiralling down or perceived to hit the ground were credited as "kills" even when the "victims" came through the encounter safely and their aeroplanes were still useable. Such were the vagaries of aerial combat success verifications on all sides in World War I.

There is no doubt that Hermann Göring waged a hard fight against the stable but hard to manoeuvre artillery spotter.[15] Proof of the British observer's tenacity was made clear less than two weeks later, when Second Lieutenant Wood, who was wounded in the fight,[16] was awarded the Military Cross.[17] The award citation noted his 'conspicuous gallantry in action. He has continually … obtained valuable information, and displayed great courage and determination throughout.'[18]

The extraordinary circumstances that Göring claimed occurred on 2 November 1916 – from flawed descriptions of a huge bomber to the film-like scenario of a fortuitous landing next to a field hospital – are examples of his embellishing (or authorising the embellishment of) an account of an already worthy achievement to make it seem to be even more significant. As will be shown, such behaviour became typical for him.

Behind the Veil

But he never admitted to his blatantly obvious self-aggrandisement, even in texts he wrote or authorised. Dismissing a short autobiography he was asked to write when first confined at Nuremberg in 1945, Göring told a U.S. Army psychiatrist, Dr. Leon Goldensohn: 'Nobody knows the real Göring. I am a man of many parts, but the autobiography, what does that tell you? Nothing. And those books put out by the [Nazi] party press, they are less than useless.'[19]

Obviously, 'those books' include the Sommerfeldt and Gritzbach biographies he approved. As will be seen, both have historical value. Further, other records and accounts exist to add balance to his early life's story and thereby help researchers determine more of the unadorned truth, despite the apparent ease with which Hermann Göring stepped away from reality and into his own fantasies.

His family background was a most sensitive area of the shining image that he sought to manipulate. Goldensohn observed, Göring 'seemed loath to pursue the story of his siblings … or of his relationship to them.' But that delicate area and its foibles is where this story begins.

Hermann Göring's father – christened Ernst Heinrich, but called Heinrich – was born on Hallowe'en, 31 October 1838 in Emmerich, a small city on the north bank of the Rhine river, a few kilometres from the Dutch border. He was descended from a line of civil servants among who include a *commissarius loci* [administrative district commissioner] appointed by the eighteenth century Prussian King Frederick the Great.[20] Born in 1649 at Rügenwalde in Brandenburg Province and christened Michael Christian Gering,[21] this ancestor changed the family name – which, as an adjective, means 'small, trifling, petty' – to Göring. Under the name of Michael Christian Göring, he became so successful at his work that he was appointed to be royal tax collector for the Ruhr industrial area, and thus his descendants lived in western Germany, where they prospered as officials and officers.[22]

The son of a judge, Heinrich Göring studied law at the universities of Bonn and Heidelberg and earned a doctoral degree in jurisprudence. He also gained a commission in the Landwehr [militia] and was called to active duty when war broke out between Prussia and Austria in 1866 and again during the Franco-Prussian War of 1870-71.[23] Between the wars, the thirty-one-year-old military officer married Ida Remy, the daughter of a prominent industrial family in Rasselstein bei Neuwied in his native Rhineland and eight years younger than he. Their first child, Friedrich Wilhelm, was born on 29 October 1870 in Heddesdorf in the Neuwied district.[24] After the war, Heinrich Göring was appointed a district judge,[25] which provided some minor prestige and a steady source of income. A second child, Ida, was born on 13 September 1872, but died seventeen days later.[26] Heinrich and his wife had three more children – Ernst Albert on 5 October 1873,

Friederike Wilhelmine Clara on 16 July 1875, and Heinrich Carl on 17 April 1879. Unfortunately, six days after the birth of her youngest child,[27] thirty-one-year-old Ida Göring died of 'maternity fever',[28] related to poor hygienic conditions where she delivered.[29]

The last three births and Ida's death occurred in Devant-les-Ponts, near Metz in the Lorraine province that had been ceded to Germany after the Franco-Prussian War. There, Heinrich Göring made slow, steady progress in the civil service,[30] until 1884, when he gave up his judgeship and put aside sad memories of Germany's new western frontier to join the consular service at the foreign office in Berlin.[31] The widower arranged for his extended family to raise his children while he pursued his new career – and an active social life. Thus, the strait-laced Prussian bureaucrat met and became charmed by Franziska (Fanny) Tiefenbrunn, who is variously described as 'a Munich beer garden waitress of uncertain descent',[32] and 'a lively, buxom Bavarian girl of Austrian origin'.[33] She was also some twenty years Heinrich's junior.

Overseas Postings

The following year, Heinrich was assigned to administer German South West Africa [now the Republic of Namibia], an area of significant German commercial and religious settlement that had become a colony of the young German empire a year earlier. To prepare for his new post, he went to London to study the organisational and administrative techniques that had made Great Britain such a successful colonial power. The trip to London came at a most fortuitous time, as Fanny had become pregnant by Heinrich and they could be married out of sight of official circles in Berlin. The 28 May 1885 ceremony in the German Chapel Royal, St. James was witnessed only by a German couple with whom the Görings were close friends.[34] Heinrich and Fanny returned to Berlin long enough to put their affairs in order and have their marriage solemnised by a Lutheran minister before Heinrich departed for Africa,[35] leaving his wife in Germany.

A few days later, on 2 June, Fanny arrived in Rosenheim, some fifty kilometres southeast of Munich, where she had family and friends. While in the picturesque town, she boarded with a local family, the Gabriels, in Kunstmühlstrasse Nr. 8, until she was admitted to the Rosenheimer Marienbad at Hausstätterstrasse Nr. 22. That sanitarium was run by an Austrian medical team 'whose skilful care … [was] so well known that patients came from all over Germany and the Austro-Hungarian Empire.'[36] The sanitarium cared for patients convalescing from illnesses and depression, and also had a maternity section.[37] After the death of his first wife, Heinrich Göring naturally sought the best care for his new, younger bride. Thus, in the Rosenheimer Marienbad, midwife Karoline Feil delivered the Görings' first child, Karl Ernst, on 3 August.[38] Fanny remained in the Gabriel family's care until 26 March 1888.[39] The two years and nine months she spent in Rosenheim may have been due to extended treatment for some post-partum medical event or simply to allow Fanny and her infant son to be comfortable and safely away from the fierce wilderness of German South West Africa.

Meanwhile, Heinrich Göring had negotiated with the indigenous Herero tribal chiefs to secure a large, safe and stable territorial stake in that part of Africa.[40] His efforts to promote growth in the country were so successful that in May 1886 Bismarck appointed him as the colony's first Reichskommissar [Reich's Commissioner]. Indeed, Göring's legacy lives on in Windhoek, the capital of today's Republic of Namibia, where one of the main thoroughfares is still named Göring Strasse.

By the time Fanny and Karl joined Heinrich at his new posting, the boy was walking and able to cope with some of the hardships of colonial life, including attacks by Herero tribesmen that forced the Görings to flee their home 'on many occasions'.[41] Fanny remained in Africa for the birth of her second child, Olga Therese Sophie, in the German settlement of Waldfischbach on 16 January 1889; Olga was delivered by an Austrian-born physician assigned to the region, Dr.med. Hermann Epenstein,[42] who later became an important figure in Göring family life. But when Fanny became pregnant a third time, she returned to her friends at Kunstmühlstrasse Nr. 8 in Rosenheim and entered the Marienbad sanitarium, where the midwife Frau Feil delivered her daughter Paula Elisabeth Rosa.[43] This time Fanny stayed with the Gabriels in Rosenheim for twenty-eight months, from 4 June 1889 through 2 October 1891.[44]

Meanwhile, in 1890, Reichskommissar Göring was granted a long vacation leave in Germany to recuperate from the strain of his African experiences. Joyful at being reunited with his wife, he volunteered for another – apparently less stressful – overseas posting as consul general and minister resident at Port-au-Prince, capital of the former French colony of Haiti.[45] Fanny and the three children accompanied him, but after she became pregnant with her fourth child, she left the disease-ridden Caribbean nation and returned alone to Rosenheim. On 10 July 1892, once again she moved in with the Gabriel family.[46] In the interim, she and her husband had remained in contact with the physician from their days in Africa, Dr. Hermann Epenstein,[47] who was made aware of the now thirty-three-year-old Fanny's visit to Rosenheim. It was no surprise when he showed up at her door and assured her that she would be under his watchful eye when it came time for her to enter the Rosenheimer Marienbad. On 12 January 1893, the same midwife, Frau Feil, delivered the Görings' second son,[48] who Fanny named Hermann Wilhelm.[49] There is speculation that the boy's first name honoured Dr. Epenstein, who had become Fanny's constant companion during the lonely days without Heinrich and the children. Further, Epenstein became godfather to Hermann and then, later, to all of Fanny Göring's children.[50]

From the beginning of his life, Hermann was a big boy, weighing some 'twelve pounds'.[51] And soon he became a neglected boy. After he was weaned, a few months later,[52] Fanny left him in the care of her friends (and possibly relatives) in the Graf family in the Franconian city of Fürth, just northwest of Nuremberg, when she returned to Haiti to rejoin the rest of her family. As a consequence of that early separation from Fanny, Hermann addressed Frau Graf as 'mother' and throughout his life held her in the highest esteem.[53] British writer Leonard Mosley, who met Hermann Göring prior to World War II and later came to know Göring family members and friends, observed about Hermann: 'He was obviously a lonely child and nothing that his surrogate parents did for him seemed capable of making up for the absence of his real parents. "It is the cruellest thing that can happen to a child, to be torn from his mother in his formative years," Hermann … [said] many years later.'[54]

Fanny did not remain with her husband and children during much of the remaining time of Heinrich Göring's assignment in Haiti. In the summer of 1894 she sailed alone from Haiti back to Germany, where the ever-helpful Dr. Epenstein got her settled in Friedenau, the Berlin suburb in which he also lived. On 9 March 1895, she gave birth to her fifth (and last) child, Albert Günter, in Berlin-Friedenau.[55] Once again, Dr. Epenstein was on hand. Eleven years younger than Fanny's husband, the physician had the means to assure that she lived comfortably during and after her confinement.

Most likely, during the 1894-1895 time span Fanny Göring and Hermann Epenstein began what would become a long-time love affair,[56] which raises questions about Albert Göring's paternity. Fanny and her husband could have conceived the boy just before she departed Haiti, but many people who knew Fanny and Epenstein were sure that Albert had been fathered by the physician. Both had similar facial features, dark hair and eyes, as well as 'a Central European physiognomy, while Hermann and the other Göring children were fair and blue-eyed'.[57] But, as a family friend noted later: 'Everyone accepted the situation, and it did not seem to trouble Hermann or Albert at all.'[58]

Back Home

In 1896, Heinrich Göring returned from Haiti, sick and, at age fifty-eight, prematurely old.[59] Life in the tropics had taken a toll on him and now he was being ushered into early retirement. He had few savings, having spent considerable sums of money to pay for Fanny's three extended visits to Rosenheim. But his friend – and Fanny's ardent admirer – Dr. Epenstein was most generous with financial support. By now, Heinrich must have realised that his wife and Epenstein were more than friends, but there was nothing he could do about it. As a consequence, he began to drink heavily to cope with the despair about his waning career and, likely, the sorry state of his marriage.[60]

One result of his son Hermann's long separation from his parents became clear when they finally travelled to Fürth to retrieve him from the Graf family. Upon being presented to his birth mother, young Hermann used his fists to 'bash … [her] in the face when she came to embrace him'.[61] It cannot be determined whether the boy sought to punish his natural mother or, not recognising her, thought a stranger was taking him away from 'Mother' Graf, with whose family he had spent such a formative time. During his post-World War II imprisonment, Hermann Göring recounted that story as his earliest childhood recollection to U.S. Army psychologist Gustave M. Gilbert. Seeking to understand what motivated Göring later in life, Dr. Gilbert made this assessment:

> '…This tendency to overt aggression manifested itself very early as one of [Göring's] chief satisfactions in life, and he undoubtedly laughed in playful glee at his mother's pained chagrin over his unruliness. At least he laughed most heartily in describing this and similar incidents to me in his cell in the Nuremberg jail …'[62]

Heinrich, Fanny and their five children settled in Berlin, where, once again thanks to Dr. Epenstein's generosity, the family lived – rent-free[63] – in a house that the physician owned in Friedenau.[64] Epenstein had his own house in Berlin, where his father, also a physician, had become wealthy through land and property speculation.[65] His largesse – especially toward Fanny and the children[66] – assured him of a warm welcome at the stylish Göring residence in Fregestrasse, a tiny neighbourhood that was an ideal location for Heinrich and Fanny to entertain civilian and military notables in a manner that would otherwise be beyond their financial resources.

Those guests and the Görings' regular Sunday visits to the Potsdam parade grounds[67] had a profound effect on young Hermann. Dr. Gilbert observed from his discussions that the boy 'became fascinated by the military display: the uniforms and parades, the officers barking orders at their goose-stepping soldiers. Prussian militarism appealed to [Hermann's] aggressive temperament in preference to the Bavarian *Gemütlichkeit* [geniality] and he soon identified himself with the aspirations common to … offspring of the Prussian Junker caste.'[68]

Part of that identification centred on the value that young Göring placed on prestige. Gilbert noted that Hermann precociously learned from his father that '[t]he lowest second lieutenant … took precedence over a minister of state in the rules of protocol at the Kaiser's court – even on the grand march into the ballroom at state receptions.'[69]

Heinrich Göring tried to maintain a semblance of normalcy in his home and indulged his children. When he presented Hermann with a Hussar officer's uniform for his fifth birthday, it was the perfect accoutrement for the boy's fantasies, as Dr. Gilbert observed:

'His childhood play was devoted almost exclusively to waging war, leading his small army of youngsters and toy cannons against imaginary enemies of *Kaiser und Vaterland* [Emperor and Fatherland]. If there was any question about his leadership … he would bash their heads together and let them know "damn quick" who was boss. For, if his beautiful uniforms and his father's position of authority were not enough to establish [Hermann's] right of dominance over his companions, his ready use of force settled any doubts on that score.'[70]

A Fortress Dream Come True

In many ways, Hermann Göring's fantasies were matched by those of his godfather and patron. A year after Hermann was born, the wealthy physician purchased an abandoned fifteenth century burg [fortress] among the Tauern Mountains in Mauterndorf, Austria, about 125 kilometres southeast of Munich, and 'spent a great deal of money on … recreating it in the heavy and pompous atmosphere of German medievalism that so stirred the young imagination of his godchild'.[71] Then, in 1897, Epenstein bought another, smaller burg in the Bavarian mountain village of Neuhaus an der Pegnitz, some thirty kilometres northeast of Nuremberg. Over the next decade, the physician used his wealth to return the 900-year-old bulwark – known as Burg Veldenstein[72] – with its commanding view high above the Pegnitz river, to some of its former glory. Meanwhile, when Heinrich Göring was finally pensioned off by the foreign office in 1898, he was enticed to leave his pleasant home outside Berlin by Epenstein's offer for him and his family to use a house built into the lower walls of Burg Veldenstein. But it soon became apparent that Heinrich and his children were living in baronial style at an emotional cost to him. They lived in one part of the old fortress while, during Epenstein's visits, Heinrich's attractive, much younger wife lived in another part, obvious to one and all as the physician's mistress.[73]

Chapter Two

From the Fortress to the Frontlines

'When I become an officer … there must also be a war right away.
I shall distinguish myself and get even more medals than Papa got.'[1]

HERMANN GÖRING

For five-year-old Hermann Göring, Burg Veldenstein – soaring majestically into the sky, secure against any threat – was a dream fulfilled. And, as with most children at that age, his young mind made little clear distinction between fantasy and reality. Consequently, on his first day at the old fortress, the imaginative would-be warrior disappeared within Veldenstein to explore its defensive structures, passageways and other secrets. And then there was the tower, offering a spectacular view of the surrounding Bavarian countryside. Dr. Hermann Epenstein owned the fortress, but young Hermann Göring must have felt as if he were master of the place.

The following day, the boy is said to have returned to the tower and taken down the ornamental broad swords and lances that had long been on the walls and arranged them in the order needed for a coming battle. Such an undertaking seems to be an incredible feat for a youngster. Thus, what happened next, as related by biographer Erich Gritzbach some thirty-five years later, is best regarded as offering the flavour, if not the actual facts, of events that may have taken place at Veldenstein:

'Under the leadership of Hermann the children play a game of "Knights and Squires". As Hermann expertly explains to his father and godfather, in the village he has rounded up all of the hardy squires and horsemen. His sisters [Olga and Paula] and the daughters of Mother Graf [Hermann's caretaker when he lived in Fürth], Fanny and Erna, who are all about the same age as his sisters, are the Knight's daughters who have found shelter under the protection of the "Lord of the Fortress". But the game lasts only a few days. He says it is too boring, that his enemies are weak-kneed and cannot even force their way into the lower courtyard.

'Now [Hermann] will "play" the enemy and conquer the fortress himself. He appoints the strongest boy in the town … who is also his best friend, as Lord of the Fortress. But, he adds, it is understood that [status] is only as long as they are playing. And now the other boys, who were given a good thrashing, man the ramparts of beautiful Veldenstein. Then Hermann withdraws with his squires. But before he goes, he calls out to the defenders: "You must wait awhile. I am not coming right away. We shall certainly come, but not where you expect us." Like a strategist firmly convinced of the seriousness of the situation, he withdraws through the village with his troop, moves stealthily through the forest and down into the lovely Pegnitz valley, out of which the fortress rises 120 metres steeply above the high crags and into the heavens. '"Here is where we will attack," he announces. While most of his squires look at him in disbelief, he calls out to them: "If you are cowards, then go away. But do not show your faces at the fortress ever again."'[2]

Gritzbach's account – surely dictated by Göring – became even more fanciful. In it, the boy warrior and five of his 'men' ascended the sheer fortress walls and, of course, only the steely-courageous Hermann completed the climb and successfully 'swung over the ramparts' in the most dramatic manner. And there only to be apprehended by a servant who brought him to his anxious parents. As Göring noted on this and other occasions, an inherent toughness enabled him to survive any punishment.[3]

There is little reason to believe that tired, old Heinrich Göring was harsh in his treatment of the 'wild child' of his second brood of offspring. Indeed, Hermann sensed favouritism in his father's eyes. As one story goes, in the days before Hermann could read, a telegram arrived when his father was not at home and the boy quickly snatched it away and kept it until his father returned. Fearing no chastisement, he surrendered it and exclaimed gleefully *'Ich bin doch Papas Liebling!'* [After all, I am Papa's favourite!].[4]

The combination of parental laxity and Hermann's wilfulness led to behavioural problems when, at age six, the boy's formal education began. At first, he joined his sisters Olga and Paula, who were only seventeen months apart in age, in a private class taught by a governess. When Hermann was added to their small classroom, however, there was more disruption than the teacher could manage.

With its scenic view over the Pegnitz valley, Burg Veldenstein was the centuries-old Bavarian fortress where Hermann Göring lived as a young boy.

As time passed, American psychologist Gustave M. Gilbert observed, Hermann became a cruel bully: 'Not content with tyrannising the boys in his neighbourhood, he turned upon his sisters …Neither his mother nor his governess could control him and the father's punishments proved to be of no avail.'[5]

When Hermann attended the village school in Neuhaus, he was just as unsuccessful a pupil.[6] So, at age seven, he was enrolled at the *Volksschule* [primary school] in Fürth.[7] There, 'he found only new outlets for his uncontrollable aggression'.[8] Under other circumstances, Hermann might have been boarded with the Graf family in Fürth, but Heinrich and Fanny may have felt that the boy's discipline problems were too much to inflict on the woman who had raised him from infancy. On the other hand, Hermann might have benefitted from Frau Graf's intuitive maternal connection. In any event, he was boarded with one of the primary school teachers,[9] a man who 'lived in modest circumstances in the workers' quarter'.[10] Perhaps the thought was to put a strong male figure in Hermann's life and discipline him properly. He was allowed to bring one luxury from home, his pet dachshund, *Waldmann* [goblin], whose energy and friskiness delighted the other boys.

Seeds of Anti-Semitism

Aside from school vacations, Hermann spent nearly four years in Fürth. That time marked an especially grim period in his young life, during which it was said he hated school and his favourite expression upon returning to school after holidays was: 'If only Fürth would burn down …!'[11] Adding to that dark thought, someone in his circle of acquaintances filled the impressionable boy's head with hate-inspired stories about Jews.

The Jewish emancipation that was granted throughout Germany in the 19th century was meant to end centuries of discriminatory societal practices,[12] but lingering feelings ranging from resentment to hatred of non-Christians were readily available to infect young minds. As Erich Gritzbach wrote, Hermann Göring hated Jews 'ever since his time in Fürth'.[13]

Hermann acted on this new turn of events by urging his little dog Waldmann to bark and snap at people he thought to be of Semitic origin. When punished for these or other misdeeds, often the boy went to bed and told everyone that he was sick.[14] Hermann was a smart boy and received good grades, but he did not care for school; as with so many other life events, he wanted school to be on his terms.

By all accounts, young Hermann was not exposed to anti-Semitism within the Göring family. He certainly did not hear about racial hatred from his much admired and generous godfather Dr. Hermann Epenstein, who was of Jewish heritage,[15] but who had been raised as a Christian.[16] Yet, it is clear that some person or persons in Fürth indoctrinated Hermann Göring into a malevolent passion that remained with him for life.

Ironically, Göring never learned of his own Jewish heritage, which was hidden from him, especially during the peak period of his political power. Prof.Dr. Hansmartin Decker-Hauff (1917-1992), a highly respected post-World War II German genealogist, wrote:

'Göring's entire genealogical chart was prepared for publication by university Prof.Dr. Otto Freiherr von Dungern [1875-1967] of Graz [Austria]. It appeared in the series *Ahnentafel berühmter Deutscher* [Genealogical Charts of Famous Germans] in about 1938. Göring was the only prominent Nazi who was from a "good" family; the paternal grandfather was a Prussian administrative district president, [and] the great-grandmother was a [member of the House of] Metternich zur Gracht. Yet, Göring's mother – and this pained Göring very much – was a Munich beer garden waitress of questionable descent. He placed all the more value on research into and publication about his paternal ancestors, especially that, in addition to many lesser aristocrats, he also had genealogically interesting "dynastic bridges" (legitimate lines of descent) to higher nobility and, in fact, was descended from almost all of the reigning royal houses of the Middle Ages. Among his patrician ancestors were many distinguished families who were written about at length. But, Dungern omitted, certainly from the publication noted above … [Göring's ancestral link to the Swiss] money-changer family Ebeler, also known as Grünzweig, which was converted from Judaism to Christianity in the fifteenth century.'[17]

As a boy, Hermann's genealogical connections meant nothing to him. Once away from school, he was happiest when he was back living in Burg Veldenstein, where his rich dream world came to life. Such a vivid excursion beyond reality occurred in about 1901, as Dr. Gilbert noted:

> '[Göring's] fantasy life was so vivid that on occasion he could actually experience life in a medieval fortress. On one occasion that he never forgot, he was looking over the countryside from the [fortress] tower. A smoking locomotive came lumbering down the valley below. Suddenly the whole scene changed and he saw Roman chariots with plumed warriors charging down the countryside while crowds roared. "But [it was] so *real*! Just as though it was all actually there like in the story books [Hermann related]. I don't know how long the vision lasted. Then I ran down all excited and told my mother and my sister about it. They only laughed …"'[18]

Most summers, Dr. Epenstein invited the Göring family to live with him in his larger and grander residence, Burg Mauterndorf.[19] There, young Hermann enjoyed a life of medieval splendour. Epenstein, whose father had been elevated to the rank of *Ritter* [knight] in the non-hereditary nobility,[20] indulged his own fantasies of a life of stately grandeur by requiring his servants to wear uniforms like those found in the elegant residences of true nobility. Further, 'meals were called by a blast of a hunting horn, and … musicians played and sang in the gallery of the great hall … [while Epenstein] strode his domain, giving orders, receiving deferential salutes from the men and curtsies from the women as if he were of royal blood.'[21]

During one visit to Mauterndorf, where Hermann's mind was excited by the burg's extensive battlements and military history dating back to Roman times, he made a prophetic remark to his parents: 'Now I want to become a soldier; for me, there is no thought of any other occupation.'[22]

Reinforcing that conviction and fuelling Hermann's imagination further, at Burg Veldenstein his family lived less than forty kilometres south of Bayreuth, where composer Richard Wagner's *Festspielhaus* offered musical works such as his four-opera cycle *Der Ring des Nibelungen* [The Ring of the Niebelungen], which was steeped in Germanic lore. On

Burg Mauterndorf in Austria was the larger of Dr. Hermann Epenstein's two fortresses and it dazzled young Göring with its old battlements, towers, passageways and defences.

many occasions Dr. Epenstein took the Göring family to Bayreuth to experience these colourful and lavishly-staged operas,[23] a main source of popular entertainment at the time that would have left Hermann enthralled. According to Gilbert:

'His fantasies were also stimulated by his early lessons in Teutonic history – the one subject that really interested him. He listened avidly to stories of … Siegfried and the Valkyrie … admiring their war dress and heroic exploits. As he learned to read, the lives of the great heroes of German history became his favourite books. Heroism, chivalry and loyalty to the sovereign became deeply ingrained as primary values of his culture. Aside from such ego-involved subjects, he cared little for learning, although he was of superior intelligence.'[24]

Back in the harsh reality of Fürth, however, Hermann's endless fighting with his peers, bullying other boys and 'causing new troubles by picking on Jews'[25] finally led to his being withdrawn from school.[26] In 1904, when he was eleven years old, he was sent – without his beloved dachshund – to an austere boarding school at Ansbach, which proved to be an even worse experience. In addition to strict discipline, at which Hermann always chafed, he became the butt of an incident of anti-Semitism.

A few weeks into his stay, his class was directed to write essays about the most admired man in their lives and young Göring wrote about his *Pate* [godfather], Dr. Hermann Epenstein, who he viewed as a model of success and a man to be emulated. Within a very short time, young Hermann was summoned to the headmaster's office, where, in an ice-cold fury, the administrator towered over him and let him know loudly and clearly that 'Ansbach boys' did not write essays that praised Jews. In his typically bold fashion, Hermann objected to the characterisation of one of his life's heroes, pointing out that Epenstein (whose mother was a gentile) was raised as a Roman Catholic. The incensed headmaster produced a copy of a large volume commonly called the Semi-Gotha, a perverse and unauthorised variation of the *Gothaer Namensverzeichnis* [Gotha Roll of Names], a respectable genealogical chronicle of noble families in the German-speaking world. The Semi-Gotha served only to identify and further stigmatise Jews who had married into titled families or who had been granted patents of nobility. The headmaster pointed out the Epenstein listing and ordered Hermann to write 100 times 'I shall not write essays in praise of Jews'. Then the boy was made to transcribe every name in the Semi-Gotha from A to E.[27]

Later that day, a deeper humiliation took place after the story was spread among the other students. Hermann was accosted outside the building and, after much kicking and punching, was subdued by three bigger boys who forced him to walk around the school's grounds wearing the crudely fashioned sign *'MEIN PATE IST EIN JUDE'* [My godfather is a Jew]. Hermann's anger remained so strong and furious that, the following morning, he arose very early, gathered up his possessions and walked to the train station to leave Ansbach for good. Later, he told his sister Olga that, on his way out, he expressed his rage by smashing a violin he had been given and cutting the strings of the school band's other instruments.[28]

A Military Education

Hermann's parents and Dr. Epenstein did not know what to do with the obstreperous boy. He simply did not seem to fit into normal society. Near the end of his life, Göring admitted that his mother once said of him: 'Hermann will be either a great man or a great criminal.'[29]

As one of his teachers recorded: 'Hermann is a good fellow – but a bit difficult. He is a born revolutionary.'[30] Heinrich Göring could not afford to continue to send Hermann to private schools and there were limits to Epenstein's generosity in an apparently fruitless venture. Thus, it seemed only logical to have Hermann compete for a place in the Prussian cadet corps, a strict educational system that prepared boys and young men for the professional military officer corps – and at no cost to the parents. Heinrich's three sons from his first marriage and his oldest son from the second union gained good secondary educations in the cadet corps. Indeed, he and Fanny noticed that whenever their son Karl was on home leave from the senior cadet

Hermann Göring in his cadet uniform while attending a military preparatory institution in Karlsruhe, capital of the Grand Duchy of Baden.

academy, Hermann made excuses to be with the older son and his friends, all dressed in their smart-looking blue and white cadet uniforms. At age eleven, Hermann was at the right time in life to enter one of eight cadet corps *Voranstalten* [preparatory institutions] located around Germany.[31] His sister Paula and the Graf sisters were already enrolled in a finishing school in Karlsruhe, the capital of the Grand Duchy of Baden in southwestern Germany, and so, to keep the children together, Heinrich applied to have Hermann admitted to the *Kadetten-Anstalt* [cadet institute] there in 1904.[32]

Heinrich knew from past experience that, while professional officer training 'had long been the province of the aristocracy',[33] the Prussian cadet corps had evolved into a true meritocracy, in which young men could gain places on the basis of success in a competitive examination. As a well-documented study of the cadet system noted: '… the academic evaluation of each cadet was a great leveller, showing commoner and noble alike to be qualified or unqualified for admission to the cadet corps.'[34] The cadet institute provided its young students with sparse living conditions, long hours of study and strict, unquestioning discipline. The uniforms, spit and polish, drills and complete surrender to the system were just what young Hermann Göring needed at this point in his life and he embraced it eagerly.

It was five years of hard work, but the Prussian cadet corps succeeded where civilian education could not. Upon completion of his studies at Karlsruhe, Hermann was given the grade of 'excellent' in discipline, English, French, history, music and riding. His parents must have been speechless upon reading his final report, which started: 'Göring has been an exemplary pupil, and he has developed a quality that should take him far: he is not afraid to take a risk.'[35]

In view of his success at Karlsruhe, on 1 April 1909 sixteen-year-old Hermann easily matriculated to the *Haupt-Kadetten-Anstalt* [senior cadet academy] in Gross Lichterfelde, southwest of Berlin in the Potsdam district he enjoyed so much as a young boy. Indeed, his return to the Potsdam area was the perfect melding of his earlier fantasies with current reality, as Dr. Gilbert observed:

'Somewhat estranged from his family by now, [Hermann] made his emotional transference all the more to the military authoritarian hierarchy with the Kaiser at the top … [H]is role as Junker-officer-in-the-making satisfied his status needs. More than that, it satisfied the heroic fantasies that had long since fixed the pattern of his desired way of life … For there could be no doubt in his mind that, just as he now showed rigid subservience to his superiors, he would someday be able to demand the same from his [subordinates] when he rose in rank, in keeping with the dual tradition of subservience and arrogance dear to the Prussian military condition.'[37]

If Hermann had little time for his family, it was because he was completely swept up in a world of smart-looking uniforms, behaviour 'based on medieval codes, and in the cadet societies – [where] he was elected to one of the most exclusive – there were rituals to be followed "that made me think I am an inheritor of all the chivalry of German knighthood", he wrote home to his family.'[38] And, of course, the off-duty time of cadet life included drinking great quantities of beer, going to the horse races, keeping fit at swimming parties, and meeting young women who were as impressed by dashing uniforms as Hermann was.[39] Lean and, at five feet ten inches, quite tall for his generation, the muscular, young Hermann Göring cut a dashing figure in those days.

The following year, Epenstein used his wealth to gain a patent of nobility from Austro-Hungarian Emperor Franz Joseph I. Thus he became known as Dr.med Hermann Ritter von Epenstein, matching his father's status achievement and becoming even more of a successful role model for young Göring. Perhaps inspired by Epenstein, Hermann let slip a criticism of his father by later vowing: 'When I become an officer – and that I will definitely be – there must also be a war right away. I shall distinguish myself and get even more medals than Papa got.'[40]

Also in 1910, Hermann came down with tonsillitis and was hospitalised at the senior cadet academy's infirmary from 13 through 26 October.[41] This occurrence was the first of several medical events that interfered with his military career. Otherwise, he was remarkably successful at Gross Lichterfelde. A sampling of his final grades shows he did 'quite good' in English, French and Latin, 'good' in map reading, 'very good' in German, history, math and physics, and 'excellent' in geography. In a letter dated 13 May 1911, his company commander, Richard Baron von Keiser, informed Heinrich Göring: 'I beg to inform Your Excellency that your son Hermann recently passed the Fähnrich [army ensign] examination with the grade of *summa cum laude*.'[42]

The senior cadet academy at Gross Lichterfelde where young Göring was moulded into a military man.

Hermann Göring's uniform would have been of the style worn by the young men seen here in a classroom at the senior cadet academy.

As a result of his high final examination scores, Hermann Göring qualified for inclusion among the *Selekta*, a special honour for the top students in his class, which would indicate that he should do well in his military career. Of the 3,290 *Selektaner* who graduated between 1871 and 1918, ten rose to the rank of Generalfeldmarschall [field-marshal], including Göring, and over 800 became generals.[43] For the moment, he held the rank of Fähnrich, a sort of 'third lieutenant' (i.e., a rank below second lieutenant), and would have been eligible for a field posting and eventual promotion to the commissioned rank of Leutnant [second lieutenant]. But, as a *Selektaner*, he was allowed to remain at Gross Lichterfelde for post-graduate study, focused on military subjects for eight months, after which he was promoted to Leutnant[44] and was on his way to a promising career path. Heinrich Göring honoured his son's achievement, according to biographer Gritzbach, by presenting Hermann with a purse of 1,000 Reichsmarks,[45] worth about £50 or $250 (U.S.) at the time.

Hermann was free to use the money as he wished and, as he was in great need of a vacation, he joined with some friends on a trip to Italy. While he learned about an officer's privileges during his cadet training, Hermann was also taught to treat his enlisted subordinates decently and so he invited his father's chauffeur, Sepp Rausch, to accompany him.[46] The group took in the best of Italian culture – including viewing works by Bellini, da Vinci, Raphael, Rubens, Titian and other famous art masters.

A Time of Change

Hermann's time at the senior cadet academy passed quickly. After completing his commissioned officer's examination and, in 1913, the *Abitur* examination [qualification to begin university studies,[47] if he desired], he was awarded his commission with a date of rank of 22 June 1912. But while he was finishing his studies and looking forward to his first duty assignment, the odd domestic situation at Veldenstein was coming to an end. In a last act of defiance, Heinrich Göring began to complain aloud about the liberties that Dr. von Epenstein had taken with his wife for the previous seventeen years. Long known as a wealthy bachelor who took his pleasure where he found it, Epenstein was taken aback at such a reaction from the man whose family he had subsidised very generously for so long. Moreover, at age sixty-two, the physician had fallen in love with a woman nearly forty years his junior and Fanny could not compete with the younger woman's charms. By the time Leutnant Hermann Göring returned to Veldenstein, eager to show off his new uniform to his long-time hero, Epenstein had gone off with the vivacious Lilli von Schandrowitz,[48] whom he later married. He left a sum of money along with a note for Hermann, inviting the young officer to visit him at Mauterndorf.[49] By the following spring, the Göring family had moved out of Veldenstein and – now relying on Heinrich's pension – settled into a modest and affordable apartment in Munich at Tengstrasse 38.[50]

The family were in their new home only a few months when Heinrich Göring died on 7 December 1913 at age seventy-five. Hermann recalled: 'His death was not unexpected as he suffered from diabetes for a few years … [He] never abided by his diet and drank wine and ate what he pleased right up to the end.'[51] At the burial service in Munich's Waldfriedhof cemetery, Hermann's usually tough composure dissolved and he wept over the grave.[52] It was only after Heinrich's death that Hermann gained an appreciation of his father and his achievements. When later asked how his parents influenced his life, Hermann responded:

'People who knew my parents and me often said that my mental abilities were from my father and my temperament and energy came from my mother. One explanation of their differences might be that my father was a northerner and my mother a southerner. The north German is very quiet and constructive. The south German is more lively and artistic … [My father] was strict and stern, but beloved by his subordinates. He was constantly planning and had a constructive, vital mind …I was more attached to my father for some reason. Mother was very good to the children, but I think I was out of the home so much [that] I lost contact with her.'[53]

The Göring family's southern influence must not have been lost entirely. Although he was born in the Kingdom of Bavaria, Hermann was registered as a Prussian citizen and, therefore, ineligible for admission to a unit of the Royal Bavarian Army. However, his attendance at the cadet institute in Karlsruhe, Baden's capital, a decade earlier, gave him more of a military connection to Baden than to Prussia. Hence, he accepted a commission into an army unit of the Grand Duchy of Baden, which bordered Bavaria. On Tuesday, 20 January 1914 he reported for duty in the 4th Badisches Infanterie-

Regiment 'Prinz Wilhelm' Nr. 112 garrisoned in Mülhausen[54] [now Mulhouse, France] in the Alsatian territory gained by Germany in the Franco-Prussian War of 1870-1871.

The young Leutnant Göring's fine record at Gross Lichterfelde made him a desirable asset to the regiment. In short order he was invited to visit the unit's commander, Oberst [Colonel] von Olszewski,[55] who was curious enough to want to determine Göring's social status and, more importantly, whether his financial status matched the intellectual resources of an officer of such promise. When his superior bluntly broached the subject, Göring later said he responded just as directly and with the requisite amount of politeness: 'I have no private allowance, Herr Oberst. I have at my disposal, Herr Oberst, a small but for me quite adequate means.' After that, he devoted a day of brief formal visits to his fellow officers and was just as candid with them. Some of them were heard to remark: 'The new-comer is snappish.'[56] Göring was only a very junior officer, but, as was his way, he acted as if he were someone special.

Frontier duties at Mülhausen early in 1914 were mundane exercises, broken only by the sound of military aeroplanes taking off and landing at nearby Habsheim airfield. Infanterie-Regiment Nr. 112's proximity to an early aviation facility may have inspired Göring to create a flight of fancy. Seeking to enhance and manipulate his image early in his career, he claimed that aviation activities were linked to his regimental duties. In the 1917 copy of his personal record form, which officers were required to maintain and update for promotion and other purposes, Göring wrote that, after arriving at Mülhausen: 'Very quickly I reported to the Fliegertruppe [flying corps] and in July 1914 was notified I was on a list to receive training as a pilot. Frequently, I took advantage of my free time to take part in [new aircraft] acceptance flights at Habsheim airfield. My interest in aviation was already very prominent.'[57] None of Göring's other official service records or career summaries mention this unlikely assignment and it is not included in any later biographies he approved. Spinning such a tale can only have been another case of Göring's mind blurring what he wished for with what actually occurred.

It is an interesting coincidence that the young leutnant who became Göring's best and lifelong friend, Bruno Loerzer, was transferred from Infanterie-Regiment Nr. 112 to the Militär-Fliegerschule [military flying school] at Habsheim six weeks before World War I began.[58] The two men met during Göring's introductory visits with fellow regimental officers and struck up a friendship. Loerzer was the older of the two, having been born on 22 January 1891 in the Berlin suburb of Friedenau, where Göring lived after his father returned from his last diplomatic posting. Upon completing studies at the Königsstädtische Realgymnasium, a prestigious old secondary school in Berlin,[59] Loerzer took a more traditional route to obtaining his commission by qualifying as a Fahnenjunker[60] [officer candidate] at a regiment, in this case Infanterie-Regiment Nr. 112, and received his commission on 27 January 1913.[61] Loerzer was introduced to flying when the early German civilian pilot Viktor Stöffler[62] offered him an aerial ride in an Aviatik biplane above Habsheim and the Alsatian countryside on a nice spring day. That was all it took to motivate Loerzer to apply for transfer to the flying corps. His request was granted, and, on 15 July 1914,[63] he moved into officers' quarters at the airfield. Perhaps Göring's growing bond with his friend at Habsheim caused him to 'draw' Loerzer's experiences into his own.

The War Begins

Unlike other, more comfortable garrison assignments within Germany, Infanterie-Regiment Nr. 112 patrolled the frontier area between Germany and France at a time of rising international tensions. The assassination of Erzherzog Archduke Franz Ferdinand, heir to the Austro-Hungarian throne, on 28 June 1914, added fuel to the fire. Consequently, Infanterie-Regiment Nr. 112 spent most of July at a troop practice ground in Heubeck, well within the Rhineland. The unit mobilised there on 1 August and returned to Alsace on a wartime footing.[64]

Elements of France's 14ème Division took advantage of Infanterie-Regiment Nr. 112's absence from Mülhausen and occupied the city on 8 August. German forces returned swiftly and fought their way back reclaiming the city two days later. For most of the next seven weeks, Leutnant Hermann Göring was involved in the kind of heavy, close fighting he had dreamed about and hoped for.[65] He acquitted himself well, serving as a company commander during fighting at Mülhausen and in the foothills of the Vosges mountains.[66] While the regiment pushed westward toward Verdun, on 15 September, Göring was awarded the Iron Cross 2nd Class.[67] Later in the war, this would become quite common, with some 5,210,000 issued by war's end,[68] but Göring's award at that early point was considered a bravery honour of high distinction.[69]

At 4:30 a.m. on Wednesday, 23 September, Göring's regiment came under heavy fire from French forces trying to secure the railway line from Flirey to Bernecourt during the battle for Baccarat. Again, Göring tenaciously led his men into the fight and by 7:00 a.m., French forces were retreating.[70] The fighting was hardly over when Göring experienced excruciating pain in his knees. A medical examination showed he had not been wounded in the morning's combat; it was determined that he could not walk as a result of the onset of severe rheumatoid arthritis. He had experienced bouts of arthritis when he was younger, but they were not as severe as this occurrence. First, he was sent to the Feldlazarett [field hospital] at Thiacourt and then to the larger Festungslazarett [fortress military hospital] in Metz-Montigny. Doctors there could not help him and the following day he was sent by train to the Klinisches Krankenhaus [clinical hospital] in Freiburg im Breisgau, a major city in southwestern Baden.

Throughout his travail Göring was given medication to ease his pain, but he must have sensed that his brief but distinguished infantry combat career could be coming to an end. Without fully functional legs, he could not lead a company of soldiers running across a battlefield and jumping over hurdles to engage the enemy at close quarters. At best, he could hope for a staff assignment at some command headquarters fairly close to the frontlines. At worst, he would be 'invalided' to a desk job back in Germany, the land he pledged to fight for and defend as a frontline soldier.

For the moment, Freiburg offered him only a course of treatment of undefined duration and a splendid view of the mountains of the southern Black Forest, rising above the picturesque Rhine river valley.

CHAPTER THREE
INTO THE AIR

'Struggle is and remains essential for [my] life, whether in nature or among people. I want to tower over the human herd, not that I will follow them; rather, that everyone will follow me.'[1]

HERMANN GÖRING

Hermann Göring's sagging spirits rose quickly when he learned that his regimental comrade Bruno Loerzer was also stationed in Freiburg. Loerzer's pilot training at the Aviatik military flying school in a suburb of Mülhausen in Alsace was interrupted on the day the war began, when all of the school's equipment was shipped by rail from the dangerous frontier area across the Rhine to Freiburg.[2]

The friends were reunited in a typically Göring take-charge manner, as his early biographer Martin Sommerfeldt noted:

'[Loerzer's] training was nearing its end. When he returned from one flight, an orderly handed him a note: "Visit me here in the hospital. Greetings, Hermann."

'Ten minutes later Loerzer stood before Göring's bed. There he lay, with his knees heavily wrapped in cotton wadding. "That is no wound; during the fighting near Baccarat I got a bad case of rheumatoid arthritis. It hurts all over," he grumbled with a grim face. "In a week I will be able to stand up. It is still uncertain how long it will take until I can get back to the regiment."

'"Do you know what you will do?" Loerzer suggested. "You will come with me to the frontlines as my observer. There you will not need legs and we can have your knees wrapped in cotton bindings – then you will be warm enough."

'"Fabulous!" [Göring replied.]'[3]

And from what Göring heard about flying, it suited him perfectly. Loerzer later recalled:

'Life at the flying school brought with it new impressions and experiences daily. The aeroplanes were ... still subject to treacherous defects that led easily to crashes. For this reason, after every fortunately completed flight, the beginners had an especially elated feeling of complete achievement. The officers and non-commissioned officers assigned there were trained by civilian flight instructors, who had been thrown together topsy-turvy from every possible line of work. The constricting bounds of military life were soon abolished. The officers and NCOs lived like sportsmen: Training during the day and [indulging in] joyful diversions in the evening.'[4]

Göring was not a total stranger to flying. He flew once in 1913, when he was a student at the senior cadet academy. While passing over Berlin, pre-war flyer Ernst Canter had landed in a two-seat Rumpler "Taube" [Dove] monoplane on one of the academy's broad lawns to offer cadets – including Hermann Göring[5] – an aerial view of their surroundings. Göring did not mention his experience in the elegant-looking, birdlike Rumpler in any of his aviation accounts. Apparently, that initial flight lacked the transformational effect that Bruno Loerzer's first 'ride' with Canter's contemporary, Viktor Stöffler, had the same year. But now Göring was eager to find a meaningful way to maintain his army career and, inspired by his friend's tales of life in the flying corps, he became enthusiastic about every aspect of flying.

Most likely, the two friends' conversations in the hospital over the next two weeks decided the course of Göring's entire military career.[6] As U.S. Army psychologist Gustave M. Gilbert observed at Nuremberg about Göring's personality: '[Aviation] no doubt … appealed more to his individualistic and recklessly demonstrative inclinations.'[7]

Toward the end of Göring's eighteen-day stay in the hospital, Loerzer was ordered to receive advanced pilot training at Flieger-Ersatz-Abteilung 3 [Aviation Training and Replacement Unit 3] in Darmstadt. He suggested that Göring join him in his two-seat aeroplane. 'As I needed an observer, it seemed more than reasonable to take an experienced ground war regimental comrade with me to the battlefield, after his health had been restored,' Loerzer wrote later.[8]

In fact, Loerzer was not responsible for supplying his own observer, but he recognised that with the fast pace of developments in Germany in the early stages of World War I, creative license could be taken with some rules and procedures. However, Göring had to request to be transferred to the flying corps and was refused by the officer in charge of his regiment's reserve battalion.

On 13 October 1914, the day after he was discharged from the hospital, Göring took matters into his own hands and went by train to Darmstadt to join Loerzer.[9] It was a risky action for a young junior officer to arrange for his own transfer and assignment – and it could have ended in his being court-martialled and punished harshly. But, by the time the military bureaucracy caught up with Göring, he had already sought help from his godfather, who had access to many influential people in Berlin. Dr. Hermann Ritter von Epenstein arranged for a speedy official medical judgement to state that his godson was 'unfit for further service in the trenches', thereby paving the way for the young leutnant to be welcomed legitimately at the Darmstadt aviation facility. By this time Göring's regiment had fought its way westward into northern France[10] and its leaders had more on their minds than the fate of one well-connected and arthritic young officer who was still back in Germany.[11] Göring's service records give the appearance that, following his medical treatment, his transfer to aviation was a routine event, with no mention of any judicial actions.[12]

Military aerial reconnaissance was in its infancy in autumn 1914, but from the beginning of the war, aerial observers were taught to augment traditional visual observation and handwritten notes with pictures made with precision photographic equipment. For a man who considered himself a 'quick study' in acquiring new knowledge, Göring became frustrated easily by his new chores. 'Damn, there is much to learn!' he exploded. In addition to photography, he had to learn how to range the big guns of his sector's artillery units and effective ways to drop aerial bombs on to ground targets.[13]

He completed the aerial observer's course in the last week of October and reported to the frontline aviation unit Feldflieger-Abteilung 25 [Field Flying Section 25], abbreviated FFA 25, on the 28th of that month.[14] Bruno Loerzer's orders to the same unit required him to be there on 3 November.[15] According to Sommerfeldt (and, as noted previously, he has not demonstrated a high degree of accuracy), the pair arrived at FFA 25 together – and expedited their travel from Darmstadt in a new aeroplane that Göring said they tricked a subordinate into letting them use.

At the time, most German two-seater pilots were enlisted men and, in the manner of aerial chauffeurs, took their direction from observers, who were always commissioned officers. The victim in this aeroplane 'loan' was Unteroffizier [Corporal] Günther Ziegler, who had a new two-seater for his pilot training until <u>Leutnant</u> Göring bluffed him into relinquishing it to him and <u>Leutnant</u> Loerzer.[16] No matter how the story played out, the Göring-Loerzer team made it to FFA 25's airfield at Stenay, some forty kilometres north of Verdun, the fortress city that some sixteen months later became the site of one of the war's fiercest battles. As for Ziegler, he completed his training a month later and in 1915 was advanced to Leutnant der Reserve [reserve second-lieutenant]. Then, perhaps calling in a favour, in 1917 he was assigned as a fighter pilot at Jagdstaffel 26, then led by Loerzer. Years later, when Göring commanded the Luftwaffe during the Third Reich, he also remembered Ziegler, whom he helped to rise from Major to Generalleutnant [equal to U.S. major general] in nine years' time.[17]

Feldflieger-Abteilung 25

FFA 25 was established on 1 August 1914 at the training facility Flieger-Ersatz-Abteilung 9,[18] which, along with FEA 3, was also located in Darmstadt.[19] At the beginning of the war, every German individual army command and corps headquarters in the field was assigned a feldflieger-abteilung of six aircraft.[20] Initially, thirty-three FFAs[21] were equipped with six two-seat aeroplanes to carry out reconnaissance and bombing missions. Due to weight restriction, the underpowered early two-seaters were, at best, armed with a rifle or a pistol and might also carry a few 3.5-kilogram, 5-kg or 10-kg bombs. After encounters with aggressive enemy aircraft in the war's early months,[22] eventually the abteilungen were assigned lightly-armed escort aeroplanes which evolved into fighter aircraft.

FFA 25's first Abteilungsführer [literally section leader, actually commanding officer] was Hauptmann Ernst Blum, a career army officer who at age thirty-five transferred from Baden's Infanterie-Regiment Nr. 114 to the flying corps. He was a capable and courageous leader whose early time in aviation was marked by being awarded the Iron Cross 2nd Class, Baden's prestigious Knight's Cross 2nd Class of the Order of the Zähringer Lion, and the observer's badge, which was presented only after making several flights in combat. After a brief tour of duty with FFA 25, Blum returned to the infantry, where he earned other high combat decorations.[23]

Loerzer had orders to go to FFA 25, but Göring once again disregarded authority and showed up empty-handed. His arrival at FFA 25 and Blum's reaction to him was related

Hermann Göring and Bruno Loerzer made their first combat flight in Aviatik B.II 36/14 (P.15) from FFA 25's airfield on 5 November 1914.

by Sommerfeldt, beginning with the Abteilungsführer's cheerless greeting:

> '"What do you want here?" the commanding officer asked [Göring].
> '"I am Loerzer's observer!"
> '"Heaven forbid," the captain exclaimed. "I have more than enough observers. No, I am afraid I have no use for you. Look and see whether the neighbouring unit, FFA 36 in Cunel, can find a use for you."
> '"Then I am afraid, Herr Hauptmann, I cannot remain here, either," [said] Loerzer, standing by his comrade. "I must remain together with my observer."
> '"Well, do as you like!" grumbled the commanding officer…'[24]

That brash action solved the pair's immediate concern, but the potentially insubordinate exchange may have put the two newcomers at odds with their new commander, as Loerzer noted later:

> 'As the last and newest arriving pilot, I received the oldest machine, one that had been declined by the senior pilots. The peak altitude of this aeroplane was 1,800 metres. I received my baptism under fire with it in the first weeks over Verdun.
>
> 'The French [anti-aircraft] artillery fired very well. Even though we were not shot down, the loud racket of the annoying shots still made a deep impression. Later, in his report, my observer [Göring] gave a vivid description of the event. The sector of the

Front on both sides of the Meuse and east of Verdun was entrusted to us. I carried out flights with the most ponderous machine and in such bad weather, while the other aircrews hesitated, and so our reputation in the Abteilung was established within a short time.'[25]

Loerzer flew Göring on their first combat mission on Thursday, 5 November, just two days after arriving at FFA 25. To prove their worth, they made a familiarisation flight over the unit's operational area. On this mission, their Aviatik B.II (serial number B36/14), powered by a 120-hp Mercedes engine,[26] was unarmed, which allowed Göring to concentrate on using his maps to identify terrain features he would need to know. Moreover, even if he were armed, the observer in a B-type aircraft sat in the front seat, surrounded by a bird cage of bracing wires that would have hampered his efforts to defend the aeroplane; Loerzer, sitting fully exposed in the rear of the Aviatik, was also unarmed. Loerzer and Göring were accompanied by another Aviatik B.II (serial number B35/14), to assist with their initial flight, which was completed without incident.[27]

The first German military pilot's badge bore the image of a Rumpler Taube, the aeroplane in which Göring made his first flight while still at the senior cadet academy.

Wreathed within the German aviation observer's badge was a black and white checkerboard surrounded by a red border, the symbol of an army group, which made use of the observer's visual and photographic reconnaissance services.

Having completed his formal training, and even though still lacking a combat flight, Loerzer had received his *Abzeichen für Militär-Flugzeugführer* [badge for military pilots] on 12 October[28] from Hauptmann Blum. The badge had been established on the birthday of Kaiser Wilhelm II, 27 January 1913,[29] and was awarded to officers and enlisted men alike. On 15 November 1914, Göring was awarded the *Abzeichen für Beobachtungsoffiziere* [badge for observation officers][30] by Abteilungsführer Blum, who would not receive his own observer's badge until the following April.[31] It was a momentous occasion for the recipient, as the award, which had been established exactly a year after the military pilot's badge,[32] was rarely seen this early in the war.

Loerzer and Göring flew their first bombing mission on the morning of Tuesday, 17 November. Their aircraft and two other Aviatik B.IIs set out to drop bombs on the citadel at Verdun, one part of the massive fortification system that had withstood invaders since it was begun in the 17th century. This day's mission seemed equal to sending gnats to pester a horse and it was diminished further when, once underway, the Loerzer-Göring aeroplane and another Aviatik were forced by engine problems to return to Stenay. The remaining Aviatik dropped twelve bombs, but recorded no discernible results. Eager to make a contribution to the war effort, Loerzer and Göring had their aeroplane repaired quickly and made an afternoon reconnaissance flight over the Caures Woods, near Fort Douaumont,[33] northeast of Verdun. The slender young Göring had to hang half out of the aeroplane, twisting around his cockpit bracing wires, to position his aerial camera for views of the area that would be useful in the eventual offensive against the Verdun salient created by the First Battle of the Marne in early September 1914.

Meeting the Crown Prince

FFA 25 was attached to the 5th Army, the nominal commander of which was the thirty-two-year-old German Crown Prince Wilhelm, eldest son of Kaiser Wilhelm II. As his headquarters was not far from Stenay airfield, the Crown Prince saw the aeroplanes taking off and landing, and became interested in their operations. That interest proved to be fortunate for Loerzer and Göring, as Loerzer related about his night-time return flight on 22 December 1914 and subsequent events:

> 'Hindered by unforeseen strong winds in complete darkness without any help from lanterns, I landed smoothly and safely at our airfield along the Meuse River. The Abteilungsführer had hurried to the field full of concern and ordered signal flares be fired from time to time to show where the field was. The leader of the 5th Army [Crown Prince Wilhelm] …had observed the signal flares, and asked about …their use this way. After everything had come to a good end, this flying achievement was fully recognised within the circle of "old pilots". The next day the Crown Prince ordered us to report to him in person and he [was generous in] his praise.
>
> 'In the following period, it became a rule that after special [flight] achievements we had to report to the Crown Prince. Thus, Göring's role as an observer led to his becoming chief spokesman [for FFA 25]. In addition to his position as an observer, he was born for the role of spokesman, favouring at that time dramatic forms in his manner of speech. Our Abteilungsführer, who was often present during the reports, did

not agree at all with this manner of Göring's strong, personally-emphasized description of overcoming difficulties. At the time, however, the Crown Prince found pleasure in the narratives of the "wild child", as he once called [Göring]. He was also greatly amused by occasional impudent comments that Göring made about superiors of all ranks. In addition to the official reporting sessions, personal invitations came from the Crown Prince, which often brought us to his table in the company of his closest associates.

'It is surely understandable that two unknown leutnants, who stood without any old army connections, were quite taken by such treatment by their Armeeführer [leader of the army]. Over the course of time the Crown Prince became a sort of protector for us. Subsequently, when I became a fighter pilot and fought over other army sectors, he continued to be kept informed [of my service activities].

'As a consequence … there arose among members of FFA 25 … a constantly increasing dislike of Göring, who they spurned primarily for his overly strong exaggeration during the formulation of reports, especially his oral statements … The critics were not without validity, and finally when I attempted to exercise moderating influence on Göring, he defended himself most fervently against such a restriction. He reproached me for my "damned objectivity" because of which it would never be possible to give a vivid description of an especially dangerous flight or overcoming difficulties.'[34]

A French postcard showed the aircraft from Feldflieger-Abteilung 25 that was captured on 12 January 1915.

Heavy rains in mid-January 1915 proved just how fragile aeroplanes were at that time. FFA 25 records show that the Loerzer-Göring Aviatik B.II (B36/14) was damaged by temporary flooding that washed through their hangar tent at Stenay airfield. The full extent of the damage was not determined until Loerzer, at considerable personal risk, took it up for a test flight on the 18th and found that he had great difficulty in controlling the Aviatik.[35]

While Loerzer was checking out his damaged aeroplane, another FFA 25 aircraft and crew became the unit's first casualty of the war. Offizierstellvertreter [acting officer] Paul Müller was flying Hauptmann Wolfgang Schmidt on a long-range mission over the lines when he became disoriented and had to land at Behonne, some forty kilometres south-southwest of Verdun. Both airmen were taken prisoner.[36] Schmidt was repatriated in a prisoner exchange on 12 July 1918, almost two months short of his thirty-fourth birthday.[37]

Aside from that loss, the slow pace of events made it seem that the war was a distant event for Loerzer and Göring. On Saturday, 23 January 1915, they travelled to Trier, Germany to obtain new photographic equipment and a replacement for their damaged Aviatik B.II. But they spent eleven days there, perhaps awaiting the arrival of their new aeroplane – Albatros B.I 990/14 – from the factory in central Germany.[38]

Hermann Göring and Bruno Loerzer wore their respective observer's and pilot's badges when they posed by Albatros B.I 990/14 outside an FFA 25 tent hangar.

During his enforced inactivity, the twenty-two-year-old Göring whiled away some of his time writing to Fräulein Alwine, a girlfriend back in Germany. He countered his frustration by penning some stirring lines that surely were meant to impress the young woman, while unintentionally revealing an inner drive that defined his life in 1915 and for decades in the future: 'I do not want to be an ordinary person. Struggle is and remains essential for [my] life, whether in nature or among people. I want to tower over the human herd, not that I will follow them; rather, that everyone will follow me.'[39]

Once Loerzer was satisfied with the airworthiness of the more powerful 150-hp Benz-engined Albatros,[40] Göring got his wish in a way. With his camera ready, he soared high above everyone else while on a series of photographic reconnaissance missions focusing on a new development in the extended Verdun fortification system. Verdun already boasted several cannon-equipped armoured rotating artillery turrets and, from 24 February through 3 March 1915, Göring tracked a special armoured turret construction at the Côte de Talon, near Douaumont. As Sommerfeldt wrote:

'According to ground troop reports, extensive preparations were in progress to install a high-calibre cannon, which the [5th Army] staff felt was a serious threat. Göring had to determine the exact situation of this so-called "armoured tower". During the first flight he succeeded in finding the site and making very good photographs of it. Then thorough preliminary discussions of ranging fire against the "armoured tower" were held.

'On the day of the ranging operation [3 March], Loerzer and Göring circled some kilometres behind the enemy lines. From directly above Göring observed the batteries' bomb craters and directed their fire with a complicated system of flare pistol shots. At the same time he made an exact sketch of the location of the shell hits.

'With this sketch done, they glided back over the position of the firing batteries and from 600 metres' altitude Göring dropped it in a report pouch so auspiciously that it fell right onto the batteries' observation post. In only an hour he had directed the devastating fire and the "tower" was completely destroyed.

'The reward followed quickly. The leader of the [5th] Army, the Crown Prince, personally presented both comrades with the Iron Cross 1st Class. In addition they received a few days' leave.'[41]

The award ceremony did not occur that 'quickly'; rather, it took place almost three weeks later, on 23 March, to allow time for the recommendation paperwork to proceed through proper channels. Göring's award for the honour was approved on 22 March[42] and Loerzer's a day later[43] – likely reflecting normal military bureaucratic processes. On the bright side, however, such presentations were usually very public events, in which the awardees were roundly congratulated by their immediate superiors and peers. Being honoured at a ceremony presided over by the Crown Prince would have reinforced Hermann Göring's sense of self-importance. In this case, the presentation was certainly consistent with Crown Prince Wilhelm's high regard for the two airmen and their unit. In his post-war memoir he wrote:

'With much anticipation, the General Staff officers maintained the closest verbal [telephone] communication with all reconnaissance units, and the splendidly vigorous flyers of … [Feldflieger-] Abteilung 25 – always ready to take-off – speedily earned [my] appreciation and deepest affection … Through their special zeal and daring the aviation Leutnants Göhring [*sic*] and Loerzer, among others, distinguished themselves.'[44]

The Crown Prince's compliment to the FFA 25 crew is all the more meaningful in that, of all the many notable aviators the heir to the German throne encountered during World War I, he singled out only four for such praise in his memoir. In addition to Göring and Loerzer, he also mentioned the forty-victory fighter ace Hauptmann Oswald Boelcke and the staff air officer for the 5th Army, Major Wilhelm Haehnelt.[45]

Between the time of the successful destruction of the armoured tower at the Côte de Talon and the medals award ceremony, however, Loerzer and Göring had a most unpleasant experience. Ignoring bad weather on the morning of Friday, 19 March 1915, the crew took off for a photo-reconnaissance and artillery-ranging mission and seemed to disappear into the mist. Their comrades became worried when the pair did not return within a normal sequence of time. Just after lunch, however, FFA 25 was notified that the missing crew of Albatros B.I 990/14 had been forced to land after the aeroplane's propeller broke. Consequently, they were stranded near the town of Mersch in the German-occupied Grand Duchy of Luxembourg. Abteilungsführer

New Iron Cross 1st Class recipients Göring and Loerzer were congratulated by FFA 25's resident physician Dr. Gimbel.

Blum sent an officer and a mechanic to drive to the site to dismantle the aeroplane and haul it to the nearest aviation facility, at Montmédy. The following day, Loerzer and Göring, apparently unaffected by the experience, resumed their normal activities in the aircraft.[46]

For the rest of March and well into April, Loerzer and Göring devoted all of their flying time to reconnoitring various Verdun-area locations. When Göring spotted new construction at the Côte de Talon,[47] he drew the 5th Army staff's attention to it and monitored the site's progress. Indeed, on 22 April, Loerzer flew Göring along the northeast portion of Verdun so that forty-five aerial photos could be taken of many fortification details.[48] Five days later, Göring made forty-three photos of the area north of the City of Verdun, the citadel and major roads in the area.

On 2 May 1915, in one of the unexplainable anomalies of the German awards system, Bruno Loerzer – but not his continually serving observer, Hermann Göring – received a

significant decoration from the Grand Duchy of Baden. As he had been commissioned into a Badisch infantry regiment, Loerzer had been approved for an award of the Knight's Cross 2nd Class of the Order of the Zähringer Lion with Swords[49] 'as a symbol of particular appreciation for outstanding conduct in the face of the enemy'.[50] In general, German officers' awards were presented more for continual service than for a single heroic act.[51] It was odd that Loerzer, who was in flying school when the war broke out, was honoured while Göring, who had gone to war in a Badisch regiment, did not receive the same award until April. Perhaps that action was a subtle chiding for the unorthodox manner in which he left the regiment to enter the flying corps.

Air to ground communication through wireless radio-telegraphy had been used by dirigibles and tethered observation balloons since 1912,[52] but light-weight transmitting equipment for aeroplanes did not reach the Western Front until December 1914.[53] Given the time needed to distribute equipment to frontline units, it was not until 29 April 1915 that Loerzer

In an early display of vanity, Göring commissioned an artist, Leutnant der Reserve Paul Birnstein (seen here), to paint his portrait after he was awarded the Iron Cross 1st Class. The work may not have been completed, as Birnstein was killed in a crash during pilot training at FEA 9 in Darmstadt on 3 February 1916.

piloted the first flight in which Göring could use that new technology to contact ground units. Radio-telegraphy represented a vast improvement in ranging artillery fire; instead of having to tuck written notes into a pouch or canister to be dropped at the artillery battery, the observer could use Morse code to transmit information to ground radio receiver units. Due to engine and wind noises, the observer could not receive radio-telegraphy messages. Loerzer and Göring continued those missions into May.[54]

War in the Air

In the 1930s Göring's first two biographers created the impression that their subject achieved FFA 25's first air combat success while flying with his close friend Bruno Loerzer. However, the unit's air combat summary to the office of the Feldflugchef [chief of field aviation], submitted on 2 June 1916, showed a different picture. According to that source, on 20 May 1915, the honour of the first aerial "kill" went to twenty-nine-year-old Hauptmann Karl Keck. His pilot, twenty-one-year-old Offizierstellvertreter Adolf Schmidt, brought their aeroplane into position so that Keck could shoot down an enemy aircraft over Fresnoy. Six days later, the same crew downed an enemy aircraft over

FFA 25 comrades Oberleutnant Hellmuth Volkmann (standing by propeller) and Leutnant Huog Weingarth (in the aeroplane) and their ground crew posed while Göring took this photo with his camera.

Vienne,[55] some thirty kilometres west of Verdun. In his nine years in Infanterie-Regiment Nr. 125,[56] Keck had had much experience with the light rifle he would carry aboard his two-seater, thereby providing the marksmanship needed in aerial combat. And his efforts were handsomely rewarded, when, on 21 December 1915, he was awarded the Kingdom of Württemberg's Knight's Cross of the Military Merit Order.[57]

Göring's most significant activity in May occurred on the late afternoon of the 29th, when he flew with a pilot new to FFA 25, Oberleutnant [First Lieutenant] Kurt Wegener, who had been a pilot with the Brieftauben-Abteilung Ostende [carrier pigeon section at Ostende], abbreviated BAO. In fact, Wegener, a pre-war civilian pilot,[58] was one of the founding members of the oddly-named unit. The BAO developed Germany's first dedicated bombing units and was later assigned to fly missions over Verdun. Wegener and Göring flew together again on 30 May in a Rumpler B.I,[59] which was Göring's first 'ride' in that type of two-seat biplane.

Göring's and Loerzer's first aerial engagement came a few days later, when French air units bombed Stenay and FFA 25's airfield. Beginning at 4:30 a.m. on Thursday, 3 June, a force of some thirty French bombers dropped sixty to eighty bombs on the town for the

next two hours.[60] The German aircrews were billeted in Stenay and had to make their way to the outskirts to reach the airfield. Bruno Loerzer described the raid and his and Göring's response in their Albatros two-seater:

'We were awakened … by muffled detonations. It was still dawn [when] the French attacked Stenay with bombs. In great haste we got dressed and set out from our individual rooms as fast as we could through the city [sic] to the airfield. The attack itself was incomprehensible to us, for at that time it was not at all common for high-ranking staff quarters or airfields to be bombarded. The flyers usually left each other's facilities in peace.

'But then it occurred to us that, on the previous day, Crown Princess Cecilie had arrived in Stenay. We found it to be the height of ungallant behaviour that this event had become the unusual cause of a bombing attack. As the bombs of one French squadron came whistling and squealing down while we were running, we jumped adroitly into the protection of a house.

'At the airfield our Abteilungsführer and the other flyers were already in a dug-out. It occurred just as the enemy squadrons had paused. A captured Russian cannon installed on a pedestal in an open square had already slipped so far backwards from the recoil that the barrel stared almost vertically into the heavens.

'We had no fighter aeroplanes at that time. But our new Albatros with its 150-horsepower Benz engine had an outstanding climbing ability. Additionally, the observer had received a [9-mm] Mauser pistol with a clip that held twenty-five rounds that could be fired only a shot at a time. Obviously, the Abteilungsführer had taken it for granted that we would take off in this aeroplane to repel the enemy. As I warmed up the engine, suddenly there appeared in the blue sky a new [French] bombing squadron. In a flash I dashed out of the machine and into a trench that was close by, while the engine continued to run quietly. The bombs fell between the airfield and the headquarters and made … an ear-splitting racket.

'After this bombing, I took off and climbed in circles above Stenay. The mere presence of a German aeroplane had a calming effect on those below, I was told. When I was at about 2,000 metres' altitude, a new formation was heading for Stenay. It was the last squadron. I went toward the enemy at full speed and, I could not believe my eyes, the squadron turned away from the target. They had no machine guns on board and must have assumed by the way I attacked them that I was an enemy with a machine gun. I came in at an oblique angle to the left behind the squadron so that Göring, who was sitting in front of me, could open fire above the propeller arc. The opponent circled high and got away. But I went after him, although I did not get at all close to him. Göring fired off the whole clip of ammunition. Based on my later experiences as a fighter pilot, I must admit that the distance of many hundreds of metres was a little too much for the likelihood of scoring a hit in the air.

'But [when we were] over the frontlines, one of the machines left the formation and made an emergency landing on the French side. Another had also been brought down. We followed the formation until it reached its airfield at Verdun, on which we dropped three small one-kilogram bombs that we happened to have aboard. As we had no bomb-sight and simply dropped them at our own discretion from 2,000 metres, I hardly believe that we hit the airfield or an aeroplane. The drop should simply be noted only as the presence of a German aeroplane over the enemy.

'After the landing we were very well recognised for our brave behaviour by the older flyers. However, when I interjected during Göring's account of the one-sided aerial combat that perhaps the Frenchman had had engine failure from having his machine strongly "forced down", [Göring] became very indignant with me.

'The afternoon brought us another – but more pleasant – surprise. We were invited to have tea with the Crown Princess. In addition to the esteemed recognition, which was expressed with it, we did not forget to devour as much as possible of the pastry and coffee offered. The Crown Princess continually asked questions, and Göring and I talked until the good stuff ran out.'[61]

CHAPTER FOUR
EARLY AERIAL COMBATS

'I seem to come alive when I am up in the air and looking down on the earth. I feel like a little god.'[1]

HERMANN GÖRING

After their audacious attack against French bombers on 3 June 1915, Hermann Göring and Bruno Loerzer were welcomed warmly by their brother airmen in Feldflieger-Abteilung 25's officers' mess, just as Hauptmann Karl Keck and Offizierstellvertreter Adolf Schmidt had been. Granted, Keck's use of a rifle had produced a more decisive outcome, but Göring's action in forcing back the attackers – with a pistol – was cause for celebration.[2] Even Göring's detractors, who considered him a loud-mouth bluffer, recognised that this time the bluff paid off.

At 3:30 a.m. the following day, Loerzer took off with Göring in their Albatros B.I (B 990/14) to bomb Beaumont, immediately north of Douaumont. In addition to demonstrating their battle readiness to their adversaries, the pistol-armed Loerzer-Göring team would be in the air to greet any French airmen intent on carrying out a follow-up raid on Stenay. The mission turned out to be uneventful, but, that evening, when a Bavarian artillery unit alerted FFA 25 that French aircraft were approaching Stenay, Loerzer and Göring set out to find them. Their search was in vain,[3] but they showed their comrades once again that they were eager to engage the enemy in the air. Consequently, when Oberleutnant [First Lieutenant] Dr. Kurt Wegener scheduled a flight to Freiburg to determine whether a captured French-made machine gun was suitable for mounting on his aeroplane, Göring was an eager companion. To Wegener's dismay, the weapon, fully loaded with 600 rounds of ammunition, weighed fifty-five kilos, which was too heavy for his lightly-powered Aviatik B.II to carry in the air.[4]

On Thursday, 17 June 1915, Göring flew with the two-time air combat victor Offizierstellvertreter Adolf Schmidt – and in a much different aeroplane, an Albatros C.I two-seater. The newer machine was the sign of things to come in German reconnaissance aviation. The pilot sat in front and the observer in the rear and was armed with a ring-mounted flexible machine gun that could be elevated and lowered and swung from side to side to fire in a wide defensive arc.

Before he became too enamoured of the new two-seater, however, Göring heard from other pilots about Dutch-born aircraft designer Anthony Fokker's new single-seat Eindeckers [monoplane fighter aircraft]. It was only a matter of time before Göring followed Loerzer's lead and become a pilot; thus, he was especially interested in the

With its machine gun synchronised to fire through the propeller arc, the Fokker Eindecker enjoyed a brief advantage over other conventional front-engine aircraft.

Fokker aeroplane's advantages over the C.I biplanes. As General der Kavallerie [equal to a U.S. lieutenant general] Ernst von Hoeppner, the World War I commander of the German Lufstreitkräfte [literally air force], later wrote:

'The true *Kampfflugzeug* [combat aeroplane] originated first with the utilisation of Fokker's invention, which made it possible to fire [a machine gun] through the propeller arc. The fixed [forward-firing] machine gun was now operated by the pilot himself. The removal of the observer produced in this new [single-seat] E-type aeroplane extraordinary speed, manoeuvrability and climbing ability; these attributes identified the dedicated combat aeroplane. In the hands of a determined pilot, the Fokker Eindeckers very soon became the real fear of our enemies.'[5]

Fokker's 'invention' – actually, a refinement of existing technology – was the interrupter gear. His engineers developed a push-rod gear that interrupted the gun's firing sequence when the propeller blade was in front of the gun's muzzle.[6] Interrupter gears were so effective that they were also applied to pilots' stations in new two-seaters.

The synchronised machine gun added to the allure of combat in the skies. Göring noted later: 'When the Fokker single-seat fighters arrived at frontline [units], I requested permission to become a pilot. [And] on 1 July 1915, I reported to the [Aviatik] flying school in Freiburg.'[7] Loerzer also temporarily departed from FFA 25 at this time, to receive fighter aircraft training at Fokker's flying school in the town of Görries in the Grand Duchy of Mecklenburg-Schwerin – also beginning on Thursday, 1 July.[8]

The Nieuport 11, a captured example of which is seen here, had no synchronisation gear and relied on firing over the propeller arc, which was not as efficient as the Fokker Eindecker it faced.

When Hermann Göring was almost three-quarters of the way through the ten-week course at Freiburg he received a pleasant surprise. In a brief ceremony at the flying school, which was located in Baden, he was presented with the Grand Duchy's impressive looking Knight's Cross 2nd Class of the Order of the Zähringer Lion with Swords.[9] As aviation awards expert Neal W. O'Connor observed: '… [It] is considered to be the most attractive of all Imperial German orders insignia because …instead of the usual enamelled arms of [the award's] crosses, they are … made of dark green crystal. The effect is further enhanced by a delicate gold filigree that appears between the arms of the crosses.'[10] The award honoured Baden's centuries-old House of Zähringen,[11] but, given Göring's love of fantasy, it is easy to see him as being quite taken with receiving such a chivalric-sounding honour, if only a second-class knighthood. He surely sensed there would be more and higher awards to come.

While Göring continued to develop his piloting skills, Loerzer returned to FFA 25 as a Fokker-qualified pilot on 2 August.[12] But, at that time, the unit had no Fokker E.I monoplane fighters and he was posted temporarily to a nearby unit, FFA 60, in hopes of finding a better use for his new talents; he did not return to FFA 25 until 2 October.[13]

A New Commander

On Sunday, 13 August, Hauptmann Ernst Blum handed over command of FFA 25 to Hauptmann Leo Leonhardy, a career officer who had recently flown as an observer with FFA 59 on the Russian Front.[14] Blum did not seem to be suited to a command position. His tolerance of near insubordination when Göring and Loerzer reported to the unit and his allowing Göring to dominate the Crown Prince's briefings were examples of the Abteilungsführer's lack of the iron-willed command ability expected of a German officer. As Blum's records show, however, he became more successful back in infantry operations. Leonhardy, on the other hand, had strong leadership and organisational skills, as well as a better sense of his immediate environment. For example, he viewed Crown Prince Wilhelm's interest in aviation as a way to improve the unit and his own career prospects and, as will be seen, Leonhardy took advantage of both.

Under Leonhardy's command, FFA 25's air operations were directed south-westward, into the 3rd Army Sector in France's Champagne region. Commenting on events prior to the next offensive, which began later in September, Leonhardy wrote:

The Knight's Cross 2nd Class of the Order of the Zähringer Lion with Swords, established on 16 December 1812, was the first non-Prussian award presented to Göring.

'A new, very interesting and highly responsible assignment developed for me from this [coming] offensive. My Abteilung, which consisted of six aeroplanes, was strengthened to twenty-two aeroplanes and assigned to Generaloberst [Colonel-General, equal to U.S. four-star general] Karl von Einem at Vouziers. This merry little throng of a single Flieger-Abteilung, thrown together without non-commissioned officers to rein it in, was at that time more difficult to look after than a sack of fleas. But, as we were all in agreement about what we had to accomplish, the inner frictions were soon lost. Among those transferred into the unit were some single-seater pilots, who brought with them the first Fokker fighters with forward-firing [synchronised] machine guns. These aeroplanes had an outstanding forward field of fire ... [that] gave us a significant technical superiority ...'[15]

The new Abteilungsführer was buoyed when, on Wednesday, 1 September, FFA 25 logged its third aerial victory. At about 6:00 p.m., Offizierstellvertreter Adolf Schmidt was at the controls of a two-seat reconnaissance aeroplane, which encountered a French aeroplane over Vauquois, west of Verdun, and shot it down.[16] As was Fliegertruppe practice at the time, Schmidt and his observer, Leutnant der Reserve Walther Wuthmann, each received credit for downing the French aircraft.[17] The twenty-nine-year-old observer and his pilot, age twenty-six, became the latest heroes of the officers' mess, but their celebrity status lasted only a week. On the following Wednesday, 8 September 1915, they were returning from an aerial combat in which their Ago C.I two-seater had been badly shot up when,

The bodies of Leutnant der Reserve Walther Wuthmann and Offizierstellvertreter Adolf Schmidt were returned to FFA 25, where funeral services were held in a hangar. The men's awards were laid out on black velvet *Ordens-Kissen* [awards pillows] that were draped over the coffins.

just as it seemed they would make a normal landing, their aeroplane suddenly crashed to the ground at Stenay airfield and both men were killed.[18]

Hermann Göring completed his pilot's qualifications a week later, on 15 September, but was not returned to FFA 25 to fill the vacancy left by the loss of Schmidt and Wuthmann. The replacement of one aircrew was not a priority matter in view of the broad changes taking place in eastern France, where German units, in full expectation of an attack, were working with feverish energy to strengthen their defences'[19]. As an earlier part of those preparations, a multi-purpose reconnaissance and bombing unit, a so-called 'carrier pigeon section' named Brieftauben-Abteilung Metz (BAM), was formed on 17 August at a key aviation depot in Döberitz,[20] outside Berlin, for eventual use in operations in the Champagne and Verdun sectors. The BAM was not yet ready for deployment and, in mid-September, elements of the original multi-purpose unit, the Brieftauben-Abteilung Ostende (BAO), were transferred from Flanders to the German 3rd Army sector,[21] to support German ground fighting in that area.

While those events were occurring, Göring was assigned for two weeks to the regional aviation depot Armee-Flugpark 5[22] at the old fortress city of Montmédy, west of Stenay. He had no real duties at AFP 5 and, hence, no opportunity to make qualifying flights for his pilot's badge. Soon he began to chafe at still having to wear 'only' an observer's badge. Inactivity and Göring's ever-busy mind were a bad combination; consequently, he caused trouble when his curiosity led him to enquire about the new Fokker monoplane's rotary engine. He was familiar with the stationary engine, which was bolted to the aeroplane's frame, with pistons driving a crankshaft that turned the propeller and powered the machine. But he had no experience with the rotary engine in which the crankshaft remained attached to the aeroplane and the cylinders and engine rotated around it; the propeller was bolted to the engine and the resulting rotation of both powered the aeroplane. Göring knew the lighter-weight rotary engine ran smoother and was cooled by its own motion, but he wanted to learn more about it.

Hermann Göring marked the completion of his pilot's qualifications by posing in his training aeroplane at Freiburg.

Munich-based journalist Walter Zuerl, who in the 1930s wrote extensively about World War I flyers and heard many stories first-hand, related the following (never refuted) anecdote about Göring's introduction to the rotary-engine Fokker aeroplane:

'One day [Göring] came … to Armee-Flugpark 5 at Montmédy and asked whether he could try the rotary engine of a Fokker. There was no opposition. Why should an observer not be allowed to try running the engine of an aeroplane that has been parked? Göring had the engine explained to him, let it run for a while, [then] had the brake-blocks [chocks] pulled from in front of the wheels, gave it the gas and flew off in the … brand-new Fokker machine, which was the gem of the Armee-Flugpark. Everyone looked into the sky in horror as the aeroplane circled overhead. The pilot came roaring down and in his mind's eye every person there could see the Fokker taking a dip [in a nearby pond]. The first attempted landing had to be aborted, the second approach was too long, but the third was perfect. [After viewing this display] the Flugpark commander was really irritated and his adjutant, Hauptmann Hans von Kloesterlein, who had given [Göring] permission, received a strong reprimand.'[23]

Göring walked from the scene of his misdeed unscathed and without a care about the condition of the aeroplane, the consequences to the officer who allowed him to 'try the engine' or the risk to his own life by flying an unfamiliar aircraft. He seemed to have no fear and, as seen on other occasions, concentrated on whatever interested him. At that moment he focused on flying because, as he commented later: 'I seem to come alive when I am up in the air and looking down on the earth. I feel like a little god.'[24]

Following a post-World War II interview with Göring, U.S. Army psychologist Dr. Gustave M. Gilbert saw such behaviour in another light:

'In examining his feelings about danger, Göring admitted that he just never believed that any harm could really befall him. His fantasy life, it seems, conveniently carried over to real life to protect him from the anxiety of dangerous realities. The insensitive extrovert could thus satisfy his drive for physical stimulation and excitement while acting out his fantasies as a fearless hero who scorned danger. Whatever the reasons, the early signs of aggressive leadership qualities were unmistakable.'[25]

Loerzer was not very busy at FFA 60 and travelled easily to Montmédy to visit his friend. Hence, on the afternoon of Friday, 17 September, they were allowed to flight test a Luft-Verkehrs-Gesellschaft LVG B.I (serial number B 294/14).[26] It was like old times, with Loerzer in the pilot's seat behind Göring, who was in the observer's front seat. Their flight was uneventful, but it was good to be in the air again. On succeeding days the two men maintained their flying proficiency in other – albeit older – B-type machines, but that slow period must have made them wonder why they had gone off for further training and when they would return to combat.

Göring got lucky on Saturday, 23 September, when he received his first 'official' assignment as a pilot.[27] He was directed to use an Albatros B.I (serial number B 106/15) to fly an important staff officer, Hauptmann Helmuth Wilberg, from Montmédy to an airfield near Metz, where he would inspect Flieger-Abteilung (A) 203, one of six new two-seater units[28] dedicated to aerial reconnaissance and wireless telegraphy-supported artillery spotting. The German flying corps was beginning a reorganisation and these units were established as part of that process.

Even though Göring completed pilot's training, when he posed for this photo, he had not yet earned his pilot's badge and, thus, still wore his observer's badge. Hauptmann Wilberg is on the left and Oberleutnant Berr on the right.

As it turned out, Wilberg became a valuable contact for Göring. The thirty-five-year-old Hauptmann[29] had commanded FFA 11 at the outbreak of the war[30] and, beginning on 27 July 1915, he became Stabsoffizier der Flieger [staff officer for aviation] for a succession of individual army staffs.[31] After Göring's second flight with Wilberg, from Stenay to Metz on 24 September, Wilberg introduced him to a pilot of rising prominence, Oberleutnant Hans Berr. A former observer with FFA 60 who had become a pilot,[32] Berr went on to command a fighter unit that Göring later joined. The German flying corps was a 'young' branch of service in 1915 and Wilberg's introduction put Göring into a network of personal connections that aided current and prospective commanders in selecting people for their units.

While serving as Wilberg's aerial chauffeur, Göring was well away from the chaos at the frontlines when the French offensive began early on the morning of Saturday, 25 September. He did not miss much, according to Leonhardy, who described part of the confusion that prevailed:

'Throughout the French surprise attack, an understandable nervousness had broken out in the trenches among our [German] brethren who blamed the activities of the enemy flyers for the bombardments and attacks. [And] our own flyers often caused a commotion among German troops. I recall that … five aeroplanes, one after another, had to be sent to [a point designated as] Kanonenberg to drive off the continually increasing and allegedly enemy aeroplanes that were circling overhead. When, after dispatching the fifth machine, yet another call for help rattled from the telephone, I flew there myself – and became the sixth "enemy" flyer [over the area].'[33]

Aviation was then a new phenomenon that was incomprehensible to many senior German officers. Consequently, they were uncertain how to make use of it in modern warfare, noted Leonhardy, who wrote:

'Incredibly, people [at 3rd Army headquarters] had not believed the assessment that the staff officer for aviation prepared based on aerial reconnaissance photographs … We flyers were very annoyed, but it should be explained that our general staff's knowledge about the flying corps had to be built up. Having them employ this new … air weapon as a [planning] factor and placing trust in the flyers' reports was something that, especially among the older general staff officers, occurred only gradually.'[34]

In any event, there was still much to do when Göring reported back to FFA 25 on 1 October,[35] the day the unit relocated to Vouziers airfield. He noted: 'During the Champagne Offensive, I flew with my observer[s] in the 3rd Army Sector and carried out long-range reconnaissance along the line from Epernay to Châlons to St. Ménéhould.'[36] FAA 25 records show that, from 2 October to 5 December, he flew with several observers on various operational assignments.[37]

Loerzer returned to FFA 25 the following day[38] and found it to be more tightly run under Hauptmann Leonhardy, whose combination of military organisational talent and personal bravery led him to become one of five bomber group commanders to earn

Prussia's [*de facto* Germany's] highest bravery award, the Ordern Pour le Mérite, in late 1918.[39] There was no questioning Leonhardy's orders or, as had occurred earlier, of FFA 25 crews (e.g., Göring and Loerzer) arranging their own flights together. Moreover, with Göring now flying as a two-seater pilot, Loerzer moved on to other assignments as a fighter pilot.

Always interested in showing his personal status, Göring took this photograph of the stately old house he lived in while based at Vouziers.

On the morning of Sunday, 3 October, Göring made his first flight over the lines in the pilot's seat, at the controls of an Albatros C.I (serial number C 486/15). By this time C-type aircraft on the Western Front had been equipped with machine guns[40] and now he had his own forward-firing machine gun to complement the flexible gun used by his backseat man, Unteroffizier [Corporal] Mayer. It was most unusual for a German officer pilot to have an enlisted observer, so Mayer may been a pilot himself, serving as an aerial gunner and back-up pilot in the event Göring had a problem while qualifying for his pilot's badge. Göring and Mayer joined two other two-seater crews in a two-hour flight along the left flank of the 3rd Army in the Champagne Sector. The three aeroplanes reported being involved in seven air combats during the flight.[41] Göring, in typically dramatic form, added to his report that he (and, presumably, Mayer) had 'fought off seven French aeroplanes one after the other'.[42]

According to an FFA 25 summary, the unit's only successful air combat on 3 October took place later that morning. To provide combat experience to newly arrived airmen from other Feldflieger-Abteilungen, mixed-unit crews were sent out on missions. Thus, FFA 25's Leutnant Ehrhardt (pilot) flew with FFA 34's Leutnant Bernert (observer) when they encountered and claimed to have shot down a French aeroplane at 11:00 a.m. near Tahure, twenty kilometres south of Vouziers.[43] However, French records list no air combat casualties that day,[44] which calls the victory into question, as French loss records needed to be accurate to justify ordering replacement aircraft and personnel. Other World War I belligerents' aircraft loss records are generally accurate for the same reason.

Göring and Mayer made an uneventful observation and orientation flight the following afternoon[45] and apparently were not involved in the encounter in which the mixed unit crew of FFA 25's Vizefeldwebel [Sergeant-Major] Schramm (pilot) and FFA 44's Leutnant Cammann (observer) attacked an enemy machine at 5:00 p.m. over Suippes,[46] about twelve kilometres southwest of Vouziers. Schramm and Cammann were credited with an aerial victory; no French losses were recorded,[47] which, once again, makes their claim questionable.

Göring flew with other enlisted backseat men in succeeding days and, while he reported some air combat activity, he did not attain the success that his FFA 25 comrades Leutnant der Reserve Schülke and Oberleutnant Veiel did on the morning of Monday, 11 October, when they shot down an enemy aircraft over Montlainville.[48] Or on the 12th, when, at 5:25 p.m., the team of Vizefeldwebel Schramm and Leutnant Cammann scored FFA 25's seventh aerial victory, an enemy aeroplane shot down south of Tahure, and, five minutes later, Leutnant Kaehler and Oberleutnant Kirsch attained the unit's eighth air combat triumph a short distance away.[49] It is likely that one of these crews was responsible for bringing down the French Voisin two-seat bomber from Escadrille VB 112 crewed by Soldat [Private] Bremond and Lieutenant du Beauviez, who were forced to make an emergency landing within German lines in that area and were taken prisoner, as confirmed by French loss records.[50]

A captured French Voisin two-seater of the type brought down by FFA 25 on 12 October 1915. Note that German national markings were applied for testing the aircraft within German-held territory.

There can be no doubt that celebration of two aerial victories in the officers' mess eclipsed Göring's own special event that day as finally, he received his pilot's badge.[51] Once again, he had attained the mark of status that he wanted.

On flights at the end of October and early November, Göring flew with Rittmeister [Cavalry Captain] Eduard Ziegler, an officer for whom FFA 25 leader Leo Leonhardy had high regard. As Leonhardy later wrote, the unit had a 'really hard worker in … old Rittmeister Ziegler, who I got from the staff of an infantry brigade. This man … secretly trained as a pilot at the nearby Armee-Flugpark and eventually flew two or three times a day as observer with … Göring against the enemy and finished off many an enemy aeroplane, which then adorned our hangars as trophies.'[52]

Leonhardy's praise was well intentioned, but Göring never attained an aerial victory with Ziegler, who went on to command FFA 25 and, later, a bomber unit.[53] Göring and Ziegler flew a series of local air defence missions that were called *Sperreflüge* [blockade or barrier flights],[54] intended to keep enemy aircraft from penetrating German lines. These flights of rotating shifts of aircraft were supposed to maintain a form of defensive perimeter in the air. Ground operations in World War I became static and led to a vast network of trenches from the Belgian coast to the Swiss border and the 'barrier flights' were seen as their aerial equivalent. Barrier flights could not and did not serve that purpose and when they were suspended temporarily, Göring was able to truly shoot down an enemy aeroplane.

Göring's First Aerial Victory

What became known as the Second Battle of the Champagne ended on 6 November 1915,[55] but German ground and air units remained on alert. Hence, on Tuesday, 16 November, Göring and an observer from FFA 34, the previously mentioned Leutnant Bernert, departed Vouziers at 1:30 p.m. on a flight to enable the observer to obtain current photographs of French positions at Tahure. Flying in Göring's trusty Albatros C.I C 486/15,[56] Bernert concentrated on the natural defences of the city's banked hills and a portion of the city with a heavily wooded area. Some thirty-five kilometres east of the great commercial and industrial city of Reims, Tahure remained a prime target in any action against the larger community. Almost an hour into the flight, the Albatros was attacked by a French Farman biplane. A fight ensued, after which German ground observers reported seeing the French aeroplane fall from the sky. The news travelled fast and upon the Göring-Bernert team's return to Vouziers, they were hailed for scoring FFA 25's ninth aerial victory.[57]

Göring and Bernert each were awarded confirmation for an aerial victory in this action.[58] That practice was deceptive, as it inflated the total count of enemy aircraft brought down; with later refinements, the system of awarding aerial victories granted each crewman in a two-seater a half-victory in such events. Whether the Farman claimed by Göring and Bernert was destroyed or put out of commission is questionable, as French records show no air combat losses at all that day.[59] It is possible the French aircraft appeared to have been hit and made it safely to a friendly landing spot. In any case, all of Göring's subsequent records listed the 16 November 1915 engagement as his first confirmed aerial victory. Under the old system, it was also the second victory for Leutnant

A popular German postcard series showed this captured Maurice Farman MF 7 two-seater of the type brought down by Göring and Bernert.

Bernert, who apparently shot down no additional enemy aircraft.[60]

For most of the following week, Göring and Rittmeister Ziegler resumed making barrier flights. As fighting intensified in the Champagne Sector, FFA 25 moved back to Stenay to make room at Vouziers for aeroplanes from the BAO[61] and other air units arriving from western France and Belgium as the force build-up continued – with a view toward the German offensive against Verdun, set to begin in just over two months.[62]

In preparation for the offensive, on 1 December, Major Hermann von der Lieth-Thomsen, the Feldflugchef [chief of field operations], ordered the establishment of two major operational units that would evolve into Germany's dedicated bombing groups. The units, designated as *Kampfgeschwader der obersten Heeresleitung* [combat wings of the supreme high command] and identified by the acronym Kagohl, were to be deployed at the discretion of the high command (rather than individual army headquarters or corps commands).

Göring was back at his old airfield when an interesting challenge was presented. He and Leutnant Emil Flörke, an observer, were dispatched to Gotha in Thuringia, in eastern Germany, to ferry a new aeroplane across Germany and back to Stenay. It was FFA 25's first two-engine G-type, the designator for *Grosskampfflugzeug* [big combat aeroplane].

Göring was a model of self-confidence when he and Flörke set out for the Gotha aircraft factory's plant. However, a day short of three weeks later, on 14 December, a telegram arrived at FFA 25 to inform Hauptmann Leonhardy that the brand-new big bomber had crashed at the factory airfield due to failure of landing gear clamps. Both crewmen had been hospitalised; Flörke lost a quantity of blood and Göring suffered a knee injury.

Göring and Leutnant Emil Flörke had high hopes of flying a Gotha G.I, such as the one seen here, but they were dashed when the big bomber crashed at the factory airfield.

Göring was subdued as he and Flörke made a quiet return to Stenay and resumed a combat flight schedule that, according to FFA 25 records, contained no major events. He was not faulted for the crash of the Gotha G.I and, indeed, would later receive a two-engined replacement aeroplane. As Abteilungsführer Leonhardy recalled, the year 1915 ended on a note of confidence and a sense of readiness for the major battle to come in the new year:

> 'Despite French efforts in December, we remained masters of the entire battle line and were released [from frontline duties] with the heartfelt thanks of the 3rd Army commander. We flew back to the Crown Prince's sector, where initial preparations for the Verdun Offensive had already begun.'[63]

CHAPTER FIVE
AIR WAR OVER VERDUN

'Göring is a daredevil of the wickedest kind.
Recently, when he was over the lines, he began to spiral down
and shoot wildly at the trenches below.'

CASPAR KULENKAMPFF-POST

It is remarkable that, in all of the coverage devoted to Hermann Göring's life events, none of his biographers has delved into his combat flights during one of the most savage battles in history: the German siege of Verdun in 1916. He was only one of many pilots in that battle, but he fought long, hard and bravely in it. In contrast to embellishments seen in some of his own accounts, Göring's service at Verdun is recorded in reliable official reports and in comments by men with whom he fought.

The Prelude
German Army Chief of Staff Erich von Falkenhayn sought to knock France out of the war early in a battle of attrition intended to inflict huge losses at a vulnerable point 'for the retention of which the French command would be compelled to throw in every man they have'.[1] He selected Verdun for its symbolic value as 'the ancient gate of the west through which the German hordes had passed to attack the Gauls'.[2] German frontline sectors had already been named after characters from Teutonic mythology, as evidenced by the combat area opposite Verdun, which bore the name of Kriemhild, the vengeful she-devil of legend. The ferocious German attack would live up to the name. Facilitating the impending carnage, the battle lines at the time placed Verdun in a salient with German forces on three sides, creating a 'self-contained slaughterhouse, the flanks of which need not be extended'.[3] Moreover, the old fortress complex had not been well maintained in the years immediately before the war and, based on early German advances in 1914, the effectiveness of such structures was questioned following the German destruction of concrete-reinforced defensive fortifications in Belgium. An abundant variety of German heavy artillery – their fire directed by wireless telegraph-equipped aeroplanes – completed what seemed to be a perfect offensive plan.

Complementing the big guns deployed at the Battle of Verdun, German air planners assigned a number of the new AEG G.II two-engine aeroplanes to units of the 5th Army. Built by the Allgemeine Elektrizitäts-Gesellschaft [General Electric Company][4], abbreviated AEG, the G.II was that manufacturer's second model in its outstanding series of bombers. Over time it 'proved to be a most efficient bombing aeroplane, easy to fly and maintain and of a robust construction that endeared it to its hard-working three- to

60

AEG G.II 27/15 (left) was FFA 25's second twin-engined reconnaissance and bomber aircraft. Göring's aircraft, serial numbered 49/15, is in the centre of this photograph taken by Göring.

four-man crews'.[5] To compensate Göring for the loss of the Gotha G.I he was supposed to fly in combat, but lost in a crash for which he was not responsible, he would be assigned to fly the first AEG G.II (G 49/15) delivered to Feldflieger-Abteilung 25 at Stenay.

Until then, Göring spent most of January 1916 flying the Albatros C.I (C 486/15) previously assigned to him. FFA 25 records show he divided his time flying Leutnants Walter Kaehler and Otto Schmidt on routine reconnaissance missions along the periphery of Verdun. During a flight with Kaehler on 29 January, French ground fire hit the aeroplane ten times but did not impede its mission.[6]

On Tuesday, 8 February 1916, the big AEG was approved for frontline service. Göring flew familiarisation missions on several occasions, preparing, as were the two Kampfgschwaders [combat wings] also assigned AEG G.II aircraft, for the battle that soldiers on both sides of the lines knew was coming. There was one slight hitch in plans for the Verdun offensive, but they were soon resolved as FFA 25's leader, Hauptmann Leo Leonhardy, wrote later:

'To conceal our advance against Verdun, the supreme high command transferred … Kampfgeschwader 1 and 2 to the 5th Army Sector, where they would be used mainly for the previously mentioned "barrier flights" [aimed at blocking allied flights over German territory]. Actually, we succeeded in keeping secret from the enemy all of our …preparations for German troops until, on 10 February 1916, the date for the beginning of the attack, an [officer] of non-German descent deserted to the enemy with a copy of the attack order.

'Then, due to heavy rain soaking the ground, the attack could not begin until 21 February and, as a result of this …delay, the French gained time to make counter preparations. Despite those efforts, the breakthrough succeeded as planned …

'Once the attack became known, the flying gangs in the skies increased greatly and there was an air battle during every flight.'[7]

The Battle Begins

The German artillery bombardment of the Verdun fortifications, as well as villages and other positions on both banks of the Meuse river, began at 7:15 a.m. on a cold, dry Monday, 21 February 1916. Some 1,250 guns of varying calibres caused nearly complete devastation along a fifteen-mile frontline.[8] Hauptmann Leonhardy, one of the first aerial observers of the onslaught on that day, reported:

'… Over Caures Wood, I saw the breakthrough site. Entire French concrete bombproof command bunkers were raised out of the ground and hurled forward. Where a dud forty-two-centimetre shell lay one could see just how the impact threw up a fountain of dirt.'[9]

The AEG G.II bomber in which Göring flew with his new crew of the past few days, Oberleutnant von Schaesberg-Thannheim and Vizefeldwebel Boje, was also in the air that morning.[10] From 10:00 a.m. until 1:30 p.m., they also observed the horrifying effects of the big shells hitting and causing the earth to vomit huge chunks of every form of material on the ground. They were back at their airfield when, at 4:45 p.m.,[11] swarms of German infantrymen advanced in a methodical battle formation four and a half miles wide, marking a stunning first day's operation.

The following morning, Göring and Schaesberg-Thannheim (generally referred to as Schaesberg) went back up over the battle area, this time with two aerial gunners, Leutnant Parisius and Unteroffizier Röder. With the aeroplane at its full crew capacity – one gunner in the forward station and one in the aft cockpit – the AEG G.II crew was ready for action when a French aeroplane tried to interrupt

Göring struck a determined pose for this view of him at the controls of AEG G.II 49/15.

the observer's aerial photography work. The intruder was warded off, but not shot down.[12]

Over succeeding days other members of FFA 25 wanted to be a part of the aerial triumph or at least to gain some experience flying over the battlefront. Thus, during the early afternoon of Saturday, 26 February, Göring flew with Rittmeister Kirchhoff in the observer's seat and *Assistent-Artz* [assistant physician] Dr. Gimbel in one of the gunners' stations. Apparently, the zeal to be in combat overshadowed the physician's commitment to the medical profession's precept 'first, do no harm'. In any event, the flight was unchallenged.[13]

For the next two weeks, Göring and his observer, Julius Graf [Count] von Schaesberg, the scion of a landed aristocratic family from the Kingdom of Württemberg, flew mostly short-range reconnaissance missions to track the progress of German ground forces.[14] Their flight on the early afternoon of Saturday, 13 March 1916, was without incident. But that was not the case with the FFA 25 crew of twenty-three-year-old Leutnant der Reserve Ludwig Kienlin and his observer, Oberleutnant Franz Freiherr [Baron] von Linden, age twenty-five, who were shot down and killed in an air fight with a French Maurice Farman two-seater near Chattancourt, a few kilometres northwest of Verdun. The French crewmen, Sergent Hott and Sous-lieutenant Naudeau of Escadrille MF 228, were credited with their first aerial victories.[15]

The following morning, Schaesberg avenged his comrade's death by shooting down a French aeroplane. The day began with a German ground assault against *Le Mort Homme* [Dead Man's Hill], an important high spot west of the Meuse river and Verdun. A few hours later, Göring flew his AEG G.II over contested territory on the east side of the river, where they were attacked by a trio of French Caudron G.4 two-engine two-seat aeroplanes. Schaesberg's combat report described the encounter:

'Aerial combat with three French big combat aeroplanes (Caudrons): After about fifteen minutes of fighting I was able to down one of these enemy aeroplanes, which, suddenly approaching from the frontlines, tried to cut us off. In a steep glide the Caudron flew back toward the French lines. The left engine was burning. Leutnant Göring pursued [it] in a dive and thereby forced the enemy aeroplane to land within our lines (southeast edge of Haumont Forest). We circled several times at fifty metres altitude over the landed opponent until its capture by speedily approaching [ground] personnel. [At] 12 o'clock [we made an] intermediate landing in Jametz and [made an] immediate report about the incident by telephone.'[16]

Göring's Second Victory

After examining the Caudron on the ground, Schaesberg also noted in his report that the French aeroplane had taken twelve hits and that the two crew men appeared to be uninjured. The downed French aeroplane was listed first as FFA 25's tenth aerial victory. Then, following the custom of the time, victory was also shared equally by Schaesberg, Göring and gunner Boje[17] – even though Göring, piloting the big AEG, was unarmed and, thus, had not fired a shot. It is listed in all of his service records as 'his' second aerial victory.

Back on the ground and quick to recognise an opportunity for personal recognition, Göring went directly from his aeroplane to Stenay airfield's motor pool, where he requisitioned a car and driver to take him to the Caudron landing site. After a cursory examination of 'his' prize, Göring directed the captured French aircrew – Sergent Gaston Depèche and Sous-Lieutenant Georges Theremin of Escadrille C 6 – into the car and had them driven to the airfield. Göring often carried a small personal camera with him and, at Stenay, he arranged for one of his friends to photograph his triumphant arrival. He had photos taken of Schaesberg and himself with the two French flyers sitting in the car's backseat, but the 'choice view' showed only Göring and the Frenchmen about to step out of the car and be welcomed by General der Infanterie [equal to a U.S. lieutenant general] Hans von Zwehl of the 5th Army staff. No doubt, Göring would have preferred to have Crown Prince Wilhelm in the photo or the 5th Army Chief of Staff, General Konstantin Schmidt von Knobelsdorf, but General von Zwehl was in overall charge of daily operations during the siege of Verdun and enjoyed considerable prestige.

Göring sat in the back seat of the car that brought his two French prisoners of war to be presented to General der Infanterie Hans von Zwehl of the 5th Army Staff (left).

The following day, 15 March, Göring had the more prosaic task of selecting a new pilot to replace Leutnant der Reserve Ludwig Kienlin, the pilot who had been killed on 13 March. Göring was driven to Armee-Flugpark 5 at Montmédy, where he met twenty-two-year-old Unteroffizier Wilhelm Hübener in whose brief biographical article the encounter was described:

'Unassigned crews which had recently completed training at the various Flieger-Ersatz-Abteilungen scattered throughout Germany were demonstrating their newly acquired avocations to a small group of [aviation] observers.

'Each of the interested onlookers was an officer sent … by a frontline flying section to use his … judgement in choosing a suitable replacement for his unit.

'After a particularly skilful "set-down" by one of the Albatros B.IIs on the hillside landing field, one of the officers … strolled out to the training aircraft. "Allow me to introduce myself," he said to the young aspirant in the pilot's cockpit. "I am Leutnant Göring. I am attached to Feldflieger-Abteilung 25 and we would like you to join us at Stenay."'[18]

After arriving at Stenay, Hübener spotted the airfield's new trophy:

'The Caudron was a prize of war and after it was towed to the Abteilung's landing field, it became a major curiosity. All of the officers of the [5th] Army Staff paid a visit to view the relic. Crown Prince Wilhelm … came several times to putter with the captured aircraft. After a few such visits the over-worked mechanics would groan at his arrival, for they were well aware that it would be they who would have to clean off the smudges of grease and the castor oil spatters that His Imperial Highness would invariably leave.'[19]

The Caudron G.IV captured by Göring, Julius Graf von Schaesberg-Thannheim and an aerial gunner was displayed in a FFA 25 hangar for all to admire.

The Caudron G.4 was powered by two eighty-horsepower Le Rhône rotary engines,[20] which were lubricated by a constant flow of light-weight castor oil, most of which was burned off by the heat of the cylinders that it lubricated. As the Crown Prince no doubt became fascinated by the sight of an entire engine that rotated, he may have been tempted to tug at the propeller to watch it turn the engine – and been less concerned about the resulting flow of liquid from the oil reservoir that accompanied each motion.

At about this time Hübener was pleasantly surprised to learn that one of his FFA 25 comrades was also a hometown friend from Bremen, twenty-year-old Leutnant Caspar Kulenkampff-Post (generally referred to as Kulenkampff). Hübener's biography noted:

> 'The fact that Hübener and Kulenkampff were new to combat flying necessitated a "switching around" in the make-up of the crews. Leutnant Göring was given the tall, blond and good-natured Kulenkampff for an observer, while Graf von Schaesberg … was assigned to "tap the helmet" of the new pilot, Unteroffizier Hübener.'[21]

Kulenkampff was a bright young man for whom the outbreak of war meant not being able to accept a Rhodes scholarship to Oxford in September 1914.[22] An avid and skilled horseman, he accepted a commission into Uhlan Regiment Nr. 15. When trench warfare obviated the need for mounted troops to cross the battle lines swiftly, Kulenkampff applied for aviation training and, in November 1915, he was assigned to the *Flieger-Beobachterschule* [aviation observer school] at Königsberg[23] on the barren Baltic coast in East Prussia. Upon completion of the course of study, he was assigned to FFA 25.

Oberleutnant Graf von Schaesberg-Thannheim (rear seat) and Unteroffizier Wilhelm Hübener seen preparing for take-off in an Albatros C.V reconnaissance aeroplane.

Kulenkampff flew reconnaissance missions with Göring in an AEG G.II for the rest of March. Although the aeroplane was, technically speaking, a bomber, it was widely successful as a flying gun platform. In the hands of a skilled pilot such as Göring, the two aerial gunners could be brought to bear very effectively against enemy flyers who might try to impede the AEG's observer.

Kulenkampff wrote home often and, as seen in a posthumously published collection of his letters, he kept his family informed on a variety of activities. On 22 March, he described his flying missions and his surroundings:

Leutnant Caspar Kulenkampff-Post, who flew as Göring's observer for a time, was also one of Göring's steadfast admirers.

'Flying goes on, in spite of radiant "heavy air" [following a rainstorm]; at the moment I am working as a machine-gunner on a giant crate. In this way one learns best about the area. It is morbidly interesting at Verdun and one really has the oddest feeling just to be able to fly there. The French scarcely let themselves be seen, especially when our Fokkers come over. When one flies then he is a free man and can do what he wants …

'Stenay is a typical small French rural city with its narrow streets with archways and gables. Really very pretty, comfortable but somewhat too old-fashioned …Our officers' mess is very agreeable and nicely appointed, and the food is first rate. Outside, on the square, we have a charming little house with many cosy armchairs and bright flowers and an enormous fireplace around which [we] gather when waiting for good weather …'[24]

At the end of March 1916, German forces were still advancing on the Verdun Sector. Even bad weather did not hamper the ground troops, but it did give the air units a needed respite and a chance to reflect on their success. On 28 March Kulenkampff wrote:

'At the moment, flying is out of the question; it is pouring rain in torrents and through the moist air the thunder booms from Verdun day and night, mostly strong, and today more furious than ever. We already know what that means and which village has been taken; great confidence prevails everywhere.'[25]

In good weather, Göring went up in the AEG with various observers and gunners, and generally returned with results. On 4 April, he made a three-hour flight with Leutnant Walter Kaehler, a seasoned observer, and Vizefeldwebel Boje and Unteroffizier Röder at

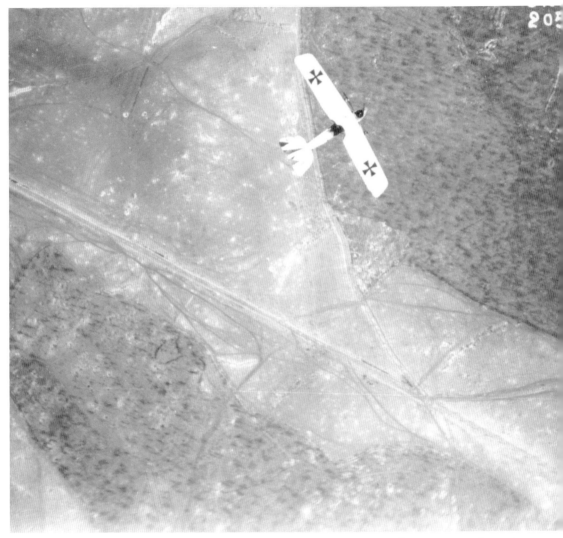

Göring's AEG G.II 49/15 was photographed in the air by another FFA 25 aeroplane on 31 March 1916.

the gunners' stations. They covered a wide area from the Meuse river to the Argonne forest and, when attacked by two French Caudrons and a Nieuport fighter, Boje and Röder drove them off and Kaehler completed his reconnaissance duties.

Göring's wartime comrades were quick to praise his flying ability, which got them to their assigned locations – or in close for aerial combat – and brought them back to Stenay. Wilhelm Hübener related an account of the Abteilungsführer's request for volunteers to fly a photo-reconnaissance mission deep into French territory:

> 'Everyone groaned when the mission was announced – except Göring. He quickly got up, tapped his observer on the shoulder and the two of them went to their aircraft and took off. When they returned several hours later their aeroplane was riddled with bullet holes, but they had the photographs. Our [Abteilungsführer] said to Göring: "… as an officer you are only a Leutnant, but as a flyer you are a General."'[27]

Caspar Kulenkampff may well have been describing the same mission when he wrote: 'And then there is Göring, the Abteilung's big gun, a master pilot. Recently he came back with fifty-nine hits on his machine.'[28]

So it is no wonder that Göring was rewarded with a brand-new aeroplane of the latest type and some time off. On 7 April, he was informed that he would be assigned an AEG G.III (serial number G 54/15), equipped with two Mercedes 220-hp engines, which would give far better performance than the two Benz 150-hp engines[29] on his older AEG G.II aeroplane. And, as part of the process, he and Unteroffizier Röder were issued travel orders to proceed to the AEG factory in Hennigsdorf, a suburb of Berlin, which happened to be one of Göring's favourite places.[30] Their mission in Berlin was to inspect the new aeroplane, but, with surface transportation being slow at that point in 1916, they were not able to return to Stenay until 17 April.[31]

Meanwhile, two days earlier, Göring was notified he had been awarded a rare distinction by the office of the Chef der Feldflugwesens [chief of field aviation]: a one-litre silver goblet to commemorate his role in the confirmed destruction of a French Farman on 16 November 1915. Simply called the Ehrenbecher [Goblet of Honour],[32] over the next three years it was presented to all pilots, aviation observers and aerial gunners after they had shot down one enemy aeroplane. The goblet became another incentive for German flyers to go after and destroy their aerial opponents.

An example of the Ehrenbecher, which Göring received. It was accompanied by a 15 April 1916 notification from Oberstleutnant Hermann von der Lieth-Thomsen, Chef der Feldflugwesens [chief of field aviation]: 'Patriotic friends of the Luftstreitkräfte have placed at my disposal a sum of money, which I used for the establishment of an Honour Goblet for the victor in aerial combat. It is a grateful pleasure for me to confer upon you this goblet in recognition of demonstrated valour in the victorious engagement.'

Fighter Units Developed

The first two Ehrenbechers had been presented at Christmas 1915 to the leading fighter aces of the time, Oberleutnant Max Immelmann and Oberleutnant Oswald Boelcke. The latter was the most prominent of the many German flyers sent to the Verdun Sector in

A photograph in Göring's album showed the top German fighter ace of the time, Hauptmann Oswald Boelcke, while test flying the LFG Roland C.II.

early 1916. Boelcke, who arrived in the area in February,[33] had nine confirmed aerial victories to his credit and now flew the nimble little Fokker Eindecker [monoplane] that Göring and Loerzer had greatly admired. Boelcke was assigned to Artillerie-Flieger-Abteilung 203, abbreviated FAA 203, an artillery-spotting unit formed on 6 August 1915 and specifically furnished with two single-seat Fokker fighters for protection. He was charged with coordinating FAA 203's Fokkers with pairs of Fokkers from other Flieger-Abteilungen to form, as needed, multi-aeroplane fighter groupings that would evolve into Jagdstaffeln [fighter squadrons].

One Boelcke FAA 203 protégé who got off to a dramatic start was Oberleutnant Hans Berr, a former two-seater pilot, who flew a Fokker to score his first two aerial victories, on 8 and 14 March 1916.[36] On the latter occasion, FAA 203's Leutnant Kommos and Vizefeldwebel [Sergeant-Major] Paulisch each scored their first victories.[37] Another FAA 203 Fokker was flown by Leutnant Bruno Loerzer, who was assigned to the unit on 9 January[38] (and would be joined by Göring seven months later[39]), and shot down enemy aircraft on 21 and 31 March.[40] Loerzer also became an early casualty for the unit when he was shot and wounded in the right shoulder during an aerial combat over Verdun on Monday, 3 April.[41] He was posted out for treatment and ended up at a facility in his hometown of Berlin.

Boelcke was also joined by FFA 25 Fokker pilot Leutnant Werner Notzke, with whom he operated out of Sivry airfield, less than twenty kilometres north of Verdun.[42] Their early flights were 'untiring [in their] …faithful watchfulness and protection of the tasks of our artillery-spotting, photographic and visual reconnaissance aeroplanes against the masses of enemy fighter [aircraft],' noted Hauptmann Leo Leonhardy.[43]

But even the most skilled airmen met with sad accidents, as happened with Notzke on Good Friday, 21 April 1916. While Göring, Kulenkampff and Boje were patrolling along a line of German tethered observation balloons, flying in AEG G.II [G 49/15],[44] one of their escorts, Notzke, was back at his base, trying to resolve a problem with his machine gun. The wind was up, Leonhardy reported, and the twenty-one-year-old Notzke misjudged his distance during a test flight and 'flew into the anchoring cable of an observation balloon and crashed to his death'[45] near Sivry airfield.

Nine days later, early on the morning of 30 April, the four-man crew of Göring, Schaesberg and the gunners Flörke and Boje set out on their first combat flight in the new AEG G.III [G 54/15]. For reasons not made clear in his report, Göring felt compelled to make an emergency landing in a meadow near Mouzay, south of Stenay.[46] Upon landing on the soft ground, the aeroplane nosed over and was badly damaged. Göring's dignity may have been bruised, but none of the crew was injured.

Not so fortunate that day was Rittmeister Erich Graf von Holck, who flew one of FAA 203's Fokker single-seaters. Holck was as bold and supremely confident a pilot as Göring, but over-extended himself on this occasion by making a one-aeroplane attack against three French Caudron two-seaters over Verdun. His demise, which demonstrates the perils of courage, was witnessed by an AEG G.II pilot, Leutnant Manfred Freiherr von Richthofen (later better known as the Red Baron). Richthofen was bucking a head-wind trying to reach the beleaguered Fokker and come to its aid when he observed:

Göring photographed two fellow officers who became casualties of Fokker Eindecker operations on the Verdun Sector, Rittmeister Erich Graf von Holck (left) and Leutnant Werner Notzke, both of whom were killed in combat in April.

'Then I saw, to my horror, that the attacker became the defender. The Frenchmen, whose strength had meanwhile been increased by at least ten aeroplanes, were forcing the German lower and lower ... The Fokker [pilot] defended himself desperately ... [as] the enemy had driven him down to at least 600 metres. Then suddenly ... he disappeared in a dive into a cumulus cloud ... When I returned home ... I learned that the unfortunate pilot was Holck, my old comrade in arms ... who had become a fighter pilot shortly before the Verdun offensive. Graf von Holck had plunged straight down with a shot through the head ...'[47]

A less sombre reaction to Holck's death – and perhaps to aerial combat in general by an eager young combatant of the time – appeared in Kulenkampff's letter of 1 May:

'Aerial combat is the most gratifying experience in all of flying. It is simply grand to be in a good machine, to dive down onto [an enemy] and send him down, and then climb again and ...leisurely go back to photographing and observing. Nevertheless, now the French again have a splendid new [Nieuport fighter aircraft], which makes many difficulties for us, and with which lately they attack us very keenly ... Some of my new acquaintances from other units here have fallen [in combat recently]; for example, yesterday Holck ...was shot down.'[48]

Much documentation pertaining to Hermann Göring's service in World War I survived the devastation of World War II due to special efforts by members of the Third Reich Luftwaffe's historical branch who wanted to assure that their leader's place in history would be secured. Some of those materials were lost in the chaos that accompanied the German empire's collapse in November 1918; but, fortunately, historians have some generally reliable anecdotal material, such as Caspar Kulenkampff's correspondence, to fill in some of the blank spots. In his letter of 7 May, Kulenkampff referred to FFA 25's change of command when he wrote: 'Now, Herr Ziegler, Rittmeister from the 12th Pferdejäger [mounted rifles], leads the Abteilung.'[49] He did not mention when or where Hauptmann Leonhardy reported to his next assignment to command an entire bomber wing.[50] But he did mention that, on 28 May, Ziegler was succeeded by Hauptmann Heinrich Claes, a pre-war observer who went on to command a unit of Kampfgeschwader 2.[51]

Caspar Kulenkampff's correspondence also left impressions of his admiration for Hermann Göring. In letters he wrote home in May, Kulenkampff referred to his pilot as 'the *Kanone* [Big Gun] Göring, really a devil of a fellow, with whom I have already made some ... [of] the most interesting flights',[52] and rejoiced: 'For the time being I will fly with Göring, which promises to be very interesting.'[53] Then, on 23 May, he wrote: 'Göring is a daredevil of the wickedest kind. Recently, when he was over the lines, he began to spiral down and shoot wildly at the trenches below. Another time we just about forced down a tethered observation balloon with machine-gun fire. With the AEG and two observers [aboard] one evening we reported [artillery hits] for 136 batteries.'[54]

Following Göring's forced landing with the new AEG G.III, that aeroplane had to be sent by rail to Flieger-Ersatz-Abteilung 1 at Adlershof in suburban Berlin for repair and

Recognising a good opportunity, Göring photographed Crown Prince Wilhelm (back to the camera, clasping his hands) before the maiden flight of the new AEG G.III G 54/15 on 30 April 1916.

testing.[55] Göring would have preferred to 'graduate' to a single-seat fighter aeroplane, but had to return to flying the earlier model AEG G.II, as well as a new Albatros C.III [serial number C 149/16], which offered 'incremental improvements'[56] over earlier B- and C-type aircraft from that manufacturer.

During all of his flights in the last half of May and well into June, Göring was accompanied by Kulenkampff. Often they had an exhausting work schedule, as Kulenkampff indicated in his letter of 5 June: 'Yesterday I made four combat flights with Göring …It was splendid, although in the evening one's rickety legs can move only with difficulty. Unfortunately, soon Göring is going on leave due to his heart.'

There is no indication in Hermann Göring's military records that he suffered from any heart-related illness, which makes Kulenkampff's reference an odd one. When Göring finally went on leave, almost two weeks later and then for only four days, his reported destination was Berlin.[57] Most likely, he visited his best friend, Bruno Loerzer, who was in a hospital in the Cöpenick section of Berlin for treatment of his shoulder wound, and was discharged on 20 June.[58] Loerzer, who had been promoted to Oberleutnant on 18 April 1916,[59] was subsequently pronounced fit to fly and again assigned to a single-seat fighter at FFA 25 – much to the envy of his friend Göring.

A Strange Occurrence

As Göring and Loerzer most likely talked about their flying activities, they may have discussed a two-seater reconnaissance flight that Kulenkampff described in an almost joking manner in his letter of 8 June (well before Göring went to Berlin):

Göring also photographed the crash of AEG G.III G 54/15 after it had landed on soft soil that could not support the aeroplane's weight.

'As you know, the fellows on the other side of the [Meuse] river have long had designs on winning … medals and, consequently, saw a favourable opportunity when, one fine morning, in complete tranquillity, I flew along from Béthincourt [a few kilometres northeast of Dead Man's Hill in the Verdun defensive line]. Without any prior notification … they put [an anti-aircraft] shell right into our propeller, which … tumbled to the ground. Now … it is not possible to fly without [the propeller] and, logically, Göring turned in the direction of Germany. Then we saw a second shell go off under the engine, which also parted company with [the aeroplane], but not before spilling all of the oil and gasoline on us … The machine, or rather, what was left of it, protested against this unfriendly and certainly disrespectful treatment by vigorously somersaulting twice and then rushed downwards. I discovered to my great joy that [the aeroplane] was on the ground … and aside from Göring and me, [only] our machine gun was also still intact.'[60]

Kulenkampff did not write down the date of this hair-raising event; only that it occurred 'one fine morning'. Göring made no mention of the incident and there is no reference to it in available FFA 25 records. However, the anecdote is reinforced by Hauptmann Leonhardy's account, which indicates it took place before his transfer from FFA 25:

'… I received as a replacement [for one crew that had perished] a two-metre tall Leutnant Kulenkampff-Post from the 15th Uhlan Regiment, who flew with a pilot … Sergeant Gehrke [sic]. Something happened to both of them that perhaps today one would chalk up as a tall tale, but it really took place. The entire engine was shot out of [their aeroplane] by two artillery direct hits while they were over enemy territory. They floated in the air, continually somersaulting with the remainder of the aeroplane back to our side of the lines, and at the last moment they so luckily succeeded in putting the landing gear onto the ground that they came away with only minor abrasions.

'The crash was observed by one of my aeroplane crews and was considered to be hopeless. I immediately communicated with the frontline sector in question to gain assurance. From there I was informed that both flyers had indeed escaped with their lives, but had gone mad.

'I immediately drove to just behind the frontlines and luckily determined that their unexpected rescue, above all on the German side, led to their performing the wildest Indian dances one could imagine because they had made it through.'[61]

The crew's temporary delirium is understandable, but it might be expected that such a 'miracle' amid the carnage of war would have been reported widely. Neither Göring nor Kulenkampff seems to have suffered any lasting effects from their uncontrolled descent. Leonhardy's mention of Sergeant Gehrke does not track with FFA 25 flight logs, which state that Göring and Kulenkampff flew together continually in Albatros C.III C 149/16 from 16 May, the day Göring took delivery of the aeroplane from Armee-Flugpark 5, to 23 June,[62] after which he and Kulenkampff were in the air together only occasionally. During some of their missions, Göring flew Kulenkampff from Stenay to Béthincourt to Cumières and back to Stenay, and they would have come under anti-aircraft fire near Béthincourt, as Kulenkampff wrote. But no records show their aeroplane sustained the terminal damage that Kulenkampff and Leonhardy mentioned. Indeed, Göring and Kulenkampff flew in that Albatros C.III for the last time on 9 July,[63] after which Göring was transferred to FAA 203 to realise his wish to fly single-seat fighter aircraft.

Published accounts of Kulenkampff's and Leonhardy's versions of the 'miracle' flight appeared in Germany during Göring's lifetime and the mystery of the occurrence is joined by a puzzle: why was Göring so uncharacteristically quiet about having enjoyed such good luck? The incident certainly fit his larger-than-life self perception.

Chapter Six
A Fighter Pilot at Last

'Yesterday … Göring came within a hair's breadth of being brought down.
He was shot through the sleeve and in every … part of his machine …'[1]

CASPAR KULENKAMPFF-POST

Initially, the German ground and air offensive against Verdun in 1916 was marked by success, but army Chief of Staff Erich von Falkenhayn did not anticipate having such a resourceful opponent as Général Philippe Pétain, commander of France's Army Group Centre. Despite fierce German artillery attacks, he organised an effective supply route that enabled him to respond with equal vigour to the onslaught.

Numerous instances on the ground and in the air demonstrate that 'both sides fought with equal bravery,'[2] but ultimate success came through the French Army Group Centre's ability to persevere until British forces relieved pressure on it by launching the Battle of the Somme on 1 July 1916.

General der Infanterie Hans von Zwehl of the 5th Army staff attributed some of the failure to 'a grievous pessimism [that] had set in'[3] among his troops. Adding to that sombre mood, while Hermann Göring was on leave in Berlin, a piece of particularly bad news circulated among German aviation units: on Sunday, 18 June 1916, fighter ace Oberleutnant Max Immelmann was killed during an aerial combat after his Fokker broke up in the air and fell 2,000 metres to the ground. It was not clear whether his death at age twenty-five was caused by some kind of failure of the aeroplane or by enemy bullets.

Throughout air corps, pilots who had hoped to emulate Immelmann's earlier well-publicised success – and that of his equally high-scoring counterpart Oswald Boelcke – had been encouraged when the pair had received the Pour le Mérite, after their eighth confirmed aerial victories. That number established a performance level at which pilots might reasonably anticipate gaining such a high honour and they were motivated accordingly. Thus, the aggressive combat pilot Hermann Göring, with two confirmed victories to his credit, could consider that he was a quarter of the way toward attaining the boyhood goal he once proclaimed – to distinguish himself and get even more medals than his father had.

Adding to the bad news within Feldflieger-Abteilung 25's area of operations, another prominent German airman became another Eindecker casualty the day after Immelmann died. On 19 June, thirty-eight-year-old Hauptmann Ernst Freiherr von Gersdorff, a seasoned pre-war pilot[4] and most recently commander of Kampfgeschwader 1 [Combat Wing 1], or Kagohl 1, was shot down while flying his Fokker near Metz.[5]

Despite worsening experiences with Fokker Eindeckers, FFA 25 retained two, which Göring photographed with a small personal camera, as seen here.

Göring, however, was not dismayed by these events. He had set his mind on becoming a single-seat fighter pilot, as had Loerzer. Since his return from Berlin, Göring flew only in the two-seat Albatros C.III [serial number C 149/16] and, most of the time, with Leutnant Caspar Kulenkampff-Post, who shared his zest for aerial combat. However, Kulenkampff's letter home dated 23 June 1916 is the only record that offers the flavour of his and Göring's dedication to finding combat opportunities at this time:

> 'Göring and I, in addition to our daily flights, still prowl for a few hours [in clouds over the lines]. This morning we photographed [French] positions from an altitude of 800 metres without being fired on. Only in a glide [with the engine turned off] does one hear the tack-tack-tack of the machine gun. But in the photos one sees every dug-out and every detail. My health is splendid again, after a few days of not feeling so well. I had an unnerving aerial combat in which the [enemy flyer] was fifty metres away from me when my machine gun jammed, which is an irritating situation, even when the [pilot's] forward machine gun still functions. Well, Göring resolved the situation by going into a dive from which [the pre-war French stunt flyer Adolphe] Pégoud could have learned something.'[6]

Two weeks passed, during which Kulenkampff was removed from flight status after cutting his hand on a drinking glass during the farewell party for Rittmeister Eduard Ziegler.[7] On 1 July, Göring flew a reconnaissance mission over Hill 304, an important high ground northwest of Verdun, with FFA 25's new commanding officer, Hauptmann Heinrich Claes, as his observer.[8] Five days later, Göring resumed flying with Kulenkampff and then, after a morning flight together on Sunday, 9 July, their partnership ended. There is no record of the administrative process that took place, but, that afternoon, Göring was detached from FFA 25 and assigned to fly a single-seat fighter with Artillerie-Flieger-Abteilung 203. Later that afternoon, Göring took off for a thirteen-minute test flight in a new biplane fighter, a Halberstadt D.II (serial number D 115/16)[9] and not one of the troubled Fokker Eindeckers. Bruno Loerzer continued to fly his Fokker until, a few days later, he crashed it while landing. He hit his head on the rear end of the aeroplane's machine-gun breech and complained of headaches for a long time thereafter.[10] Only a sturdy flight helmet saved Loerzer from more serious injury.

Göring's camera also recorded Bruno Loerzer's Eindecker crash in July 1916.

Built by the Halberstädter Flugzeugwerke, Göring's D.II offered speed and climbing ability that was only slightly better than the Fokker Eindecker's. But the Halberstadt was powered by a stationary engine, versus a rotary engine with its inherent torque considerations, and was manoeuvrable and strong, with very good diving ability.[11] In the hands of an aggressive pilot such as Hermann Göring, the Halberstadt was a good air fighting weapon.

Frustrating Air Combat Results

Fast paced events on Saturday, 15 July 1916, convinced Göring that he had scored his third aerial victory overall and his first in a fighter aeroplane. While flying the new Halberstadt over Marre Ridge, a natural defensive barrier for Fort de Marre, a smaller fortification less than seven kilometres northwest of Verdun, Göring spotted a Voisin *Gitterrumpf* [lattice fuselage] aeroplane. This was a common German description for French and British aeroplanes in which the rear-engined fuselage was connected to the tail surfaces by wooden longerons that were reinforced by bracing wires. As Göring knew from his early successes over Farman and Caudron aircraft of that configuration, the so-called 'lattice fuselage' aircraft gave their crews excellent visibility and, with the fuselages placed ahead of the engines, a wide firing arc for their machine guns. But he had defeated them before and he felt triumphant about this morning flight. Upon returning to his airfield, he reported encounters with three French aircraft in just over an hour:

> '1) 8:15 a.m. aerial combat with Voisin over Marre Ridge. After discharging approximately 500 rounds, I saw it plunge into the clouds. I do not know where it went. Observer was already dead (apparently hit by one of the first shots).
>
> '2) 9:00 a.m. aerial combat with Caudron, which fled. At the same time saw five [other] lattice tails.
>
> '3) 9:10 a.m. a Nieuport attacked me from above. I turned away.'[12]

After expending so much ammunition on the Voisin, Göring was not in a position to fight the diminutive but rugged Nieuport. The Halberstadt's 120-hp Mercedes stationary engine could easily outpace the Nieuport's 80-hp Gnôme (or Le Rhône) rotary engine[13] and Göring wisely declined this invitation to an aerial combat in which he was in danger of running out of ammunition.

Often, confirming aerial victories was a difficult task. Other members of Göring's patrol could verify what they had witnessed, but the best, most often accepted accounts came from German ground forces, which had no vested interest in a fighter pilot's success or the lack thereof. Fighter pilots, generally very eager to add to their scores of defeated enemy aircraft, often drove to crash sites within their own lines, seeking proof of their handiwork or telephoned frontline artillery and infantry units, looking for witnesses to their achievements. Hence, Göring must have been very happy when, the following day, FAA 203 received a telephone message from the commander for heavy artillery of the 7th Reserve Corps, who must have recognised his aeroplane and reported: '[A]t about 9 a.m., Leutnant Göring attacked a French biplane over the Marre Ridge and forced it to land.'[14]

Despite that testimony, Göring was denied credit for a claim that may have been tenuous, at best. French records show no loss of aircraft or airmen at the time and in the area in question.[15]

That frustration only drove Göring to make greater efforts to shoot down enemy aircraft. He maintained contact with his FFA 25 comrades and, always a 'talker', he expounded on his work, which became focused on French Nieuport biplanes, which he wanted so much to engage (as long as he had a full load of ammunition). Many German pilots of the time wanted to fight with the Nieuport 11, which 'had a fine rate of climb and was very manoeuvrable',[16] but the Nieuports' popularity came with a certain price when they became targets of special interest, as Kulenkampff related on 20 July: 'The Nieuports, they are the delicate ones, have also become considerably more cautious. Göring storms about vigorously among these worthy [opponents] in his single-seater …'[17]

Two days later, evidence of Göring's tenacity came via another telephoned message from the commander for heavy artillery of the 7th Reserve Corps. At this point, Göring had no distinctive markings on his Halberstadt, so it must be assumed that he had alerted the 7th Reserve Corps staff that he would be operating over their positions, as their message was very clear: 'Leutnant Göring had four aerial combats [and] two French biplanes were chased away…'[18]

On Sunday, 23 July, two FAA 203 single-seat aircraft were sent eastward to Metz,[19] where their pilots – Leutnants Hermann Göring and the now fully recovered Bruno Loerzer[20] – were assigned to defend the city against air attacks. Located at the confluence of the Moselle and Seille rivers and some fifty-five kilometres east of Verdun, Metz was then a major city in the Lorraine territory that Germany gained after the Franco-Prussian War of 1870-1871. At the beginning of World War I, Metz became one of four *Festungs-Städte* [fortress cities] that were slated to receive aeroplanes, airships and anti-aircraft batteries to fend off anticipated enemy air raids. Metz was assigned Festungs-Flieger-Abteilung 2 [Fortress Flying Section 2], which became Feldflieger-Abteilung 71 [Field Flying Section 71],[21] but did not receive all of the aeroplanes promised[22] and therefore had to draw on resources from frontline units for its aerial defence.

The following day, 24 July, Kulenkampff kept his family apprised of Göring's progress by writing:

> 'Göring flies a new single-seat biplane, which is somewhat similar to the French Nieuport, but is better. It climbs as high as you want it to, which means to the limit of being able to breathe, for at 4,500 [metres] one must gasp for air, especially when one works a lot in aerial combat.'[23]

That day, Göring reported encounters with French aircraft during three different flights in the vicinity of his airfield at Jametz, north of Verdun, and the embattled city itself. From his initial report, the incidents seem routine. Only the day's final flight, from 6:20 to 8:00 p.m., produced 'three aerial combats against Nieuport and two-seat Caudrons – both chased off.[24] Yet, he filed a victory claim that had to be tactfully deflected by Feldflugchef Hermann von der Lieth-Thomsen, so as to not discourage the eager young Göring. Indeed, Thomsen waited until he could confirm a subsequent air combat triumph, as noted in his 9 August 1916 response to the claims for both victories submitted via the Stabsoffizier der Flieger [staff officer for aviation] for the 5th Army, Hauptmann Wilhelm Haehnelt:

> 'I regret that I am not in a position to confirm the aeroplane [claimed to be] shot

down on 24 July by Leutnant Göring. The downing of a biplane by … Göring on 30 July is confirmed as his third aerial victory.

'I convey to Leutnant Göring my particular appreciation for his brave and unhesitating daring during the attacks on 24 and 30 July.'[25]

Göring's Third Victory

The combat report for Göring's third victory does not appear in any known holdings of German air combat documents. However, a report by General der Infanterie Adolf von Oven, governor of the fortress of Metz, was accepted as proof of Göring's success in defending his city that day:

'On 30 July at 10:30 a.m. Leutnant Göring attacked five aeroplanes from an enemy formation over La Côte. West of the Moselle [river] he brought one of the enemy aeroplanes – a two-engine Caudron – crashing down. The remaining enemy aeroplanes flew back over [to their own] lines. I convey to Leutnant Göring my complete appreciation and my thanks for his repeatedly outstanding conduct here.'

A captured Caudron G.IV of the type that Göring was credited with shooting down on 30 July 1916.

The Caudron G.IV two-seaters retreated south along the Moselle – with Göring and Loerzer after them in hot pursuit. Göring shot down one of the attackers over Mamey, some thirty kilometres southwest of Metz within French territory. French records show that the pilot, Sergent Girard-Varet of Escadrille C 10,[27] was wounded; no mention is made of the Caudron's observer, who most likely was uninjured.

Even when Göring did not succeed in knocking down his target, he earned praise, as seen in this 2 August communiqué from FAA 203 to the commander for heavy artillery of the 12th Reserve Corps: 'Yesterday, the combat single-seat aeroplanes of the Abteilung made nine fighter flights. There were three aerial combats in the morning; one in the afternoon, all by Leutnant Göring. The enemy aeroplanes were dispersed.'[28]

Göring and Loerzer were ordered back to FFA 25 on 31 July[29] and must have taken a well-deserved short leave, as they did not return to the unit until 5 August.[30] Göring continued to pursue French aeroplanes at every opportunity. Indeed, on the day of his return he made nine flights and became involved in three aerial combats.[31] During the following three days, Göring made eleven to fourteen flights per day and drove off French aircraft attempting to cross into German territory.[32]

Göring's aggressiveness was not without cost, as Kulenkampff noted in his letter of 10 August: 'Yesterday, the good Göring came within a hair's breadth of being brought down. He was shot through the sleeve and in every … part of his machine's [fuselage].'[33] FFA 25's war diary offers only a hint of the superior airmanship and daring that Göring showed that day, attacking three Nieuport fighters so he could get at the Caudron reconnaissance aeroplane they were escorting. Apparently, he drove them off, but, among other damage he sustained, his Halberstadt – a newer D.III model – was hit in the fuel tank and engine.[34]

During an aerial combat with three Nieuport fighters on 9 August 1916, Hermann Göring's Halberstadt D.III was badly shot up. He took this photograph of some of his comrades inspecting the damage. The tall man at left is Leutnant Caspar Kulenkampff-Post.

Two days later, with his aeroplane repaired and test flown, Göring was back in the air, charging after French aeroplanes but having no luck in shooting down any of them.[35] Essentially, the German offensive at Verdun ended on 11 July and further actions in this area only tied down French forces that otherwise would have gone to the new battleground in the Somme Sector.[36]

At this time, the German Fliegertruppe reorganisation was still in progress. That development did not yet affect Göring and Loerzer, who continued to fly with FFA 25's Kampfstaffel [combat detachment], even as the Abteilung eliminated its Fokkerstaffel [Fokker detachment], which was redundant, on 14 August.[37]

To refine and strengthen the role of single-seat combat aircraft for offensive operations, Feldflugchef Thomsen ordered the establishment of Jagdstaffeln [literally hunting units, but equal to Allied fighter squadrons], abbreviated as Jastas. Hauptmann Oswald Boelcke was charged with establishing the first such unit. In a peculiar sequence driven by immediate need rather than numerical order, on 10 August 1916 Boelcke was appointed commanding officer of Jasta 2, while Jasta 3 came under Hauptmann Hermann Kohze; and, on 22 August Jasta 1 was led by Hauptmann Martin Zander.[38]

As those developments were taking place during a slow and uncertain period, Göring flew a battlefield 'tour' of part of the Verdun area that had once been so hotly contested. Kulenkampff wrote home that, on 21 August, he, Leutnant Winand Grafe and Leutnant Konstantin von Kleist-Retzow accompanied Göring – most likely in the old AEG G.II. Kulenkampff wrote that the four flyers:

> '… made a review of our troops in the forward-most trenches … It was a relatively calm day. We came up to *Côte de Froide Terre* [Cold Earth Ridge], saw Douaumont off to the left, the French trenches at Thiaumont, Souville and the entire Marre Ridge. One just could not believe the devastation and destruction. Each particle of earth was disturbed not just once by a big shell; on the contrary, it was churned up day in and day out! As I said, it was a quiet day and, in spite of that, there was such a racket and uproar … Fort Douaumont is a big, high trash heap from which isolated fragments of armoured towers and stonework protrude. The village of Douaumont is, unfortunately, no longer to be found and its earlier position can be determined only in old maps …'[39]

Kulenkampff further described a panorama of destruction within the small area over which he and his comrades flew; he was stunned by the enormity of the wasteland created by General von Falkenhayn's failed plan to 'bleed' the French army at this battle site. The German lack of success at Verdun also reflected poorly on the nominal area commander, Crown Prince Wilhelm. Hence, on 23 August, General Konstantin Schmidt von Knobelsdorf, the 5th Army chief of staff and the officer generally responsible for the overall Verdun campaign, was quietly reassigned to a less important post as commander of the 10th Army Corps in Alsace. Six days later, General Erich von Falkenhayn was relieved as chief of the general staff of the German army. He was appointed commander of the 9th Army in Transylvania and was succeeded in the German army's top position by Generalfeldmarschal [Field Marshal] Paul von Beneckendorff und von Hindenburg, the hero of the Battle of Tannenberg in 1914. Popularly known as Hindenburg, he and his deputy, General Erich Ludendorff, directed the German army for the remainder of World War I.

On 6 September, Göring and Loerzer were again posted to Jametz airfield, northwest of Metz, where FFA 71 still maintained an air defence Kampfstaffel. In an odd nuance of the Fliegertruppe reorganisation, the Metz Kampfstaffel was declared an independent entity on 9 September.[40] The unit was placed under the command of the pre-war aviation veteran Hauptmann Kurt Schmickaly,[41] who was aided by Oberleutnant Stefan Kirmaier, who had scored three "kills" while flying with FAA 203[42] and who brought with him Halberstadt D.II D 109/16. Göring and Loerzer arrived next along with their newer Halberstadt D.IIIs (serial numbered D 392 and D 393).[43] The only air action recorded for the pair's brief stay occurred on 14 September, when Göring fought with two 'lattice-fuselage' aircraft in the vicinity of Nancy,[44] some fifty kilometres south of Metz.

Due to reduced French air activity near Metz at that time, on 28 September, Göring and Loerzer were transferred to Jagdstaffel 7.[45] The newly-formed unit was based at Martincourt-sur-Meuse, north of Stenay, still in the 5th Army Sector,[46] with which they

The first pilots assigned to the Kampfstaffel at Metz posed for this group shot at Jametz airfield. Known members are (from left): Offizierstellvertreter Jakob Wolff, a former pacifist who learned to fly at age forty-six; unknown; unknown; Leutnant Hermann Göring; unknown; Oberleutnant Stefan Kirmaier, who had attained three aerial victories flying with FAA 203; pre-war aviation veteran Hauptmann Kurt Schmickaly, commanding officer; and two unknown members.

were so familiar. But this assignment was during another quiet period, which only frustrated experienced and aggressive members such as Göring and Loerzer. Ultimately, however, they would benefit from the air units' reorganisation, which was finalised on 8 October. On that day, Generalleutnant Ernst von Hoeppner, a long-time cavalry officer,[47] became Kommandierende General der Luftstreitkräfte [commanding general of the air force]. The old Fliegertruppe's loose command structure was replaced by a unified command, comprising 'what had been under the Feldflugchef [Thomsen] for aviation: captive balloons, army airships and the army weather service, as well as the anti-aircraft and home defence units.'[48] The Kogenluft, as the office was known in its abbreviated form, expanded some units and reassigned or consolidated others. The Jagdstaffeln, which had grown to fifteen at this point, were to be expanded to thirty-seven for the spring 1917 offensive.[49] While German fighter pilots would continue to fly lone aircraft patrols, seeking targets of opportunity, there was increased emphasis on developing strategies and tactics for massed air strength.

Göring and Loerzer were transferred to a new Jagdstaffel when on Friday, 20 October 1916, they were sent westward to Jasta 5 at Gonnelieu, fifteen kilometres southwest of Cambrai; they flew in support of German 1st Army forces engaged in the Battle of the Somme. Jasta 5 was commanded by the up-and-coming air fighter Oberleutnant Hans Berr, whom Göring had met in late September 1915 at Stenay airfield. Berr would have been pleased that the pair arrived in their Halberstadt fighters, the same aircraft type then used by Jasta 5.[50] It has been noted that they were transferred 'together because of Göring's severe rheumatoid arthritis' so that Loerzer could stay 'close to assist his friend with mundane tasks [such as] getting in and out of a cockpit should Göring …have a severe recurrence'.[51]

Upon their arrival, they learned that Berr, their new Staffelführer [squadron leader] had shot down his fifth enemy aeroplane[52] that afternoon and was, therefore, a man to be emulated. Based on his recent performance, Göring was eager to add to his victory score and be as successful as his new leader. Thus, he must have been dismayed when, the following afternoon, he was assigned to a patrol making a barrier flight between Gueudecourt and Ruyaulcourt, a distance of some ten kilometres. The reason for such a tightly prescribed area became apparent when the patrol observed much larger formations of British 'lattice-fuselage' aeroplanes over the nearby city of Bapaume.[53]

On Sunday, 22 October, prospects for aerial victories – the measure of achievement for fighter pilots – improved as Göring and Loerzer flew two patrols. On the morning patrol, they joined with other Jasta 5 aircraft, and in a later afternoon patrol they set out individually to 'hunt' for opponents.[54] Two successes were achieved that day, one by Staffelführer Hans Berr, his sixth victor;[55] and one by Vizefeldwebel Hans Karl Müller, his seventh.[56]

The 22nd was noted as 'the last fine day of the month',[57] indicating that flight operations on the following day were carried out during diminishing weather conditions. Göring flew with the afternoon patrol on the 23rd (from 4:34 to 5:53 p.m.) and the results were as drab as the view from the air. According to Jasta 5's war diary:

'Patrol in the sector Thiepval-Sailly-Péronne. No enemy air traffic, only balloon defence. From 4:30 p.m. to darkness by order of the Kommandeur der Flieger der 1. Armee... [Jasta 5] is to fly air alert in the sector Thiepval to Gueudecourt. Very few enemy aeroplanes [observed] at low altitude. High altitude patrols [observed] far behind their own lines. Very good fire by enemy balloon anti-aircraft [units].'[58]

Three days later, the skies in that sector were filled with activity. The official British history recounts:

'The 26th, although again squally, brought two big air fights. The first one began at 7:15 a.m., and was waged near Bapaume by five deHavillands [D.H.2s] of No. 24 Squadron against about twenty single-seaters, most of them Halberstadts. The [D.H.2] pilots found that although the Halberstadts were faster and could out-climb them, they had the disadvantage, as compared with the British fighter, that they lost height in turning, a fact of which the [D.H.2s] made full use. The struggle was kept up at a fierce pace until the British pilots were left with only enough petrol to get them home, and by this time half the German formation had disappeared. As the [D.H.2s] turned for home, impeded by a strong headwind, the [German] pilots increased their attacks, but they had no success and gave up the fight before the [front] lines were reached ... The second fight, in the afternoon, was more favourable to the [Germans] ...'[59]

Jasta 5's two victories from the latter flight were both scored by Oberleutnant Hans Berr for his seventh and eighth victories.[60] The last victory, of course, qualified him to receive the Pour le Mérite, which he was awarded on 4 December.

But Hermann Göring was long gone from Jasta 5 when Berr was honoured with that high award. Surrounded by the high achievers in Jasta 5 in late October and seemingly unable to keep up with them, he must have been in quite a determined state when he focused on a British aeroplane over Combles late in the afternoon of Thursday, 2 November 1916. That aerial combat is described on pages 12-16.

The weather over the Somme Sector posed its own challenges, as one British source recorded: 'Low clouds and rain in the morning, clearing a little in the afternoon.'[62] By late afternoon, any cloud clearing was soon filled by approaching autumn darkness. Hence, by his own admission, Göring was so intent on shooting down his target that he did not see the patrol of British Royal Flying Corps Nieuport fighters until they were almost on top of him: 'Göring fail[ed] to ascertain ... that about 1,000 metres above him there was a squadron of at least twenty enemy fighter planes.'[63] There can be no doubt that he was overwhelmed by a numerically superior formation and that one or more British pilots peppered him with gunfire. The RFC war diary account for that date lists only two claims for German aeroplanes shot down – and neither was a Halberstadt.[64]

In any event, Göring's injuries put him in field and civilian hospitals for nearly six weeks. He already had recurring rheumatoid arthritis, as evidenced by candid photographs that show him relying on a cane to walk, and then a severe hip wound from his recent fight with the Nieuports; hence, he must have had considerable mobility problems. After he was discharged from the St. Elisabeth's hospital in Bochum on 12 December 1916,[65] he was ordered to light duty status at a training and replacement facility in Böblingen, near Stuttgart, in the Kingdom of Württemberg.[66] Later, he offered a more colourful account of his recovery, as his biographer Erich Gritzbach wrote:

'For four months [Göring] lay severely wounded in his homeland. Impatience gnawed away at him. In accordance with the regulations, he was – like all other wounded [flyers] – supposed to report to Flieger-Ersatz-Abteilung 10 in Böblingen. Instead, he sent the following telegram to the Inspektion der Fliegertruppen [Inspectorate for Aviation] in Berlin: "As I have not found Böblingen in either the railway guide or on a map, I returned immediately to the frontlines."'[67]

That bit of bravado is surely a fabrication. But it is interesting that Göring, the professional officer and strict disciplinarian, sought to create an image of himself as an insubordinate maverick, displaying behaviour he would never have tolerated from anyone junior to him. Contrary to Gritzbach's boldly-stated account, Göring's service records show he remained at FEA 10 for over seven (most likely uneventful) weeks and did not return to flying until mid-February 1917.[68]

Immediately following Göring's departure from Jasta 5, Loerzer was transferred back to the Kampfstaffel at Metz.[69] The latter unit needed combat-experienced patrol leaders, as top pilot Stefan Kirmaier had been transferred to Jasta 2 on 2 October,[70] and then, Staffelführer Kurt Schmickaly was wounded in an air fight near Malzéville on 22 October and died of his wounds the following day in Metz.[71]

Among Loerzer's protégés was Vizefeldwebel Jakob Wolff, who, aged forty-eight,[72] was one of the oldest fighter pilots in World War I. Wolff went on to score four confirmed victories and Loerzer's leadership skills were recognized on 18 January 1917, when he was assigned to command Jasta 26[73] – where he would once again take care of his friend Hermann Göring.

Chapter Seven
A Dream Come True

"We are bound together by something stronger than chains, Loerzer and I.
I know that in my hour of need he will never let me down."[1]

HERMANN GÖRING

Between his already arthritic knees and the hip wound from his 2 November 1916 air combat, Hermann Göring's therapeutic exercises and daily walks were very painful. But he knew that he had to improve his mobility in order to return to flying. A fine opportunity to be up and about came when he was formally discharged from convalescence at a military hospital in Munich on 15 January 1917[2]; his godfather, Dr. Hermann Ritter von Epenstein, invited him to Burg Mauterndorf.[3] Göring returned to his boyhood fantasy world and he did it as a decorated and honourably wounded war hero. The visit was a dream come true in many respects.

Epenstein's young wife, Lilli, had settled into her new life and felt quite secure in her position as mistress of the fortress. Indeed, she enjoyed being addressed as *'Frau Baronin'* [baroness][4] and responded to the honorific title with grace and charm. A source with connections to the Göring family noted:

'… throughout the castle and beyond it there was evidence of [Lilli's] lightness of spirit. She had thinned out the heavy Gothic furniture … and brought light, colour and gaiety into dark and musty corners. She had also done much to ease the heavy-handed, feudal manner in which … Epenstein had always controlled the lives of the families on the estate, and [she] moved among the woman and their children no doubt as the lady of the manor, but one wishing to be friendly and helpful.'[5]

When Göring arrived at Mauterndorf, a pleasant surprise greeted him: his mother had also been also invited to visit her former homestead. Lilli had contacted Fanny Göring 'and indicated in every way possible that she wished to be friends. It was if she were making amends for the way in which, through her marriage [to Epenstein], the Görings had lost their family home.'[6]

Unlike her reserved and often pretentious husband, Lilli von Epenstein also opened the old fortress to 'farmers and landowners in the neighbouring countryside, inviting them to meals and celebrations … and to hunts over the Mauterndorf estate'.[7] During a party in his honour, Hermann Göring met and immediately was attracted to Marianne Mauser, the pretty 'daughter of solid, well-to-do parents … [who was] dazzled by the wounded flyer'.[8] By the end of his two-week short stay in Mauterndorf, Hermann and Marianne felt they were in love with each other and Hermann called on her father to ask formally for Marianne's hand in marriage. Herr Mauser, it was reported, was 'less impressed by Göring's record than by his family's lack of land or money … but because he did not wish to offend … Epenstein by turning down his godson, he temporised, and consented to a secret engagement. He evidently reasoned that life on the Western Front was too short for the arrangement ever to lead to marriage.'[9]

Herr Mauser might have taken more interest in his daughter's suitor had he known about the conversation that took place between Hermann and Fanny Göring and Lilli von Epenstein just before the young Leutnant returned to duty. Fanny later told her daughter Olga that, as they surveyed the estate, Lilli said to Hermann: 'One day all this will be yours again. And so will Mauterndorf.[10] And, in fact, following Lilli's death, Hermann inherited much of his godfather's wealth.

Assigned to Jagdstaffel 26

With three confirmed aerial victories to his credit, Göring seemed to have emerged from the shadow of his best friend and aviation mentor, Bruno Loerzer, who by the time of their most recent flight had shot down only two enemy aeroplanes. But during Göring's extended convalescence Loerzer's career made great strides. By virtue of his rank as a regular army oberleutnant and his varied combat experiences, Loerzer was assigned to command a new fighter unit, Jagdstaffel 26, which had been established on 14 December 1916 at Flieger-Ersatz-Abteilung 9 in Darmstadt.[11] It took five weeks to gather the aeroplanes, men and equipment needed to furnish the unit and then, on 18 January 1917, the Staffel was shipped by train to its first airfield, just outside the Alsatian city of Colmar. Operating from that location, some sixty kilometres northeast of an important French airbase at Belfort, Loerzer and his men interdicted French aeroplanes intent on attacking German troops in the area and bombing cities in German-occupied Alsace and sites east of the Rhine.

As a Jagdstaffel commanding officer, Loerzer was able to request capable pilots he knew from previous assignments. If their unit commanders did not object, air force policy was flexible enough that transfers were easily arranged. Hence, it was no surprise that Loerzer requested Göring, who had no lingering ties to Jasta 5 and was now fit for duty; he duly reported to Jasta 26 on 15 February 1917.[12] Once again, Göring and Loerzer made a good pair – as long as Göring's wishes were accommodated. His dominating personality enabled him to influence many people, including Loerzer, from whom he came to expect a certain deference. Of course, Göring saw that influence in a different light and once summed up his relationship with Loerzer: "We are bound together by something stronger than chains, Loerzer and I. I know that in my hour of need he will never let me down.'[13] Their close friendship was to last until Göring's death in 1946.

Jasta 26 was equipped with the new Albatros D.III, a sleek 'winning fighter with improved performance and hitting power compared to the … Fokker and Halberstadt D-types'[14] and built by the company that produced the fine Albatros two-seat aircraft Göring had flown a year earlier. He flew Albatros D.III 2049/16 in combat from the day of his arrival in the Staffel, but with no immediate air combat successes. However, he witnessed

Early members of Jagdstaffel 26 posted for this photograph in late February 1917. They are, seated (left to right): Offizierstellvertreter Fritz Loerzer, younger brother of Bruno Loerzer; and Leutnant Karl Wewer. Standing (left to right): Offizierstellvertreter Rudolf Weckbrodt; Vizefeldwebel Langer; Gefreiter Hansen; Oberleutnant Bruno Loerzer; unknown; unknown; Leutnant Hermann Göring; Vizefeldwebel Richard Linke; Leutnant der Resereve Walter Blume; Leutnant der Reserve Hans Auer and Leutnant der Reserve Theodor Rumpel.

the third and fourth victories of Bruno Loerzer on 6 and 10 March 1917,[15] as well as the second victory of the Staffelführer's younger brother, Vizefeldwebel Fritz Loerzer on 16 March.[16]

Göring's combat report following the latter fight provided sufficient detail to help his new Staffel-mate receive credit for his aerial victory over Alsace:[17]

'I took off with Oberleutnant Loerzer and Vizefeldwebel Loerzer on a fighter patrol. About 4:30 p.m. I saw three Nieuports in the direction of Ober-Asbach. The [other] two German biplanes attacked. I immediately dived on the closest opponent, who had already been attacked by Vizefeldwebel Loerzer. I fired a few … shots at him and then attacked the second Nieuport, which after a short fight turned downwards and flew low towards home. Earlier I noticed heavy smoke coming from the Nieuport that had been attacked by Vizefeldwebel Loerzer and that the machine went downwards vertically. Despite the haze, I could see the increasing smoke all the way to the ground. The downed opponent lies in the large group of trees south of Sennheim. Because of the very strong easterly wind, we were blown several kilometres behind enemy lines during the fighting.'[18]

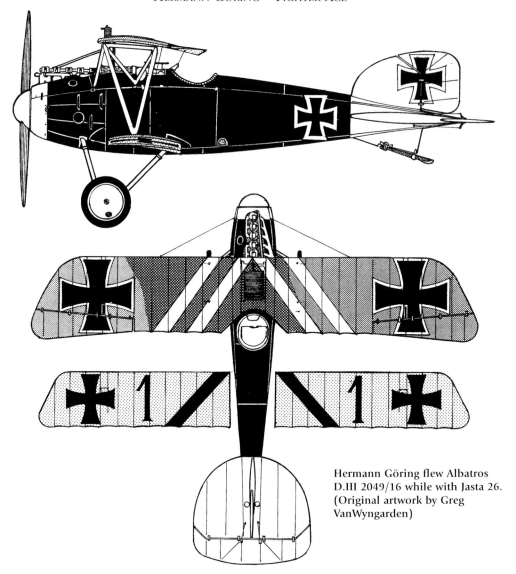

Hermann Göring flew Albatros
D.III 2049/16 while with Jasta 26.
(Original artwork by Greg
VanWyngarden)

During a late morning patrol two days later, Göring came close to success near Mülhausen, the city near which he had been stationed just before the war. His flight attacked a two-engined French Caudron and two Nieuport fighters that had penetrated German anti-aircraft fire outside the city. Approaching the Caudron at 4,000 metres' altitude, Göring forced it down to 1,800 metres and was about to close in for the kill when, at the edge of his field of view, he caught sight of another aeroplane. He wisely hesitated when the other fighter entered the fray. Early Nieuport and Albatros D.III aeroplanes were similar in appearance, as both were sesquiplanes (biplanes with lower wings shorter and narrower than the top); in fact, the evolution of the Albatros D.II to the D.III design was inspired by captured Nieuports and the greater manoeuvrability offered by their narrower bottom wings.[19] As he later reported, he stopped firing 'because of confusion [between] an Albatros with the Nieuport, [and, consequently] the heavily damaged Caudron escaped'.[20]

Göring did not determine the identity of the other aeroplane, but, in any event, he would not have wanted to shoot down one of his comrades. After that incident, however, it would be another month before he succeeded in claiming another enemy aeroplane.

Meanwhile, on 11 April, Jasta 26 was ordered to relocate to an airfield east of Guise,[21] in the Somme Sector. The prospects for air combat success were much higher in the new area, where German air units were using the vastly superior Albatros D.III fighters to inflict huge losses on Britain's Royal Flying Corps and Royal Naval Air Service. In that month alone – which has become known in aviation history as "Bloody April" – Britain lost one-third of her airmen then at the front, 912 pilots and observers in fifty squadrons.[22] Conversely, German airmen increased their scores significantly. Probably the best known example of German success in April 1917 was that of Rittmeister Manfred Freiherr von Richthofen, commanding officer of Jasta 11, who in that month added twenty-one enemy aeroplanes to his personal victory list, which rose from thirty-seven to fifty-two confirmed aerial victories.[23] Richthofen, who five months earlier trailed behind Göring in aerial kills, had become Germany's undisputed ace of aces.

Overall, Germany was in a much better position in early 1917 than it had been a year earlier. Its army had the advantage of having withdrawn behind strong defensive positions to reorganise its forces in anticipation of an impending British offensive. The air force had superior aircraft with which its pilots could fight or withdraw at will,

An aerial view of a Jasta 26 Albatros D.III on patrol.

generally over their own lines. Conversely, Major-General Hugh M. Trenchard, general officer commanding the Royal Flying Corps in France and Belgium, had to conserve his forces for the offensive, continuously and effectively countering German air units while trying to disrupt German communications.[24] Further complicating these difficulties, Trenchard's airmen had to meet these challenges in a month that was unusually stormy, with many snowfalls.[25]

Göring's Fourth, Fifth and Sixth Victories

Clear weather on Monday, 23 April 1917 favoured a major British infantry attack along a fifteen-kilometre line from Gavrelle to Croiselles[26] just west of Arras. The attack included a range of aerial activities, which had British squadrons up in strength from morning until evening.[27] To meet that challenge, Jasta 26 was ordered to advance its operations some fifteen kilometres northwest from Guise to Bohain,[28] which was an incremental step, but placed the unit closer to the fighting for Arras. During the move, Loerzer sent out a two-hour late afternoon patrol that departed Guise at 4:30 p.m. After flying westward to St. Quentin, then north to Cambrai, northwest to Arras and then southeast to St. Quentin, the patrol landed at Bohain at 6:30 p.m. It had covered nearly 200 kilometres during the flight and, about halfway through it, Göring shot down a rear-engined British F.E.2b. Although the aeroplane (serial number A.823 of 18 Squadron, RFC) returned to British territory, it was seen to crash by enough German witnesses for Göring to receive credit for his fourth victory. This aerial triumph was also noted in a new weekly publication that was instituted in March by the office of the commanding general of the Luftstreitkräfte.[29] Previously such successes appeared only in air activity summaries that the various army corps circulated within their own units. The new communication – titled Nachrichtenblatt der Luftstreitkräfte [intelligence summary of the air force] – assured that all air units would be made aware of the successes (and some failures) of their peers. Its recognition and motivational value to German airmen was as obvious as the highly-prized "Mentioned in Dispatches" (MiD) was to British Commonwealth military personnel.

Of course, there was more to that air action than the terse note in the Nachrichtenblatt and a description of the fight appeared in Göring's combat report:

'At 5:29 p.m., aerial combat with British lattice-fuselage two-seater from a [flight] of four [aircraft]. After a short fight I set fire to the opponent with [phosphorous] ammunition, [resulting in a] burning crash northeast of Arras at 5:30 p.m. Shortly thereafter, [I had] two more aerial combats with a lattice-fuselage [two-seater] and a single-seater. Without result. About 6:00 p.m. [I had] aerial combat with six [normal] fuselage biplanes which came from Guise via Hancourt.'[30]

According to British records, the downed aeroplane was scrapped.[31] The pilot, Second-Lieutenant Edmund L. Zink,[32] was wounded in the shoulder during the fight, while the observer, Second-Lieutenant George B. Bate,[33] was uninjured. Bate was fatally wounded in another aerial combat six days later.[34] A British account of Zink's and Bate's air fight with Jasta 26 appeared in a post-war memorial book published by the observer's school:

A captured Royal Aircraft Factory F.E.2b of the type claimed to be shot down by Göring on 23 April 1917.

'On April 23rd [1917], acting as observer, [Bate] went for his first flight over the German lines. In the engagement that followed he displayed great skill and gallantry, and brought down one of the enemy machines. His pilot was wounded and his own tunic was torn by a bullet, though he remained unharmed. The … [patrol] to which he was attached accounted for eleven enemy machines, without losing any of their own.'[35]

The RFC war diary entry for 23 April mentions only the crew of Second Lieutenant Reid and Lieutenant Fearnside-Speed of 18 Squadron as having 'driven down a hostile machine, which is believed to have fallen out of control'[36] and Jasta 26 suffered no casualties that day.[37] Hence, this British claim is questionable.

On 28 April, fighting at Arras was renewed and resulted in British gains.[38] Correctly anticipating that the British action at Arras would be accompanied by air attacks further south, German planners ordered fighter units, including Jasta 26, into action between Bohain and St. Quentin. Göring scored the Staffel's only victory of the day when his patrol attacked a flight of Sopwith two-seaters. Göring described the fight thus:

'About 6:30 p.m. [we had] aerial combat with a [flight] of six Sopwiths over St. Quentin. I shot down one Sopwith, which crashed behind our lines northeast of St. Quentin. After it tumbled over continuously, I followed close to my opponent. Shortly thereafter, a second Sopwith came spinning down, tumbling over and over, followed by one of our Albatros machines. I also went after the opponent down to 1,000 metres' altitude and saw him crash south of St. Quentin, apparently behind enemy lines.'[39]

Two German pilots claimed Sopwith two-seater victories that day, Jasta 26's Leutnant Hermann Göring and Offizierstellvertreter Edmund Nathanael of Jasta 5,[40] even though British records show only one such aircraft was lost. Nonetheless, both fighter pilots'

A Sopwith 1¹/₂ Strutter two-seat reconnaissance aeroplane, a type which Göring engaged on several occasions.

claims were confirmed. Possibly, Göring accounted for the Sopwith that landed within German lines, where its crewmen – Second-Lieutenant Clifford M. Reece,[41] pilot, and Aircraftsman 2nd Class William E. Moult,[42] air gunner, of 43 Squadron, RFC – were taken prisoner. A view of their aircraft is seen above.

The following day, Sunday, 29 April 1917, there was no doubt that Göring scored Jasta 26's only victory for the day, a Nieuport brought down near Ramicourt, some ten kilometres southwest of the Staffel's airfield at Bohain. To validate his claim, his combat report contained allegedly complete information about the downed aeroplane and the identity of its captured British pilot. Following his third patrol of the day, Göring wrote:

'About 7:45 p.m. [I had an] aerial combat over Ramicourt with a Nieuport single-seat fighter. I shot it down. [The pilot] tried to land southwest of Ramicourt. [The aeroplane] tumbled over on landing. The pilot, Lieutenant Flescher [*sic*] was severely wounded by a richochet shot to the lower calf.

'As I flew at 100 metres' altitude to Bohain, a second enemy single-seater came down from above, pursued by an Albatros. The Englishman attacked me shortly and hit my [aileron cable]. He himself was then pursued by an Albatros and forced to land. I could not observe any further developments since I had to fly without lateral control, which demanded my entire attention. The [captured] Nieuport bore the serial number 2745 (17bis) Engine number 2813 Type 9B.'[43]

Göring brought down Flight Sub-Lieutenant Albert H.V. Fletcher,[44] a twenty-three-year-old South African, who was taken prisoner at the crash site of his Nieuport 17bis (serial number N.3192) of 6 Squadron, Royal Naval Air Service. However, no British Nieuport ever bore the serial number 2745, as indicated in the combat report.[45] Göring duly received official credit for his sixth aerial victory.[46]

Göring's Seventh Victory

Existing documentation does not include a copy of the combat report for Göring's next victory, an Airco D.H.4 two-seat reconnaissance and bomber aeroplane he shot down on the afternoon of Thursday, 10 May 1917. While that event was reasonably fresh in his mind, however, he wrote at length about it – with typical dramatic flair – for an anthology of German airmen's experiences that was published in 1923. Göring recalled:

Göring took this photograph of Nieuport 17bis (N.3192), which he brought down on 29 April 1917.

'May 1917! It is a splendid spring day, trees in full bloom, the radiant blue sky extends over the … Somme countryside. Only lightly attired, I lie under the wondrously flowering apple tree, let the burning afternoon sun shine on my body, stretch myself in the pleasant warmth. Now and then there is a gentle breeze; then white and pink blossoms flutter down on to me. Everything around me, as far as the eye wanders across the broad countryside, breathes of peace. It is also quiet today at the frontlines. Silently our sleek [Albatros] aeroplanes stand in front of their tent-hangars; they are also sunning themselves. Down below, the Oise river winds its way to the south west; its waters shimmering. I stare into the endless sky, which shows not even the smallest cloud, and dream. High in its zenith stands the sun, sending out incandescent fire, everything draws closer beneath the shady canopy of blossoms.

'Suddenly harsh thuds pierce the peace of the spring day; in the north there are white shrapnel clouds in the blue heavens, at high altitude the sound of engines is as faint as the hum of bees. "Enemy flyers in sight", calls out the sentry. With one blow the numbness dissolves, we jump up and get dressed. The dreams are forgotten, the weariness is gone, muscles and senses become taut. The engines of our aeroplanes thunder into life – we are ready.

'"All clear" is the last command. My machine races across the grass, after a few seconds I take off from the ground. I am flying. The pitching and vibrating has stopped, my bird calmly climbs on high, towards the sun. I look around me; following close behind me, the [patrol] leader, are three other aeroplanes. They depend on me to lead them into battle and to victory, just as I trust them to follow me wherever I lead them. Higher and higher we climb, farther and farther the countryside stretches below us. There is nothing more of the oppressive mid-day heat to be felt; cold, fresh currents of air rush by us. The 160-horsepower engine works calmly and surely; at 130 kilometres per hour we climb southward toward the sun in order to remain unseen to the enemy, lying in wait within its powerful rays …

'Now the altimeter shows 5,000 metres. We are high enough to be able to reach the enemy bombers, which at this altitude intrude deeply into our rear. I throw my machine onto one wing and steer a northerly course. The others follow this manoeuvre as quick as lightning and the swarm is again gathered tightly. Restlessly, eyes search the horizon to find our opponent. We are approaching Cambrai. Then, suddenly, again there are exploding puffs from our anti-aircraft guns; they are at about 4,000 metres. Right after that I catch sight of the enemy: four big bombers hastening back to their frontlines. But they are not alone; several single-seat fighters are advancing across the frontlines to make contact with their returning comrades and cover them. Now … lightning-quick, the decision must be made as to which of the two groups is to be attacked. A battle against the bombers – with the enemy single-seaters behind us – promises little success. Therefore, first [we go] against the single-seaters. We have higher altitude and dive with greater speed onto the smaller machines and at the same time cut off the line of retreat of the big planes coming from the east.

'Unexpectedly, we break out of the cover of the sun and open fire. Our [single-seat] opponents are confounded, bring their machines about and flee behind their own frontlines. They are beaten in the field of battle and now can only follow the main attack of the bombers, which are still over our territory. We hurry after [the bombers] in a dive and in tight turns each of us gets behind his opponent. By this manoeuvre I have come out slightly ahead of my comrades and in the blink of an eye, as I charge into the formation, I am alone for a few seconds. Fierce machine-gun fire from four aeroplanes crackles towards me; an angry rattling resounds unpleasantly in my ears. The smoke streaks of the incendiary ammunition come whistling close by me. Gritting my teeth, I get closer to them. To the right and left, my people now appear and bring relief. I still have one opponent to deal with. Infuriated, he hurls his bullets at me, I dive below him and gain momentum so that I can pursue him like an arrow. The enemy observer stretches far out of his cockpit to be able to shoot more easily at me; just then I also open fire. At the same time my two machine guns hurl a hail of metal into the enemy aeroplane. From thirty to fifty metres' distance, I am now right at his fuselage, while his stream of fire comes right by me. But I do not let up and soon the observer slumps over. Just after that an enormous flame of fire bursts out of the machine and … the enemy aeroplane explodes. Wood and metal splinters fly everywhere and endanger my machine; quickly, I pull up to climb above the wreckage swirling in the air. Below me, the brightly flaming fuselage and its crew plunge to the ground. The wings break off and follow slowly smouldering, leaving behind a black ribbon of smoke. This all took only a few moments, but it was an experience of great stress! The enemy is demolished. I look around me and a thousand metres below me I see a comrade in battle with an opponent which he forces lower and lower until finally … [it] hits the ground and smashes to pieces.

'Less successful were both of our comrades: each of their opponents just barely got away. The four of us formed up tightly together, set a course for our airfield and a few minutes later I am again lying under my blossoming tree – it has not even been an hour since we were resting here.

'Again I stare into the sky, in which everything is now calm, and think about my brave opponents – Englishmen – who now find their graves in France's soil. My nerves tingle faintly [from the recent excitement] while a steamy oppressive humidity spreads over the countryside. "My second victory," says my comrade, who is stretched out contentedly in the blazing sun. I reply: "My seventh". Tranquillity rules again, as we dream on. Strong thunder rumbles and black clouds move in from the south, lightning flashes, the relief of thunderstorms draws near. Gusts of strong wind disrupt the oppressive humidity of the late afternoon. Heavy drops of rain come pelting down. We hurry inside. Refreshed by the stormy air, we sit in the garden of our quarters in the evening twilight and there the Staffelführer [Bruno Loerzer] raises his glass. We drink to the victors: "*Vivant sequentes!* [Long live those who are to come!]".

'Lightly we clink our glasses together, the ice-cool wine relieves the burning thirst of the hot day. Yes, *vivant sequentes!*'[47]

The RFC war diary entry for 10 May offers another albeit less dramatic view of the quartet of D.H.4s that Göring's patrol engaged:

'A photographic reconnaissance of No. 55 Squadron had heavy fighting during the whole time they were over the lines. As a result of the combat, one German machine was destroyed by Lieut. Pitt and 2nd Lieut. Holroyde, and two were driven down out of control – one by Capt. Rice and 2nd Lieut. Clarke, and the other by 2nd Lieut. Webb and 1/AM Bond.'[48]

There were no German fighter aircraft losses corresponding to these claims; indeed, there was only one fighter loss that day – Leutnant der Reserve Werner Albert of Jasta 31 – and it occurred over Vaudesincourt[49] in the Champagne Sector. It took place too far east to be connected to 55 Squadron's operations.

However, a British source confirms the loss of 55 Squadron's D.H.4s over German lines that day, while making a photographic reconnaissance of a seven-kilometre area from Caudry to Neuvilly, northwest of Le Cateau:

- The crew of Second-Lieutenants Bevan W. Pitt and John S. Holroyde[50] in D.H.4 A.7416, whose aircraft, according to RFC records, was last seen going 'down in flames and … [was] seen to crash at Le Cateau … A German publication states that both pilot and observer were killed.'[51]

- Captain H. Senior and Corporal P.H. Holland, R.E.[52] in D.H.4 A.7413, whose 'machine [was] brought down at Gouzeaucourt … pilot wounded, observer killed'.[53]

- Second-Lieutenant Trevor Webb and Aircraftsman 1st Class (Sergeant) Walter Bond[54] in D.H.4 A.7419, whose 'machine was seen to fall in pieces at Le Cateau as a result of a direct hit by A.A. fire… A German publication states that both pilot and observer were killed.'[55]

In addition to Göring's claim of credit for a D.H.4 that exploded in the air over Le Pavé, just over twenty-five kilometres west of Le Cateau, there were two other German participants in this fight: Leutnant Walter Blume, also of Jasta 26, who claimed a British two-seater northeast of Gouzeaucourt, some thirty-two kilometres west of Le Cateau; and Vizefeldwebel Fritz Krebs claimed a British normally 'fuselaged' biplane north of Le Cateau. All three claims were approved.[56]

Sorting out the claims, it seems most likely that Göring shot down the two-seater that exploded; despite the RFC contention that the Webb-Bond aeroplane was hit by anti-aircraft, no German anti-aircraft [*Flug-Abwehr-Kanone*, popularly known as *Flak*] unit claimed a two-seater in that area on 10 May.[57] Blume's claim of a two-seater northeast of Gouzeaucourt was almost certainly the aircraft in which Captain Senior and Corporal Holland were brought down. And, Krebs' claim of a victory north of Le Cateau surely involved the Pitt-Holroyde D.H.4.

The unnamed comrade with whom Göring chatted lightly after the fight was Leutnant Walter Blume, who achieved his first (not second) aerial victory that day. Blume had been a successful combat pilot in Feldflieger-Abteilung 65 in Alsace and, on 31 January 1917, became among the first pilots to join Jasta 26. He made steady progress in his air fighting career and, after he shot down twenty-seven enemy aeroplanes, on 2 October 1918 he was awarded the coveted Pour le Mérite.[58]

Command of Jagdstaffel 27

A week after Göring scored his seventh aerial victory, the commanding general of the air force appointed him as Staffelführer of Jasta 27. Established on 5 February 1917,[59] the Staffel was initially led by Leutnant Hans von Keudell, a founding member of Jasta 1 and an eleven-victory ace; he started with four pilots, mechanics and fighter aircraft (older machines used by Jastas 8 and 18) and three aeroplanes and pilots from Armee-Flugpark 4 [Army Air Park 4] in Gent. Keudell led this battle force to its first airfield, at Ghistelles[60] in the 4th Army Sector in Flanders,[61] where the next Allied offensive was anticipated. Keudell scored Jasta 27's first aerial victory, on 15 February, but was himself shot down and killed the same day.[62] He was succeeded by Württemberg native Leutnant der Reserve

Göring kept Albatros D.III 2049/16, seen here at far right, when he transferred from Jasta 26 to Jasta 27.

Phillip Wieland, who had scored an aerial victory while with Feldflieger-Abteilung 6 and went on to fly with Jasta 8 before joining Keudell's crew.[63] In late March, Wieland moved the unit[64] southwest to an airfield at Iseghem, in the 6th Army Sector.[65] The new airfield was even closer to the battles that would mark Bloody April, but Jasta 27 faced a daunting task: it was the only mid-to-high-flying single-seat fighter unit assigned to Gruppe Souchez,[66] one of five aircraft unit groupings in the 6th Army Sector. Jasta 27 and three Schutzstaffeln [protection flights] of low-level two-seat ground attack aircraft[67] were responsible for four two-seat reconnaissance / artillery cooperation units.[68] Additionally, Jasta 27 lacked new aeroplanes – and an aggressive Staffelführer with more combat experience.

By mid-May, 'such Allied types as the Spad, Sopwith Pup and [Sopwith] Triplane, and S.E.5 [were] each able to out-fly the Albatros D.III'.[69] In the face of that situation, it was clear that Hermann Göring, an accomplished Albatros pilot and flight leader, was definitely the man to command Jasta 27. Leutnant der Reserve Helmuth Dilthey, a seasoned combat pilot newly assigned to the Staffel,[70] noted:

> 'Our fighter aeroplanes were mostly technically inferior to those of the enemy. Speed and ceiling were too low. When I came from Feldflieger-Abteilung 50 to Jagdstaffel 27, we had only three combat-ready aeroplanes there, instead of the eighteen planned. Thus, with its technically inferior single-seaters at the time, the Staffel had no aerial victories at all. When we got Leutnant Göring as Staffelführer, it became better, for not only did he already have seven confirmed aerial victories, but also pleaded our case very energetically to the higher-ups.'[71]

As the records shows, Göring's combat experience and knack for connecting with senior officers would lead Jasta 27 to greater success in the battles to come.

CHAPTER EIGHT
THE TEST OF COMBAT

'The victory is finally mine and the Englishman is taken prisoner …
But my strength is at an end, my knees shake, my pulse is pounding,
my entire body is soaking wet because I had to work so hard during the battle.'[1]

HERMANN GÖRING

By the time Hermann Göring arrived at Jagdstaffel 27, the unit had moved southward from Iseghem to an airfield at Bersée, outside of Lille, the key industrial city in German-occupied northern France. The movement of their air units was a consequence of the German high command's receiving only scant information about Allied intentions following Britain's disappointing results in the Battle of Arras.[2]

H. A. Jones, the official Royal Air Force historian noted why German planners were strengthening their air units in Flanders:

> 'When the Arras offensive began to slacken [in late April], a general move north had begun. Between the 4th of May and the 7th of June, [General der Infanterie Friedrich Sixt von] Armin's Fourth Army along the front from the River Douve to the sea was increased from fifteen air units (ten reconnaissance and artillery flights and five fighter flights) to forty-four (nineteen reconnaissance, eight protection [Schutzstaffeln], eleven single-seat fighter, and six bomber-fighter flights). These units represented a nominal strength of about 300 aeroplanes of which half were fighters. That is to say, the German air strength from Messines to the sea was approximately the same as the Royal Air Force strength available for the ten-mile front along the Messines ridge.'[3]

Messines, only eighteen kilometres northwest of the centre of Lille, was the focal point of the coming Allied offensive. For almost a year, British sappers had tunnelled to prepare for 'the simultaneous explosion of nineteen great mines, containing 600 tons of explosives' under the Messines ridge at 3:10 a.m. on 7 June 1917.[4] The explosions and attendant artillery barrage led to the successful British infantry assault at Messines, and later Wytschaete, but German air operations were unaffected by that event.

Indeed, if one were to believe Hermann Göring's 1930 account, all of the action in Flanders took place in the air:

> 'Again it is a clear June day in the year 1917, not even a small cloud in the heavens. In the early morning hours, I gathered my officers and pilots about me and impressed on them all of the regulations about flying and fighting as a formation. Then I assigned

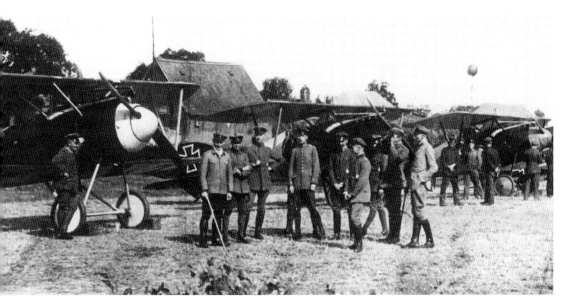

Hermann Göring, far left, often walked with a cane due to flare-ups of rheumatoid arthritis. His distinctively marked Albatros D.III 2049/16 is seen behind him.

each one his place in the formation and gave the final orders. I believed the new Staffel to have been sufficiently trained and I firmly decided to lead them into battle this day and ... let them show proof of it.

'Soon after take-off the formation was assembled and we set out in the direction of the frontlines. In order to fly and fight in a more mobile way, I had the Staffel separated into two flights of five units each. I led the lower one and the upper one had to stay closely above us and follow. In the sector from Lens to Lille a relative calmness prevailed. From time to time a lone artillery spotter aeroplane moved about with great effort far behind its own lines. We flew on and on northward toward our chief objective, the Wytschaete Salient.

'When we arrived at Ypres, we were at 5,000 metres altitude. A marvellous view of Flanders was spread out below us. In the distant background gleamed the coast of France, stretched along the sea; we could clearly recognise Dunkerque and Boulogne; we knew that in the pale mist at the end of the horizon were the chalk cliffs of the British Isles. Below us lay Ypres and the enemy positions, which were situated around the heavily shelled city in a salient opening to the west. To the north the Flanders coast stretched on from Ostende to the mouth of the Schelde river. The Schelde itself glistened in the sunshine on to Holland. From 5,000 metres the eye took in a view of this piece of the earth, above which arched the sky in light blue.

'But danger also lurked here and we had to ... examine everything carefully. A sudden flash in the sun could betray us or the enemy. Despite having dark-green lenses in our goggles it was difficult to make out objects in the blinding flood of sunlight ... Just then I recognized that six enemy fighter aircraft were above us and ... flying with us. Blue-white-red cockades clearly shone on their silver-grey wings. Yet they did not attack us, as we were too many for them; they simply followed at an ominously close distance. For the present, we ... could do nothing other than be careful.

'Then I sighted more opponents. A formation of enemy Spad single-seaters approached from the rear left, another of [Sopwith] Triplanes from ahead on the left, both still some kilometres away, but heading towards us. At this moment, coming from in front of us, there suddenly appeared a squadron of British Sopwith [Pup biplane] single-seat fighters. Now they had to be dealt with. If I were to attack them, I would immediately have the six Nieuports soaring over us and down on our necks and a few minutes later both of the other enemy formations would be rushing toward us, as well. If I were to avoid them, then I must abandon the frontlines altogether, and the airspace would be free for the Englishman; he could do whatever he wanted over our lines.

'I decided to attack immediately, no matter what the cost. Now everyone had to show what he could do and what he was good for. There was no longer any thought of retreat; we had started a fight against a force four times greater than ours, now we battled desperately for our survival. This is how I wished to put the Staffel to the test. The aerial battle was upon us. I gave the signal to attack – nosed over steeply with my machine – and charged into the Sopwiths. Immediately, they dispersed and the field of combat went downwards. There was wild firing all around me. From all sides you could see smoke trails of one's own and enemy incendiary bullets; tracer ammunition flew past me. Machines turned wildly, reared up, dived down, and looped.

'The enemy had now thrown himself into the battle in full strength; we duelled against thirty to forty enemy single-seaters. The greatest danger was [that we would] ram into each other. I sat behind a Sopwith that tried to elude my field of fire by desperately twisting and turning. I pushed him down ever lower as we came ever closer to enemy territory. I believed I would surely shoot him down, as he had taken some hard hits, when a furious hail of machine-gun fire opened up behind me. As I looked around, I saw only cockades; three opponents were on my neck, firing everything they had at me. Once again, with a short thrust, I tried to finish off the badly shot-up opponent ahead of me. It was too late. Smack after smack the shots from behind hit my machine. Metal fragments flew all around, the radiator was shot through; from a hole as big as a fist I was sprayed in the face by a heavy stream of hot water. Despite all that, I pulled the machine about and upwards and fired off a stream of bullets at the first fellow I saw. Surprised, he went into a spin. I caught up with the next opponent and went at him desperately, for I had to fight my way back across the lines. He also ceased fighting. It was a decisive moment. My engine, which was no longer receiving water from the radiator, quit and with that any further fighting by me was over.

'In a glide I passed over the lines and our positions. Close behind them I had to make a forced landing in a meadow. The landing proved to be a smooth one, and the machine stayed upright. Now I saw all of the damage. My worthy bird had received twenty hits, some of them very close to my body. I looked around me apprehensively; what had happened to my Staffel? There was a noise above me and shortly thereafter one of my pilots landed in the same meadow. His machine looked pretty bad too; various parts were shot to pieces. Another two pilots also had to make forced landings with shot-up machines. But the pilots were safe and sound. The Staffel had prevailed in the toughest battle. Despite its numerical superiority, the enemy had quit the field of battle. Everything had been observed from down below and we reaped our rewards of recognition. Far more important for me, however, was the feeling that I could depend on my Staffel. During this violent Flanders battle the Staffel had delivered on what it had promised on one fine June day – to fight and to be victorious.'[5]

Hermann Göring had such a good sense of history that, after he took formal command of Germany's military air arm in 1935,[6] he directed the Luftwaffe's historical branch to review all records and reports pertaining to his military activities from 1914 through 1918. Ultimately, a daily summary of all his operational flights and other materials was compiled for use in a planned biography of him that would have been longer and more detailed than the 349-page volume[7] his aide Dr. Erich Gritzbach had written. Had that project been completed, Luftwaffe archivists documenting Göring's World War I service would have faced the challenges this author found in trying to reconcile Göring's post-1918 writings with the official records so carefully preserved. In the case of the preceding account about 'a clear June day in … 1917,' Jagdstaffel 27's daily reports for June do not include a single day in which all of those actions occurred or of his leading two flights of aeroplanes 'of five units each' at the same time, as claimed in the article.

Daily Operations in June
Perhaps that 1930 text is a compilation of several air combats and related actions that occurred in June 1917, as seen in the following examples.

According to Jasta 27's daily report for Saturday, 2 June, late in the morning, during clear weather in the Ypres Sector,[8] Göring led five other Albatros D.III fighters from Bersée

Sopwith Triplanes were encountered by Jasta 27 at this time.

airfield southwest to Arras, then northward along the frontlines to Ypres at 5,000 metres and back southeast to the airfield.[9] His Staffel's mission was well defined:

'On the telephoned orders of the Kommandeur der Flieger 6, Jasta 27 is to depart as circumstances require on a special request by the Kommandeur der Flieger 4 in the sector of the 4th Army, particularly in the Wytschaete Salient. In accordance with Heeresgruppe [Army Group of Bavarian Crown Prince] Rupprecht I c order 18562 of 2 June 1917, Jagdstaffeln 30 and 27 are to shift the point of emphasis of their combat activity exclusively to the Wytschaete Salient.'[10]

The following evening, Göring did not score, but at about 6:50 p.m., Offizierstellvertreter Klein attacked and was credited with shooting down a Royal Naval Air Service Sopwith Triplane.[11]

On Tuesday, 5 June, Göring led a late morning flight, after which he reported:

'Combat with two Sopwith single-seaters [over Wytschaete[12]]. I pressed one down all the way to the trenches, where it suddenly disappeared from before my eyes. The last I saw of him he was weaving back and forth, tumbling like a falling card. British single-seaters coming from above to assist were no longer able to help the Sopwith.'[13]

Apparently, the British pilot's manoeuvres fooled Göring and the aeroplane returned to its own aerodrome, as the Royal Flying Corps combat casualty list contains no mention of a destroyed or damaged Sopwith single-seater arising from this encounter. Likewise, there was no German confirmation of a kill by Jasta 27 on this day.[14]

While leading an evening flight of four aeroplanes over the same area on Friday, 8 June, Göring shot down a British Nieuport single-seat fighter and received credit for his eighth aerial victory.[15] That aerial battle is discussed in detail on page 107-109.

The next afternoon, Göring and five comrades encountered British aircraft, two of which they attacked. Göring reported that 'the opponent was driven off', yet, in his own combat report, he claimed to have hit a B.E.2 reconnaissance plane east of Roulers at about 5:00 p.m. He said he was stopped from finishing off the two-seater when the empty portion of his ammunition belt came loose and jammed one of his machine guns. He made 'an intermediate landing at Abeele … [to] Jagdstaffel 26 to refill … ammunition'.[16] He was not credited with shooting down the B.E.2.

Based on verbal orders from its army corps aviation commanders, on Saturday, 16 June, Jasta 27 prepared to move fifty kilometres northward from Bersée, France in the 6th Armee Sector to Iseghem, Belgium in the 4th Armee Sector. Leutnant der Reserve Karl Riehm, the Staffel adjutant, organised transportation and other arrangements while Staffelführer Göring led seven of the unit's Albatroses along the frontlines from Lens to Roulers and then to their new airfield. No aerial combats were reported and, upon reaching Iseghem, they were greeted by members of Jasta 26, still under the command of Göring's closest friend, Oberleutnant Bruno Loerzer.[17]

There were no flight operations on Friday, 22 June, but Jasta 27 was identified in the 4th Army weekly report as being attached to Gruppe Jeperen [Ypres],[18] marking a shift in operational emphasis (within a very tight air defence boundary) from Wytschaete to Ypres, just over five kilometres to the north.

In the course of Jasta 27's afternoon patrol, between Ypres and Wytschaete, on Sunday, 24 June, Göring and three other pilots spotted isolated British aircraft within their own lines. Apparently the aeroplanes were protecting a British tethered observation balloon, one of several such craft in use to help range the guns of British artillery units. Göring and his men approached the frontlines, were greeted by red warning rounds of presumably phosphorous ammunition and did not proceed further.[19] That reticence was an odd reaction by the usually aggressive Staffelführer Göring and his not crossing the lines allowed British forces to hit German ground gunners in his sector. As one Allied source reported that day: 'Artillery of the [British] Second Army successfully dealt with nineteen hostile batteries, damaging ten gun pits and causing thirteen explosions.'[20]

Finally, continued rain on 30 June no doubt led to the cancellation of Jasta 27's flight operations for that day and the next. The Staffel did not report flying again until 2 July. While there is no evidence that Hermann Göring experienced a single day like that in his description above, he did have a hard-fought and successful engagement of a different nature on the morning of Friday, 8 June.

Göring's Eighth Victory

He wrote about that day when his recollection of events was sharper, for an anthology of German wartime aviation reminiscences that appeared in 1920:

'It was on 8 June 1917. The unnatural heat of early summer … still weighed oppressively over the countryside. The sun stood brightly in the sky, yet it was just six o'clock [in the morning] and therefore still somewhat cool. I wanted to make the most of it. A few minutes later the entire Jagdstaffel flew closely together under my leadership towards the northwest. I went by our actual Front to the left, because we had been assigned to fly in support of the 4th Army in Flanders. There, the battle in the Wytschaete Salient had flared up and with it the beginning of the great British offensive in Flanders, which amid violent battles would continue on into the winter.

'Bathed in a torrent of sunshine, Lille lay before us. There was clear visibility as far as we could see; there was heavy haze only in the south near Arras. It was a glorious feeling to fly through the radiant morning, full of eager expectation about what the next hours would bring. Behind me followed a group formation of ten aeroplanes of my Staffel. I'd been their leader for just a few days and had not yet tested the pilots sufficiently. So it was all the more urgent to make sure that the enemy would not come up from behind and pounce on them and slaughter them before I could speed back to help them, as they were all still new as fighter pilots. Yet I was in good spirits and full of fervour to train this good material into a dashing, battle-ready Staffel.

'We were up to about 4,000 metres when we flew over the Lys river and had thereby reached our hunting ground, which lay about sixty kilometres away from our airfield. Below on the battlefield there was a wild battle going on; very heavy mortar and barrage fire was falling onto already battered positions. But I did not have time to observe this enormous battle; I had to search for the enemy and hit him. I did not have to wait long: above us appeared a Nieuport formation of twelve units. They were hard to see, these small, silver-grey fighting machines; cleverly, they sat [with the sun behind them] and from there dived onto us. The … battle began. My formation split up too early and could no longer fight in a unified way. I was as wary as a lynx whenever one of my men was in danger and dashed over to him to give him room to manoeuvre. Then I had to go after this one and then that opponent to support those being harried. But my pilots struck back well and threw the opponent back behind his own lines.

'During this engagement all the action drops down lower. I had just taken a deep breather from the wild mêlée when suddenly I see an opponent above me. Carefully, he stalks me from out of the sun in order to surprise me and shoot me down from behind. I realise his intention, let him approach and know that it will come to a decisive battle. He has the tactically better position and I have the stronger machine and a favourable wind. The duel can begin. Now he believes that he has seized a favourable moment and comes down on me like a hawk. That is what I am waiting for; I push my machine down a bit to pick up momentum, pull it around in a flash and powerfully rise up towards him, at the same time opening fire with both machine guns. Instead of his catching me from behind and surprising me, I hit him from the front and parry his thrust, surprising him. He has gone from the attacker to the attacked. My burst of fire is on the mark, for immediately he goes into a spin to get away from it … and now I am on his heels and forcing him down with my machine-gun fire. A frenzied mêlée begins. Around to the right, around to the left, loops, turns, pulling the machine up high and at the same time letting it side-slip again. Every feint and trick is used in an attempt to get behind the other, to get above him to get on the inside of a turn in order to bring to bear a burst of fire right on the target. Often we rush so closely by each other that [we] believe we are going to crash into each other.

'The Englishman flies splendidly, skilfully and smartly; I see him clearly, sitting in his machine. The battle is furious, exciting and strenuous, neither of us wants to give up, each hopes resolutely for victory. I skid into a turn and my opponent has already spotted his advantage and in a rage pounds away at me with his weapons. Several hits strike my aeroplane close behind me. Again I bring my machine up as straight as a candle and fire at the Englishman. He has also taken some hits. In a nosedive he roars by me and tries to make good his escape from me. I put my bird on its nose and chase after him. He begins anew to twist wildly in order to get away from my fire. Now we are at no more than 2,000 metres' altitude. Once again he furiously takes up the battle and tries to attack me. Now I have only a few bullets, they must be expended carefully. The decision must come quickly, for I have become sick of the idiotic turning. Yet he defends himself desperately. I must exert myself to the utmost. With my last bit of resolution I throw myself at him and at extremely close range I drive my shots into his machine. He goes tumbling down, his engine is off; he is shot to pieces.

'Just above the ground he starts his engine once again and tries to land, but the landing goes badly, [and] his machine is smashed to bits. He himself is hurled out, but remains uninjured. The victory is finally mine and the Englishman is taken prisoner … But my strength is at an end, my knees shake, my pulse is pounding, my entire body is soaking wet because I had to work so hard during the battle. It was a tough struggle.

'The gruelling battle had lasted ten minutes. The Englishman was an evenly-matched opponent. A few minutes later I landed near my friend Loerzer [commander of Jasta 26 at Iseghem] in order to recuperate and to fortify myself with a hearty breakfast. The telephone reported from the frontlines that my opponent was taken prisoner. He was an experienced fighter pilot, who had already shot down five German aeroplanes. I was able to speak with him and … we both made flattering comments about this difficult battle. In the afternoon I returned to my airfield. Thank goodness, I said to myself, it is better that Mister Slee[21] is on my victory list as the eighth[22] instead of my being on his as Number Six!'[23]

Göring's opponent was Australian-born Second-Lieutenant Frank D. Slee of 1 Squadron, RFC, who flew one of four Nieuport 23 fighters that departed at 5:25 that morning on a two-hour offensive patrol (O.P.) from Poelcapelle to Passchendaele to Wervicq. According to an RFC report:

'Between Poelcapelle and Becelaere, at 14,000 to 18,000 feet, six H.A. [hostile aeroplanes] were engaged by patrol. Lt Hazell drove one down in a series of rolls – Decisive. Confirmed by 2/Lt Fullard. He also drove one down vertical – Indecisive. 2/Lt Fullard sent one down in flames – Decisive. One of the H.A. was painted black fuselage with white band and red crosses on band.

'2/Lt Fullard saw a Nieuport going down vertical with an Albatross [sic] on its tail.

'2/Lt Nuding made a forced landing … owing to [his] engine being hit by a bullet – machine turned over on landing. Pilot unhurt.

'2/Lt Slee fell behind enemy lines.'[24]

Despite the RFC claims, there were no matching German fighter casualties that day.[25] However, another view of Slee's encounter with Göring was made public in 2003, when the Australian pilot's son, John, released part of his father's wartime memoir. That text revealed that, despite Göring's contention that Slee was an RFC ace, the Australian was on his first mission over the lines when the Jasta 27 Albatroses struck. Slee wrote that his flight commander, Lieutenant Tom Falcon Hazell, instructed him: 'Don't join in any scraps this trip. Just pull out to the side and watch, then rejoin us.'[26]

Apparently, the twenty-three-year-old Nieuport pilot could not resist going after Göring's aeroplane, which was below him and seemed to be an ideal target. Slee dived on it and opened fire. Later he wrote: 'I will swear I hit his machine. I could see my tracer bullets.'[27] But as Slee pursued his intended victim eastward, into German territory, he was attacked by two other Albatroses and, eventually, his Nieuport's engine was knocked out and Slee had to head for the ground. He found a flat meadow and landed, after which he was captured before he could set fire to his aeroplane.

When he was in German custody, Slee was visited by three German pilots, with whom he 'had a broken conversation in schoolboy French'. After reading an account of the fight in a 1950 Göring biography by Willi Frischauer, the Australian learned who his opponent had been.

Slee's French-built Nieuport 23 fighter was the fifth aeroplane that Göring shot down while flying the Albatros D.III (serial number 2049/16)[28] that he had brought with him from Jasta 26. Despite Slee's best efforts to destroy or disable that Albatros, it was none the worse for wear and Göring went on to use it five weeks later, when he scored his ninth confirmed aerial victory.

Göring posed in the cockpit of Albatros D.III 2049/16 for a picture that eventually appeared on a popular Sanke postcard.

High-quality postcard photos of aviators had begun to appear before World War I. After hostilities began in 1914, however, a small industry of postcard providers saw profits to be made by offering the likenesses of flyers and other national heroes. Thus, Göring's Albatros served as the setting for his first exposure to national fame. After his fifth victory, a view of him – which he captioned 'I in my fighter-machine, Albatros D.III 2049'[29] – appeared in June[30] as Postcard No. 535 in the series of views offered by Berlin-based *Postkartenvertrieb* [postcard sales by] W. Sanke. That company specialised in airmen's likenesses and distributed their images nationwide. The cards were widely collected by Germans young and old to show support for their country's aviation heroes.

Now Göring could consider himself to be a success. Loerzer outranked him, but he had shot down more enemy aeroplanes at the time – eight to Loerzer's five – and his picture had appeared on a postcard. Just like Manfred von Richthofen and the major aces and Pour le Mérite recipients.

It was small glory, perhaps, but it was important to Göring.

Chapter Nine

In Flanders' Skies

'Again and again new forces from both sides arrive and at times
over 100 aeroplanes can be seen above the ... ground fighting.
It is a mad Witches' Sabbath in the skies.'[1]

HERMANN GÖRING

Once the Messines ridge was cleared of German troops in early June 1917, British ground forces advanced their campaign to drive back the German army in Flanders. But, as an eminent British historian observed: 'Nearly two months passed before ...preparations for the main advance were completed, and during the interval the Germans had ample warning to prepare counter-measures.'[2] The coming event would be known as the Third Battle of Ypres because of its focus on the commanding heights of the German salient opposite that city. But even before the campaign began, on 31 July 1917, Oberleutnant Hermann Göring and Jagdstaffel 27 were aggressively – and successfully – challenging their Royal Flying Corps adversaries in the skies above and around the centuries-old city (see Appendix I).

Two weeks before the battle started – on the evening of Monday, 16 July 1917 – the Albatroses of Jasta 27 tangled with S.E.5 fighters of 56 Squadron, RFC. The British aircraft were escorting a bomber formation when they were attacked by Göring and ten of his comrades.[3] Following that encounter, the Staffelführer gained his ninth aerial victory,[4] but, as Göring noted in his combat report, one of his foes got in enough good shots to knock loose the engine of his Albatros D.III:

'At 8:10 p.m., northeast of Ypres I attacked a single-seater formation, [and] shot down one, which ... crashed. Immediately thereafter, I had to turn against a second opponent, whom I forced down to 200 metres. As a result of [that] aerial combat, suddenly the engine dropped off [its mountings] and hung only loosely in the fuselage [in such a way] that I immediately went into a spin and [had to] land the machine behind the third row [of trenches], where I nosed over. By that [action] the second opponent got away.'[5]

Apparently, Göring's first opponent was Second-Lieutenant Robert G. Jardine[6] of 56 Squadron, RFC, whose aircraft reportedly was disabled. Back on the ground, Göring's Albatros D.III (serial number 2049/16) – in which he had scored his fourth, fifth and sixth victories – was beyond salvaging and was scrapped. His new aeroplane, an Albatros D.V, was fitted with a more powerful engine than his D.III.

He flew Albatros D.V 2080/17 when he scored again, on the evening of Tuesday, 24 July 1917. Earlier that day, a Göring protégé, Leutnant der Reserve Helmuth Dilthey, scored his first victory – which was also Jasta 27's first triumph over a Royal Naval Air Service Sopwith Triplane fighter. Dilthey wrote:

After being badly damaged in aerial combat, Göring's Albatros D.III 2049/16 carried him back to his airfield and then was finally scrapped.

'I was ordered, with two other machines, to keep enemy aeroplanes far from the frontlines and to protect our own flyers there. At the frontlines I encountered seven Sopwith [biplane] single-seaters that withdrew as I turned towards them at about the same altitude. After that, above them appeared three triplanes, [employing] … what was for them the usual and … relatively safe tactic of diving down on us from above, firing, but before coming close, pulling up … Thanks to their tremendous climbing ability, [they] were again immediately several hundred metres above us. After this manoeuvre, one of them flew by us and off to the side. I also pulled right up and fired at him … until my machine side-slipped, which occurred after a short time as I had to put my

This captured S.E.5a was the same type as that flown by Second-Lieutenant Robert G. Jardine, and was also from 56 Squadron, RFC, but was not flown by him.

machine into an extremely steep angle in order to get the higher flying triplane in my gun-sight.

'Just as my machine went into a side-slip … I caught it again, I thought: "He was, of course, probably too high to hit and the time was too short." Then I saw individual pieces of the aeroplane falling by me … I recognised the British cockade. I made note of the place where the main piece fell, which took a relatively long time, and then gathered again … the other members of my swarm.'[7]

The Sopwith Triplane could 'out-climb and out-turn the Albatros and was fifteen miles per hour faster'.[8] This time, however, the Sopwith 'Tripehound', as it was nicknamed, perished under the guns of a more experienced Albatros pilot. A British source noted that nineteen-year-old Canadian Flight Sub-Lieutenant Theodore C. May, RNAS[9] 'was last seen folding up and falling near Moorslede when diving to attack [enemy aircraft]. An unconfirmed report in [the] German press states that "J.C. May [sic]" is dead.[10]

Twenty minutes later and about three kilometres to the west, Staffelführer Göring (in his new Albatros D.V) and seven of his men attacked a flight of British two-seaters. Göring wrote in his combat report:

'At about 8:30 in the evening ... my Staffel [engaged in] aerial combat with an enemy formation. Quickly, I attacked the enemy machines ... after which they disappeared in the extraordinary haze and clouds; at 3,200 metres' altitude I cornered an opponent – apparently a Martinsyde – which I forced down in a spiral fight. The opponent spun often and lastly crashed from a 200-metre altitude north of Polygon Wood (south of Passchendaele). I circled the area several times and then flew back. I had come down to about 200 metres. The opponent had a large C or G on the upper wing. Time of crash 8:40 p.m.'

A formal view of Second-Lieutenant Robert G. Jardine, fatally wounded in an aerial combat with Hermann Göring.

The British source that confirmed the loss of the Sopwith Triplane recorded no casualties of Martinsyde or any other two-seaters in the area northeast of Ypres that day. Yet, Göring was credited with his tenth victory.[11]

Hermann Göring (second from right) and Helmuth Dilthey (far right) at the crash site of the 10 Squadron, RNAS Sopwith Triplane that Dilthey shot down on 24 July 1917.

Striving for the Pour le Mérite

After his tenth air combat triumph was confirmed, Hermann Göring sought to fulfil one of his boyhood ambitions alluded to earlier: To distinguish himself and earn more (and presumably higher) medals than his father had received in the Franco-Prussian War. In World War I, the zenith of German military recognition was Prussia's highest bravery award, the Pour le Mérite, established by Prussian King Frederick II in June 1740 and conferred upon officers for 'truly brave conduct in battle' in every major Prussian, or subsequently German, conflict up to the end of World War I.[12] After Boelcke and Immelmann became the first flyers to receive the award, in 1916, Göring eagerly followed succeeding reports of fellow fighter pilots who also earned it. But, without understanding the award's criteria, he now considered that his achievements were such that he deserved this significant honour and he acted accordingly. As he could not propose himself for the award, he persuaded some of his superiors to present a case for recognition of his combat achievements. Göring's approach was naïve, but no one seemed to be willing or able to sharpen his perspectives.

He initiated the process by urging his immediate superior, Hauptmann Percy Baron von Ascheberg, to write a letter of recommendation for him. Ascheberg, a pre-war flyer,[13] had been appointed to the new post of Gruppenführer der Flieger 15 three months earlier.[14] He was responsible for coordinating the missions of groups of 4th Army air units and his letter carried significant influence as it was forwarded up the chain of command – and endorsed at every intermediate level – to the overall regional authority. Thus, within a few days Ascheberg's letter of 28 July 1917 was on the desk of Generalleutnant Freiherr von Stein, commander of the Royal Bavarian 3rd Army Corps. It recounted Göring's achievements since the beginning of the war and concluded:

> '[Göring] is an excellent Staffelführer, who by his ability and accomplishments serves as a special example for his Staffel. He understands how to motivate his Staffel through his [strong] personality and thereby have them perform in a superior manner. Being such a young officer, he nevertheless commands his Staffel even under the most difficult flying circumstances and has proven himself, especially as a Staffelführer. Thanks to their commanding officer, the Staffel maintains a good and daring spirit. I consider Leutnant Göring to be worthy of every decoration.'[15]

Generalleutnant von Stein endorsed the recommendation, which was followed two weeks later, on 13 August, by an even more important and equally enthusiastic recommendation of Göring for the Pour le Mérite. That letter – signed by General der Infanterie Friedrich Sixt von Arnim, commanding general of the 4th Army – drew attention to Göring's leadership, bravery and resilience despite his serious combat wounds. Further, Sixt von Arnim wrote, 'Leutnant Göring has served continuously on the Western Front as a fighter pilot and distinguished himself as the leader of a Jagdstaffel … by prudent leadership and personal spirit … Under his leadership, his Staffel has achieved forty-nine aerial victories … Therefore, I propose most humbly that this proven, extremely efficient and excellent officer, who has served continually in the field for four years of war, be awarded the high decoration of the Pour le Mérite.'[16]

A Sopwith Camel of the type Göring claimed as his eleventh aerial victory.

Despite a glaring factual error – Jasta 27 had a total of only ten (not forty-nine) confirmed aerial victories as of 5 August 1917[17] – Sixt von Arnim's letter was sent to Generalleutnant Ernst von Hoeppner, commanding general of the Luftstreitkräfte, by the newly appointed officer in charge of aviation for the 4th Army, Hauptmann Helmuth Wilberg – a friend Göring had made during the Battle of Verdun over a year earlier.[18] There can be little doubt that Göring provided the information for Sixt von Arnim's letter. That no one checked the figure before the general signed the letter is another example of Göring's incredible good luck, which only fuelled his brazen self-confidence.

In fact, Jasta 27's tenth victory was also Göring's eleventh individual confirmed victory,[19] which was scored on Sunday evening, 5 August. In that fight, his patrol attacked nine Sopwith F.1 Camels, among the Royal Flying Corps' newest fighter aeroplanes. South of Houthulst forest, Göring got on the tail of one Camel and opened fire from a distance of fifty metres. 'Suddenly, flames … and heavy smoke came out of the machine and the opponent went [down] into a deep spiral in the dense cloud mass',[20] he reported. Göring's opponent, Lieutenant Gilbert Budden[21] of 70 Squadron, RFC, made it back to British lines, where he was reported as: 'Wounded in left arm. Forced landing near Bailleul owing to machine being damaged during combat.'[22]

Surely, the nomination process for Göring's Pour le Mérite award was aided when, on 15 August, Generalleutnant Freiherr von Stein praised Jasta 27's most recent efforts in the Battle for Ypres. Published in the daily report of the Ypres battle group (and widely circulated within the 4th Army), Freiherr von Stein's letter commended Jasta 27's Leutnant der Reserve Ludwig Luer and Vizefeldwebel Max Krauss for each shooting down a British tethered observation balloon northwest of Ypres. He also praised Vizefeldwebel Alfred Muth for attempting to shoot down yet another balloon, which 'was prevented … by balloon defence aeroplanes and [then Muth] became engaged in intense aerial combat'.[23] All of these actions reflected favourably on Göring's leadership capabilities.

Command responsibilities were much discussed among career officers such as Göring and Loerzer, as new levels of opportunity were opening in the Luftstreitkräfte. On 23 June 1917, the chief of the general staff announced the formation of Germany's first Jagdgeschwader [fighter wing] composed of Jagdstaffeln 4, 6, 10 and 11[24] in daily flights and led by Manfred von Richthofen, the highest-scoring fighter pilot of the war. The success of Jagdgeschwader I's joint operations led to the establishment of four Jagdgruppen [temporary groupings of fighter units] in the 4th Army Sector. One of them, Jagdgruppe 15, was composed of Jastas 3, 8, 26 and 27,[25] with Jasta 8's commanding officer, Hauptmann Constantin von Bentheim, in charge of the grouping. Bentheim was senior to Göring and Loerzer, but he had only one aerial victory to his credit, which robbed him of the prestige advantage that Richthofen and other group leaders enjoyed. Surely, Göring could imagine succeeding to Hauptmann von Bentheim's position.

Göring's ambitions must have been fuelled further when he was promoted to Oberleutnant on 18 August and, a week later, on Saturday, 25 August, he scored his twelfth confirmed victory.[26] Leading an evening patrol, this time in concert with Loerzer's Jasta 26, Göring went after an F.E.2 two-seat reconnaissance aircraft, but broke off the chase when his twin Spandau machine guns jammed. After he had cleared the jam, he attacked a lone Sopwith Camel flying at 4,200 metres' altitude south of Ypres. Göring reported that he drove the British fighter down to 1,800 metres, firing steadily until his opponent 'fell downward, turning over several times and rearing up … [and then] crashed in the haze'. Most likely, his prey was Second-Lieutenant Orlando C. Bridgeman[27] of 70 Squadron, RFC, who returned to British territory and was reported as being 'wounded during combat with E.A. [enemy aeroplane]'[28] at the time and in the area Göring reported.

His luck changed in early September, however, when he was informed of General von Hoeppner's memorandum to the chief of the military cabinet, composed of Kaiser Wilhelm's closest advisers. Dated 1 September 1917, it read: 'I cannot at this time approve the [Pour le Mérite] proposal, since the award of an additional decoration for Leutnant Göring, after [having attained] only ten aerial victories, would show preference compared to [the achievements of] other fighter pilots.'[29] Hoeppner referred to the ten confirmed victories that Göring had scored at the time he was proposed for the high award and not the twelve that he had to his credit by the time this decision was made.

But even a ten- or twelve-victory score was no longer relevant to what Göring hoped to achieve. By August 1917 the number of confirmed aerial victories needed to qualify for the Pour le Mérite had risen to over twenty. As Neal W. O'Connor, a leading authority on German aviation awards in World War I noted, honouring airmen with this high bravery award 'relied heavily on a statistical approach to their accomplishments and for fighter pilots this [standard] meant the number of their confirmed victories'.[30] When Oswald Boelcke and Max Immelmann became the first aviation recipients of the award, on 12 January 1916, each had shot down eight enemy aeroplanes. Exactly a year later, Manfred von Richthofen had sixteen confirmed kills when he became the thirteenth recipient. By the time Göring's nomination was advanced, the twentieth aviation Pour le Mérite recipient, Leutnant Carl Allmenröder, had received the award on 14 June 1917 – with twenty-six confirmed victories to his credit.[31]

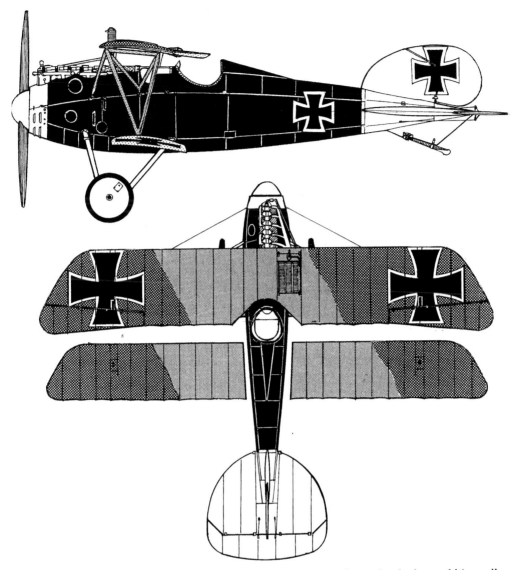

Hermann Göring's first Albatros D.V (1027/17) retained the colour scheme that had served him well since his Jasta 26 days. (Original artwork by Greg VanWyngarden)

Perhaps Göring had not paid attention to the fighter pilots' scores published in popular German news media several times a month. But his adversaries did. Thanks to the brisk trade in Allied and German magazines and newspapers in neutral countries, items from these media, as well as captured documents, were re-printed in widely-circulated intelligence summaries. Thus, British airmen learned that Göring had eight victories to his credit in early August 1917,[32] two weeks later that he was commanding officer of Jasta 27[33] and, a week after that, that he had become a ten-victory ace.[34] It is more likely that, viewed through the lens of his own egocentricity, Göring considered *his* ten or twelve victories as qualitatively superior to other pilots' achievements. In any event, the Luftstreitkräfte's rejection of his nomination for the Pour le Mérite made him work harder to earn the 'prize' he thought he deserved.

Göring's Thirteenth Victory

Consequently, when the staff of his old friend Hauptmann Wilberg, the officer in charge of aviation for the 4th Army, did not confirm Göring's 3 September victory claim in their weekly report,[35] he must have complained. And Wilberg must have taken action, as Göring's victory over an Airco D.H.4 two-seater north of Lampernisse, on that date, appeared in the Luftstreitkräfte's weekly summary. Göring's report was convincing, as he and eight Staffel comrades attacked five D.H.4s heading east from Dixmuide and Göring reported going down after one of the two-seaters and chasing it until it crashed. His victim was probably an aircraft from 57 Squadron, RFC, which reportedly returned from a mission in this area with a wounded observer, twenty-seven-year-old Lieutenant Georges W. Guillon.[36] The incident was counted as Göring's thirteenth victory.[37]

Despite considerable effort by Göring and his men, the Jasta 27 victory score rose only slightly in September. In addition to confirmed victories by Leutnant der Reserve Ludwig Luer on the 9th and Leutnant der Reserve Fritz Berkemeyer on the 15th, there was the disappointment of a rejection of Vizefeldwebel Willi Kampe's claim of another Sopwith during the same fight in which Berkemeyer had scored. On the following day, 16 September, the Jasta 27 war diary noted Leutnant Rudolf Klimke's claim for a Sopwith over Ypres, but no ground confirmation supported his claim.[38] On Thursday, 20 September, claims by Göring and Vizefeldwebel Krauss were denied for the same reason.

Often, it was difficult to confirm aerial victory claims due to the inability of ground personnel to distinguish the colour schemes used by the different Jagdstaffeln fighter squadrons, to say nothing of the variations within the units. Consequently, a new aerial combat report form was instituted to ease the identification of pilots and units. For example, Göring's report for his combat activity on 21 September noted he flew Albatros D.V 4424/17, which bore a 'black fuselage, white nose and white tail'.[39] His first patrol of the day was successful, as he noted:

> 'Shortly after 9 a.m., I sighted an enemy formation of 14 units (bomb droppers), which were returning in the direction of the frontlines from Torhout. I attacked with my companions at an altitude of 4,500 metres. I positioned myself closely below the tail of an opponent and opened fire at it. I followed it closely with one of my other aeroplanes. Near Sleyhage, west of Roulers, the aeroplane crashed. Pilot and observer were injured. The machine was completely destroyed.'[40]

Göring's victims were most likely Second-Lieutenants R.L. Curtis,[41] pilot, and D.P. Fitzgerald-Uniacke, observer, in a Bristol F.2B of 48 Squadron, RFC. They reported taking off at 8:00 a.m. on a bombing mission and were 'last seen going down overwhelmed by E.A. ten miles northeast of Roulers'.[42] The same two-seater was also claimed by Leutnant Fritz Kieckhaefer of Jasta 29 and, once again, the office of the commanding general of the air force awarded full credit to both claimants of the Bristol Fighter: Göring's for his action over 'Sleyhage, west of Roulers' and Kieckhaefer's for combat over 'Hooglede', three kilometres northeast of Sleyhage.[43] This author has reviewed many hundreds of World War I air combat victory claims for more than forty years and is still at a loss in trying to understand – much less explain – the chaotic credit methods used by all belligerents in

A Bristol F.2B of the type Göring shot down on 21 September 1917.

The Great War. The best that can be said is that many claims were valid and others were subject to an almost whimsical interpretation that lacked consistency, reliable standards and accuracy.

Other factors in assigning Jasta 27 victory claims were Göring's domineering personality and overly aggressive way of pressing for credit. His bad behaviour was not often discussed in Germany up to and including the World War II years and even anecdotal information about him did not begin to circulate publicly until after his death in 1946. Thus, pre-World War I flyer[44] Rudolf Nebel's second-hand account of one instance appeared only in 1972. Nebel and Göring served briefly together in Jasta 5 in 1916 and, as Nebel had many friends in his country's small community of fighter pilots, he heard stories such as this one:

> '[Göring] was very standoffish toward his [Jasta 27] comrades. He was a good pilot, but was disliked by his men due to his high-handed manner. Often, after obscured aerial combats, there were disputes about who had really shot down this or that machine. If it could not be ascertained incontestably, it was decided by a toss of the dice. Of course, the victor in this game must give up the next one and be the "loser" without using the dice, so that over time everyone had the same chance. Only Göring did not agree with such a solution. In doubtful cases he always maintained that he had shot down the enemy machine and did not understand why he should not participate in every toss of the dice.'[45]

Nebel's anecdote could be contested in this instance by the fact that it was over four weeks before Göring received credit for another aerial victory – his fifteenth – during which time Jasta 27 recorded seven victories (and claimed two more) by other pilots.[46] Further, Staffel records show that, aside from a five-day furlough in the second week of October, Göring took part in every patrol and obviously had not altered the reports in his favour.

Irrespective of his methods, Göring's efforts were rewarded on 8 October, when he was proposed for what might be considered the second highest Prussian bravery award, the Knight's Cross with Swords of the Royal Hohenzollern House Order.[47] This award, which was bestowed by the Kaiser's own royal house, 'came to be the customary intermediate award for officers between the Iron Cross 1st Class and the Order Pour le Mérite itself'.[48] He received it on 20 October 1917.[49] Thus, Göring could be reasonably assured that, with continued valorous service and effective leadership, he was on track to receive the higher award and thereby be among the most exclusive élite of German military aviation.

Great Battle Day in October

In the late autumn, hard-won British advances in Flanders slowed down. Then, as a British historian noted, 'the High Command decided to continue the pointless offensive during the few remaining weeks before the winter, and thereby used up reserves which might have saved the belated experiment of Cambrai [in November] from bankruptcy'.[50]

Typically, when Göring wrote about his Flanders experiences in the late 1920s, he considered this time of difficulty for both sides as a triumph of German military might and a time of glory for Loerzer's and his air units:

'For months the violent battle continued; month after month the fertile ground of Belgium was assaulted and ripped apart by landmines and artillery shells; for months British troops laboured in a tenacious, dogged fury to move forward and to reach their objective. But for all of those months German will and German fortitude … pushed them back. For just as many months the iron wall of German heroism and German sense of duty neither wavered nor faltered. For months the battle in Flanders raged and roared.

'The enemy was exhausted; his initial advance, with momentum [from the victory at Messines], had been halted and shattered by the stiff-necked defence and splendid attitude of our troops. Day after day, often week after week, the enemy drew his breath, gathered new forces, [and] once again prepared everything in the best possible way in order to overthrow us with an enormous fresh assault. Yet this lasted only one or two days until, at the point of the highest intensified pressure of battle, it collapsed under the fire of our counter-attack. This most dreadful and most grandiose spectacle of all the months of the raging Battle of Flanders was called a *Grosskampftag* [great battle day].

'… Victory or destruction was the watchword! And now a story about… the *Grosskampftag* in October 1917.

'The stars in the heavens are still sparkling and in the east the new day is dawning feebly. There is booming and thundering throughout the air. A heavy rumbling and a muffled howling sound drifts through the departing night. A violent tremor runs through the ground and shakes the houses to their foundations. There is an almost supernatural clattering of window panes and from time to time one hears the terrible strike of artillery shell and a thundering, deafening noise, as if all hell is let loose. The heavy drumfire of thousands of big guns of all calibres has begun and brings with it an intensifying momentum of death and total destruction. The awful explosions come from direct hits on ammunition dumps where all at once thousands of shells burst.

'Instinctively, I sit bolt upright in my bed and, as happens so often, am amazed at the enormous gunfire. Then the telephone rings and rings: "Loerzer here! Good morning. You can hear that we are having a *Grosskampftag* today. Therefore, our mission is to [fly] in waves, as usual." I answer that in all of this noise no one will sleep any more, but otherwise all that is missing is the obligatory foul weather by which the British great battle days are always distinguished.

'As quickly as possible, however, I am present with my Staffel at the airfield, where discussions take place. "*Auf wiedersehen!* Hopefully, we will bring down some Tommies." As usual … we declare it will be a great day for our Staffel … today will be looked upon as accomplishing something extraordinary. *Grosskampf, Grosskampf* roar the big guns at the frontlines uninterrupted. Again quickly, a cup of hot coffee and then we pile into the lorry and are off to the flight line. In the east, the first rays of sunlight flicker upwards as we, shivering in our fur-lined flight suits, arrive at the flight line. A light haze billows across the airfield while in the west heavy cloud banks draw near. Bad weather is approaching. Cannons thunder mightily from the frontlines. The infantry attack must come soon and, with it, the enemy air force. Our job begins.

'The air defence officer, who has a good view from his post a few kilometres behind our lines, informs us by telephone that enemy flyers at low altitude will open fire on our positions. Immediately afterwards our artillery units call for aerial protection, as British artillery coordination flyers are directing their batteries against ours. And yet a third call for help comes by radio telegraph; it is from our two-seater patrols, requesting assistance against enemy fighter aircraft, which are hindering them from carrying out their missions.

'Again and again the telephone rings and brings new calls for help up at the battle lines. Now the moment has come for us to attack, to gain aerial superiority and sweep … the enemy out of the air space over our hard-fighting troops. Strong action appears to be requested and, accordingly, I immediately order the entire Staffel to take off, as always split into two flights in order to remain flexible and yet work together.

'From all the reports flowing in I try to form the clearest picture possible of the air and ground situations. After that I will take action. I ask the neighbouring sectors to inform me quickly which Jasta forces have been deployed in their areas. Then we take off. Everything proceeds smoothly and, after a few minutes, I gather my Staffel around me. Close together, twelve Albatroses storm against the hotly contested frontlines with firm wills to be victorious. A not too disdainful battle force of twenty-four machine guns.

'The closer we come to the frontlines, the worse the weather becomes. Over the lines … the clouds are unbroken down to 1,000 metres. Intense activity prevails. Great numbers of German and British flyers swirl about on all sides. In between them are bursts of shells and the shrapnel of defensive batteries on both sides. Wherever we encounter the enemy, we attack him. In furious dogfights he is pushed back behind his own lines or forced down. Repeatedly, we push forward into enemy territory in order to clear the airspace for our aerial reconnaissance crews.

'Meanwhile, the battle below rages on. The ground is splattered and ripped apart by shells battering down on it, masses of earth and stone spray high into the air, in between one sees the long trails of poison gas fumes moving over the ground. Mighty jets of flame shoot up and out from the exploding ammunition dumps. A gigantic wall of smoke, gas, iron and chunks of earth identifies the battle line; in their shelters the British divisions form up for the attack, accompanied by enormous battle tanks. Our infantry grapples with them. The obstacles and barbed wire entanglements lay torn apart and demolished. No trench or dug-out offers protection, as they are filled with rubble. Yet, our own [troops] tenaciously defend themselves in individual shell craters. Murderous machine-gun fire … hits the attackers from hidden nests and earthen mounds and permits them to move forward only slowly. But soon they will be thrown back by a fresh counter-offensive led by our reserve troops. With the cold steel of bayonets there are man-to-man duels; hand grenades are hurled; the flame-throwers issue forth black dense smoke and annihilation.

'And above this horrible mass killing are the aerial machine guns of airmen, who grapple for supremacy in furious engagements. Again and again new forces from both sides arrive and at times over 100 aeroplanes can be seen above the … ground fighting. It is a mad Witches' Sabbath in the skies. There, some go rushing down in steep dives; here, others pull up their machines so that they shoot their bullets upward like arrows. In frantic haste some turn tightly around others, eagerly taking great pains to get the opponent in his field of fire. Others rear up, tumble over or lightning quick go into a spin; still others succeed by going inverted or attempt to get away from the opponent in grotesque, desperate turns. Down below, the big guns roar and thunder, the shells burst and crack; up above, the engines, strained to the limit, thunder and rage, and the machine guns clatter and fume. Aeroplanes break apart, machines enveloped in flames and smoke plunge straight down and, far below show the results of total destruction in the air …

'Storming rain soaks the ground, fills the craters and trenches, and hinders the attacker. It lashes the pilot sharply in the face and obscures his vision, making aiming his weapon almost impossible. In addition to all the other dangers, now there is that of ramming into each other in the rain and misty clouds. Now one can only see the other aeroplanes as shadows..... a crash fragment suddenly appears for a few seconds and just as quickly disappears in the black clouds. Flying in the storm and rain, fog and mist is almost supernatural. One comes back to the airfield half-dead, exhausted and worn down by inhuman exertion and nerve-racking agitation. There are only a few hours of rest, and then the awful battle goes on anew. No weather is able to restrain us fighter pilots.

'We want to do our part in defence of the mighty battle, the *Grosskampf* in Flanders.'[51]

Göring's Fifteenth Victory

Göring did not date the events in the preceding text, but, given the intensity of the fighting, it probably took place about the time he was victorious in an air fight on the afternoon of Sunday, 21 October 1917. According to the Jasta 27 war diary summary, at 3:45 p.m., Göring and five other pilots – joined by aircraft from Jastas 4 and 26 – saw five 'Sopwiths' attacking an LVG two-seat reconnaissance aeroplane and went to the aid of the German aircraft. In the course of the fight, Jasta 27's Leutnant der Reserve Fritz

Berkemeyer shot down a 'Sopwith' over Rumbeke, a few kilometres southeast of Roulers, and Göring sent one down near Bondues, just north of Lille.[52] The British aircraft were misidentified; they were, in fact, two S.E.5s of 84 Squadron, RFC, which fell in combat while attacking a 'red and yellow two-seater' over Roulers.[53] A third S.E.5 from the same squadron was credited to Oberleutnant Kurt von Döring of Jasta 4 as his ninth victory.[54] Berkemeyer's victim was confirmed as his fourth and Göring's as his fifteenth.[55]

It is reasonably certain that Göring brought down Australian Second-Lieutenant Arthur E. Hempel,[56] who was captured uninjured and sent to a prisoner of war camp in Germany.

CHAPTER TEN

SHIFTING WINDS

'I have been flying at the frontlines for three years without having had a compassionate or homeland command. Now, I feel a certain exhaustion, especially after the heavy fighting in Flanders.'[1]

HERMANN GÖRING

In World War I, airmen experienced little sense of relief at the end of ground fighting in their sectors. Air operations continued, even when new forward ground positions were established. And, of course, fighter pilots relentlessly attacked opponents trying to fly over their territory to gather information before the next battle. Accordingly, Hermann Göring's Jagdstaffel 27 fought hard during the final struggle at Ypres, even strafing Allied ground troops at Passchendaele on the morning of Tuesday, 30 October 1917.[2] But Staffel flights were not immediately affected by the successful British-Canadian capture of Passchendaele on 4 November,[3] which ended the often rain-soaked Battle of Flanders.

Line-up of Jasta 27 aircraft at Iseghem, Belgium. Göring's Albatros D.V appears at far left, with the fuselage in solid black and not numbered, as were other Staffel aircraft.

As H.A. Jones, the Royal Air Force historian, noted: '[A]nother attack, immediately following the Flanders offensive, would … create a feeling of uncertainty and so make the [Germans] uneasy throughout the winter. [They] would realise the danger of withdrawing too many troops to back areas for rest and training.'[4] Thus, while the four Jagdstaffeln of Manfred von Richthofen's highly successful Jagdgeschwader I were transferred southward to the Somme Sector[5] to aid the 2nd Army in the Battle of Cambrai, Oberleutnant Hermann Göring's Jasta 27 and most other air units in Belgium and northern France remained in place to help the 4th Army maintain its perimeter.

Heavy, low-hanging clouds on the morning of Thursday, 1 November, caused a lull in air activity[6] that provided cover for Jasta 27 as it moved back slightly – some eight kilometres southeast – from Iseghem to Bavichove. As he did not fly that day, Göring had time to draft a report justifying his taking five days' leave during the fighting in Flanders. Directed to his immediate superior and sometime patron, Hauptmann Percy Baron von Ascheberg, the Gruppenführer der Flieger 15, Göring wrote:

'The five days of furlough I requested in October were used merely to settle a family matter. Because of the long distance and poor train connections to Upper Bavaria, at that time I was on the train four days and at home only thirty-seven hours. Before that my last convalescent leave was in January 1917 in conjunction with my discharge from the field hospital (recovery from my severe wounds). Although I had four weeks of leave at that time, I interrupted it two weeks early in order, as the only senior Jagdflieger [fighter pilot], to help with the establishment of the new Jagdstaffel 26. I have been flying continually at the frontlines since January 1917. In my capacity as Staffelführer I must fly many times a day in order to lead my Staffel …Since January 1917 I have made over 200 Jagdflüge [fighter flights]. In so doing, once I was shot down and had to land in a loose [wire] entanglement. I have been flying at the frontlines for three years without having had a compassionate or homeland command. Now, I feel a certain exhaustion, especially after the heavy fighting in Flanders.'[7]

His report was essentially true, but as he often did Göring took some liberties with the facts. He did cut short his leave earlier in the year and, when he joined Bruno Loerzer's Jasta 26 on 15 February 1917[8] (not in January, as stated), Göring was the senior Jagdflieger in terms of enemy aeroplanes shot down. He had three to his credit, Loerzer had two,[9] as did new arrival Leutnant der Reserve Friedrich Weitz and Offizierstellvertreter Rudolf Weckbrodt had one.[10] And, while Göring had been shot down into some frontline barbed wire 'entanglements,' that incident occurred in late May 1916, as recounted on pages 75-76 of this book. Surely, Göring's mention of 'a certain exhaustion' relates to the toll taken by recurrences of his rheumatoid arthritis. No doubt aggravated by the many recent cold and rainy days, the episodes would have been painful and debilitating – and would have affected his ability to fly.

Göring's Sixteenth Victory

Despite his continuing ailments, Göring led Jasta 27 in the air in early November and, on the 7th of that month claimed his next victory. During a morning flight, from 8:30 to 9:45 a.m. that day, he led nine Albatros fighters over Houthulst Forest, northwest of Poelcapelle. He reported encountering four Airco D.H.5 single-seat fighters behind British lines and claimed to have shot down one of them.[11] The visibility was poor, according to the six D.H.5 pilots of 32 Squadron, RFC,[12] who were in that area at that time. The British pilots' report further noted: 'Five [enemy] scouts over Poelcapelle, one attacked, indecisive, at 2,000 feet, at 8:15 a.m. by Lt. Glentworth'.[13]

From the German and British accounts, it is clear that Jasta 27 and 32 Squadron, RFC skirmished briefly at that time – listed as 9:15 a.m. (German time) and 8:15 a.m. (British

An Airco D.H.5. Göring claimed to have shot down one of these on 7 November 1917.

Summer Time, still in effect) – over or near Poelcapelle, Belgium. Due to the poor weather conditions, the encounter most likely ended quickly, with no losses on either side. Nonetheless, Göring pressed his claim and received confirmation for a D.H.5 in that brief encounter.[14] The object of his attention, most likely Lieutenant Viscount Glentworth (Edmund William Claude Gerard de Vere Percy), reported exchanging fire with a German aeroplane, but the young Irish aristocrat returned safely from that flight in D.H.5 A.9282.[15]

The remainder of November must have frustrated Göring, as Jasta 27 records show that, despite their various aggressive actions, he and the comrades had few combats. Thus, fewer prospects for Göring to gain the victories needed to earn the coveted Pour le Mérite. With little activity in the skies over Flanders, Jasta 27 patrols reported only a steady litany of 'Luftkampf hat nicht stattegefunden' [aerial combat has not occurred].[16]

Gale force winds on Saturday, 24 November[17] probably created enough of a distraction for Göring to slip away quietly and go on leave.[18] He should have been embarrassed, as he had publicly insulted Leutnant der Reserve Willy Rosenstein and thereby tore a bond of comradeship necessary to maintaining the *esprit de corps* of a frontline fighting unit. A pre-war flyer, Rosenstein was a highly experienced pilot and air combat veteran. He was a founding member of Jasta 27 and scored the first of his nine confirmed victories on 21 September 1917,[20] thereby gaining the admiration of his comrades.

But as Göring was a long-time and ardent anti-Semite, he made it his business to determine Rosenstein's Jewish heritage. Initially, he controlled the hatred he had learned as a schoolboy in Bavaria, but Jasta 27's recent lack of success may have made Göring irritable or perhaps something else caused him to lose his self discipline and make Rosenstein the focus of his rage. Rosenstein later wrote:

'I had a personal quarrel with Göring, caused by an anti-Semitic remark [he made] in front of all [of our] comrades in the officers' mess … I felt compelled to demand its retraction. These circumstances caused me to apply for… transfer to a home defence unit, which was granted after a short time …'[21]

Rosenstein did not record the exact words of the remark, but the implication was odious enough. Once Göring was in a more rational state of mind, he tried to gloss over the incident by leaving what might be considered a favourable recommendation for the departing pilot:

'Ltn.d.Res Rosenstein was a member of Jagdstaffel 27 from 12 February 1917 through 10 December 1917. During this period he has won the confidence of his Staffelführer due to his aggressiveness in aerial combat and the affection of his *Staffelkameraden* [squadron mates] because of his fine comradeship.

'Lately, he has shown signs of some nervous exhaustion, which must be the consequence of his nearly six years of continuous activity as a [combat] pilot.

'Therefore, I suggest [that] an assignment at a KEST [Kampfeinsitzerstaffel – home defence single-seat fighter unit] may be useful for his recovery, enabling him at the same time to remain current in his flying ability.

'I am confident that, in view of his [tough] … constitution, he will be fit for deployment at the frontlines next spring.'[22]

Oberleutnant Hermann Göring and Leutnant der Reserve Willi Rosenstein in happier times, discussing air operations with Leutnant Curt Rabe (right).

Göring was too stubborn and arrogant to admit he was wrong and that he owed Rosenstein an apology. But to save himself an awkward moment, as the incident was discussed by the pilots in private, the Staffelführer made sure he was away from the unit when Rosenstein bade farewell to Jasta 27 in early December.[23]

It is noteworthy that Göring considered Rosenstein to have 'shown signs of some nervous exhaustion' at a time when it was he who displayed instances of irrational behaviour. A few days later, for example, Göring sought an odd favour from the Kommandeur der Flieger der 4. Armee. While still on leave, he applied for reimbursement of expenses incurred when he had visited Mauterndorf a year earlier. In his 1 January 1918 letter, intended to be approved by Kofl 4 and forwarded to the Inspektion der Fliegertruppen in Berlin, Göring stated:

> 'While on my four weeks of convalescent leave in order to regain my health, I travelled to the mountain health resort at Mauterndorf in the Austrian Alps. On the long and cumbersome trip back and forth and while staying there, as well as necessary purchases I needed for [the trip], I had large expenses.
>
> 'I humbly request, therefore, to be granted assistance from the support fund. I possess neither my own fortune nor any allowance; no other funds for this purpose have been claimed.'[24]

Göring's request contradicted his report of 1 November 1917 (quoted above), which made no reference to expenses. As he had received other help from his godfather, surely Dr. Hermann Ritter von Epenstein would have provided the funds needed to his favourite godchild. Further, it was an outright lie for Göring to claim he was at a health resort in January 1917 when, in fact, he had lived at no cost in Epenstein's restored fortress.

As it turned out, the officer in charge of aviation for the 4th Army, Göring's valued contact Hauptmann Helmuth Wilberg, had begun his own extensive recuperative leave on 3 December. In Wilberg's absence, his office was administered by Hauptmann Percy Baron von Ascheberg,[25] to whom Göring had written the 1 November report about his convalescent leave. The current letter offered an opportunity to catch Göring in a lie, but in view of Ascheberg's admiration for his brash subordinate – as evidenced by his support for Göring's earlier nomination for the Pour le Mérite – Ascheberg took no action. There is no record of Göring receiving the requested funding, which suggests the matter may have been quietly dropped.

Aside from routine personnel transfers, Jasta 27 was not mentioned in 4th Army records until 17 January 1918, when it was announced: 'During Oberleutnant Göring's leave, Leutnant der Reserve Dilthey is in command of Jasta 27.'[26] During most of that month and into February, Göring was at a ski resort and spa at Bayerischzell on the Austrian border, which might explain his need for extra funds. Photographs he took at the time show him on the ski slopes and in the spa. He was joined by his mother and his sisters Olga and Paula, as well as Bruno Loerzer,[27] who had gone on leave at the same time as Göring. Loerzer had to break away from the pleasant Alpine vacation when he was among the Jagdstaffel leaders summoned to Berlin[28] for an important event beginning on 19 January. He left to attend the aircraft type tests organised by the aircraft test establishment for competitions between fighter aircraft manufacturers for production contracts. Under other circumstances, Göring might have been invited, too, but he was in great need of physical therapy for his rheumatoid arthritis and perhaps some relaxation to ease his emotional state.

Göring and Loerzer were close friends, but they were also competitors of sorts, with Loerzer usually gaining awards and choice assignments ahead of Göring. On 11 February 1918, however, Göring was the first of the two men to receive the Grand Duchy of Baden's premier bravery award, the Knight's Cross of the Military Karl Friedrich Merit Order. Baden's honour was significant, as only 288 were awarded in World War I and of that number only eight were bestowed upon airmen.[29] For the moment, Göring had the satisfaction of knowing he had received a prestigious award that had thus far eluded Loerzer.

But his time of glory was short. The following day, Loerzer was awarded the top prize –Prussia's and Germany's highest bravery honour – the Pour le Mérite.[30]

Upon receipt of Baden's Knight's Cross of the Military Karl Friedrich Merit Order, Göring posed wearing it in an odd spot (centre of his chest) and below Prussia's Hohenzollern Order. The rank order is understandable, but these awards were not worn along the button line of a tunic.

He had attained the requisite twentieth victory on 19 January 1918. Additionally, he was appointed commander of Germany's newest fighter wing, Jagdgeschwader III. Based on the same four-unit organisation that Richthofen established with JG I, JG III was composed of Jastas 2, 26, 27 and 36.[31]

Jasta 27 changed airfields on 13 February and moved about nine kilometres southwest from Bavichove to Marcke, southwest of Courtrai, Belgium. The relocation meant that, once again, Göring would live in baronial splendour. Seven months earlier, the estate of Belgian Baron Jean de Béthune had been occupied by the German local command and converted to military use. The broad lawns, the baron's castle and other buildings in a nearby area called Marckebeke became the central location for von Richthofen's JG I.[32] Following the Geschwader's departure for the Somme Sector, Hermann Göring became the new temporary lord of the manor at Marckebeke castle.

Göring's Seventeenth Victory

The unit's first contribution to JG III was a pair of S.E.5 fighters brought down on the morning of 21 February by Oberleutnant Hermann Göring and Leutnant der Reserve Rudolf Klimke. The nine-plane patrol was less than ten kilometres from its airfield, when,

Göring wrote (in 1933), they were 'attacked by two English fighting aeroplanes' that he had observed flying above them.[33] He said he identified the patrol leader (but does not say how) and then 'he and I closed in battle'.[34]

The encounter developed quickly into a fierce fight, going from 4,500 metres to 2,000 metres and then back up to 3,000. Göring judged his adversary to be an experienced, highly capable fighter pilot and wrote:

> 'I was very soon conscious of the fact that my plane was riddled with bullets. Providence or miracle must have …saved me from getting wounded. Never in all my four years' experience as a fighting aviator had I met with such an adversary … In the space of that few minutes' fighting we went through all the possible experiences of flying – we stalled, we looped, we side-slipped – and always we stuck together, neither of us leaving the other for a moment's respite.'[35]

Then, Göring managed to make a very tight turn that put him right on his opponent's tail. Firing both of his machine guns into the S.E.5, he sent his opponent down with 'his engine going full out as he plunged headlong to earth'. The dead pilot, identified as 'the famous Captain Craig, known all along the [battle] line for his audacity and daring', was pulled from the debris of his aeroplane and was found to have 'three shots through the head and no fewer than seven through the chest'.[36]

British records show that Göring's victim was Second-Lieutenant George B. Craig in S.E.5a C.5325 of 60 Squadron, RFC. His companion, most likely brought down by Leutnant Klimke, was Second-Lieutenant William M. Kent in S.E.5a B.4860 of the same squadron. Craig[37] and Kent,[38] both Canadians, reportedly left their aerodrome at 7:40 a.m. (British Summer Time) and, two hours and fifteen minutes later were 'last seen near Houthulst' and later confirmed as having been killed.[39] Those facts match Jasta 27's claims of downing Craig's aircraft near Ledeghem, and Kent's near Rolleghem-Kapelle, at 10:00 a.m. (German time, an hour ahead of BST) or shortly thereafter. Göring received credit for his seventeenth victory and Klimke his sixth.[40]

Second-Lieutenant George B. Craig of 60 Squadron, seen in the seat of his S.E.5a, possibly the one he was flying when Göring claimed to have shot him down on 21 February 1918.

Once again, Göring indulged in his characteristic hyperbole by identifying Craig as a captain who had a reputation for 'audacity and daring', as the pilot had not yet distinguished himself. According to noted Canadian World War I aviation historian Stewart K. Taylor, who had access to the airman's family records, Craig died the following day and, therefore, could not have been killed immediately, as Göring contended. Further, Taylor's research shows that Craig and Kent collided and may not have been shot down by Göring and Klimke at all.[41]

Before Göring could score again, his childhood tonsillitis returned in a severe form. He developed a tonsillar abscess (or quinsy) and, three days after his latest aerial combat success, he had to be sent for treatment to a field hospital in Deynze,[42] northeast of Marckebeke. His malady was 'serious, sometimes life threatening due to swelling of the throat and interference with breathing; it necessitated incision and drainage of the pus … sometimes warranting morphine' to alleviate pain, notes World War I historian and physician Dr. M. Geoffrey Miller. This medical condition may have occasioned Göring's first use of narcotics, to which, later in life, he became severely addicted. He did not return to Jasta 27 until 7 March and, in his absence, Leutnant der Reserve Helmuth Dilthey again led the Staffel.[43]

While Göring was being treated, plans for Germany's spring 1918 offensive were being finalised. The Bolshevik Revolution of 1917 and the subsequent cessation of hostilities assured that German forces in France and Belgium would be reinforced by fresh troops from the Eastern Front,[44] where an armistice had gone into effect on Sunday, 3 March 1918. Thus, German ground and air units in three broad operational areas entered the final phase of preparations for their spring offensive on the Western Front; Jasta 27, for example, left the comforts of Marckebeke in the 4th Army Sector on 12 March for a journey of some fifty kilometres southeast to an airfield at Erchin,[45] not far from Douai in the 17th Army Sector. Richthofen and JG I were a short distance away at Awoingt[46] on Thursday, 21 March, when 'Operation Michael' was launched on both sides of St. Quentin[47] in the German 18th Army Sector.

Jasta 27 enjoyed a relatively quiet time on the day the offensive was initiated. Göring led afternoon and early evening patrols that went unchallenged.[48] For the remainder of the month, the Staffel reported little activity and, when aerial skirmishes occurred, there were no successes.[49]

On Monday, 1 April 1918, when Britain's Royal Flying Corps and Royal Naval Air Service were amalgamated to form the Royal Air Force,[50] Hermann Göring received a congratulatory telegram from Generalleutnant Ernst von Hoeppner, commanding general of the Luftstreitkräfte, noting that in an 'unflaggingly pressing attack [Göring] raised the number of his aerial victories to seventeen in recent days'.[51] One has to wonder when that message was composed, as Göring's seventeenth air combat triumphs had been attained on 21 February, well over a month before the telegram arrived.

Göring's Eighteenth Victory

In any event, during a mid-day patrol on Sunday, 7 April 1918, Göring raised his score again, when he and nine comrades attacked a British R.E.8 two-seat reconnaissance aircraft and fighter aircraft some twenty-five kilometres within British lines, between Merville and Hazebrouck.[52] Göring went after the more dangerous target, the two-seater – in which the pilot and observer were armed with machine guns – while his men

A captured Royal Aircraft Factory R.E.8 of the type that Göring claimed as his eighteenth victory.

attended to fighters that arrived on the scene while he was chasing his target. Apparently, Jasta 27's Leutnant der Reserve Stoltenhoff also attacked the R.E.8 and claimed it as his first victory, but credit was awarded to Göring as his eighteenth.[53] It is likely that Göring – perhaps aided by Stoltenhoff – sent down R.E.8 B.876 of 42 Squadron, RAF.[54] The fight took place less than fifteen kilometres north of 42 Squadron's aerodrome at Choques, which the R.E.8 reached following a running battle with 'six [Fokker] Triplanes and four Albatros scouts in the pursuing group, which agrees with the Jasta 27 numbers'.[55] During the fight, R.E.8 pilot Second-Lieutenant Harry W. Collier[56] was uninjured, but his observer, Lieutenant Eric C. Musson,[57] was wounded.

In attaining that victory, Göring and his men ended up some fifty kilometres northwest of their airfield and back in the Flanders Sector. Hence, it is not surprising that, after the German offensive began in Flanders on 9 April,[58] six days later Jasta 27 was relocated from Erchin to Halluin, less than ten kilometres from its former airfield at Marckebeke.

Troublesome Triplanes

Having fought against Sopwith Triplanes in the summer of 1917, Helmuth Dilthey and other Jasta 27 pilots had high regard for the three-winged aeroplanes. Consequently, German fighter pilots were eager to have aircraft manufacturer Anthony Fokker's Triplane fighters when they became available some months after the British aeroplanes appeared. Unfortunately, operational and production problems delayed wide use of the Fokker Triplane until spring 1918. Thus, by the time Jasta 27 began to receive its allotment, it 'never received enough … [of them] to equip the entire unit, and it operated a mix of Triplanes and Albatros fighters for a period'.[59]

As Dilthey noted:

'It became somewhat better when we received [Fokker] Triplanes. At that time they were no longer as good as the British single- and two-seaters; above all, they were too slow and the engines were too temperamental. Other than that, they were quite nice. Our Triplanes had yellow cowlings, yellow interplane struts, yellow tails and were in other respects in natural colours. Only the leader's aeroplane, Oberleutnant Göring's [Triplane] had a white tail and a white cowling.'[60]

By then, however, the rotary-engined Fokker Dr.I Triplanes were due to be replaced by Fokker D.VII biplanes, which, with more powerful stationary engines, were less tricky to fly than Triplanes. But it was ominous when, on Sunday, 21 April, Germany's highest-scoring fighter ace, Manfred von Richthofen, was killed in combat[61] while flying a Fokker Triplane. The following day, Hermann Göring flew a Triplane – Dr.I 496/17 – on a patrol with nine of his men and, upon returning to Halluin airfield, he was apparently caught by a cross current of wind and flew into a hangar. Göring was uninjured, but the aeroplane was listed as 'damaged'[62] and was not mentioned in further reports.

Despite ground fighting on both sides of the lines during the next phase of the spring offensive, generally unfavourable weather conditions kept air units in the 4th Army Sector from making gains for the remainder of April.[63] Indeed, Kofl 4 reported only one victory in its entire sector, on 25 April,[64] while Jasta 27's log[65] noted an absence of aerial combats for the period.

That relatively calm time gave way to disappointment and loss in May. During good weather on the morning of the 3rd, Göring and seven comrades attacked a flight of British two-seaters behind their lines near Tournai,[66] but had to give up the chase when their Fokker Triplanes and Albatroses ran low on fuel.[67] Four days later, five of Jasta 24's six-plane afternoon patrol returned without success.[68] The missing pilot, twenty-three-year-old Offizierstellvertreter Waldemar von der Weppen, had been shot down and killed near Ypres.[69]

On Tuesday, 21 May, Göring led Jasta 27 to yet another new airfield, further south and east, at Vivaise in the 7th Army Sector. He could only hope that a new location would bring new luck and success.

Oberleutnant Hermann Göring at the controls of his Fokker Dr.I Triplane in late spring 1918.

CHAPTER ELEVEN
RISING TO THE TOP

'The enemy Caudron formations carry out their assignments oblivious to German fighter pilots. During an attack on a Caudron … I fired almost all of my ammunition into it at close range. The Caudron flew on calmly … A serious combat with these armoured and well-armed aeroplanes would demand great sacrifices.'[1]

HERMANN GÖRING

After Hermann Göring attained his eighteenth confirmed victory on 7 April 1918, Jagdstaffel 27 went into a slump. It is difficult to understand how his Staffel, operating in the same sector as the four Staffeln of the Richthofen Jagdgeschwader and flying the same type of aeroplanes, could be so lacking in success. To be sure, Göring and his men flew two or more patrols a day, but they did not seem to have 'the knack' for engaging their opponents as readily as did the heirs to the Red Baron.

From mid-April through the end of May 1918, one Richthofen Staffel, the Red Baron's own Jasta 11, logged twelve victories.[2] During the same period, Jasta 27 would have been without claims if not for the one submitted by Oberleutnant Maximilian von Förster on the 31st. And, for reasons that were routinely not explained, the office of the commanding general of the Luftstreitkräfte, or Kogenluft, denied the Förster claim, which was recorded by Jasta 27 as its fifty-first victory.[3] However Staffel-level recognition had no official standing.

Despite that disappointment, Friday, 31 May 1918 became a special day for Hermann Göring in another struggle.

Göring again appeared as the subject of a Sanke postcard, this time wearing his Pour le Mérite. The photograph was taken in July, but the card was not released until September 1918.

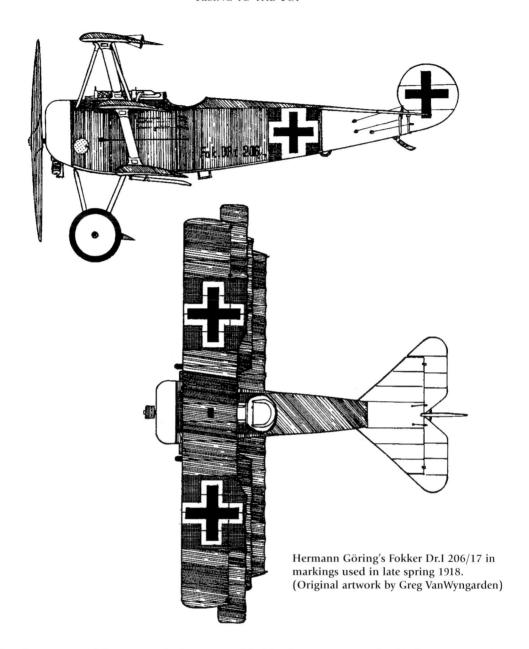

Hermann Göring's Fokker Dr.I 206/17 in markings used in late spring 1918. (Original artwork by Greg VanWyngarden)

Following a second bureaucratic 'campaign' led by his superiors, finally he was awarded the Pour le Mérite. The recommendation citation was approved by the Kogenluft himself, Generalleutnant Ernst von Hoeppner, who hailed Göring as an:

'… outstanding flying officer, who, by his reconnaissance and long-range flights during the … war, delivered exemplary support materials [needed] for critical decisions by his then commanders-in-chief. [After] recovering from a serious wound, he again distinguished himself with personal daring in the latest great offensives of the 17th and 4th Armies as the leader of a Jagdstaffel, which, under his prudent leadership, attained forty-nine aerial victories. He alone conquered eighteen enemies in aerial combats.'[4]

While no written records have come to light regarding questions raised in German army command circles about General von Hoeppner's decision to recommend Göring for the award, surely there were whispered comments about the level of the Jasta 27 leader's achievement. His eighteen victories were below the standard of the time, as German aviation awards authority Neal W. O'Connor observed:

> 'During the first six months of 1918, a Pour le Mérite generally went to a [fighter] pilot anywhere from two to six weeks after his 20th victory. That meant that … most of them … had posted additional victories in the interim. The highest number of victories … [for] a man before the award caught up with him during this period was 27 [for Leutnant Hans Kirschstein].'[5]

Fortunately for Göring, the course of his Pour le Mérite nomination had been overseen by Hauptmann Helmuth Wilberg, the 4th Army's officer in charge of aviation (abbreviated in German as Kofl 4), who was well connected in the chain of command. Following Jasta 27's move to the 7th Army Sector on 21 May, Göring's new immediate superior, the Kofl 7, was Hauptmann Hugo Sperrle, who did not have Wilberg's influence or capability as a bureaucratic advocate.

After World War II, retired General der Flieger Hermann Dahlmann offered another version of how Göring was awarded the top bravery honour. Dahlmann, who succeeded to the post of adjutant of Bruno Loerzer's Jagdgeschwader III in 1918[6] (after Göring received the award), admitted to being 'dubious … of Göring's qualities both as a flyer and an officer'.[7] He claimed 'that it was Loerzer who brought pressure to bear to get Göring awarded the Pour le Mérite before he had in fact shot down the required twenty-five [sic] enemy planes, a score he never achieved'.[8] In this author's view, Loerzer – like Hugo Sperrle – would not have been able to make the high-level connections that Wilberg already had.

Göring's Nineteenth Victory

On Monday, 3 June, the Staffel changed airfields again, setting up facilities on a meadow at Mont de Soissons farm, just southeast of the city of Soissons.[9] Two days later, Göring took off from that airfield in a Fokker D.VII (serial number 278/18) that bore a variation of his usual fighting colours over the standard camouflage: a white engine cowling and tail.[10] He led four other Jasta 27 aeroplanes over the northern part of the woods at Villers-Cotterêts. At about 10:00 a.m., they saw a French A.R.1 two-seat reconnaissance biplane that was 'adjusting artillery fire' and flying westward toward its own lines as the German patrol moved in to intercept it. Göring reported that he chased the enemy aircraft and expended 240 bullets (about a quarter of his ammunition), and shot it down over the northern part of the woods at Villers-Cotterêts.[11] His comrades saw the Frenchmen go down and Göring's claim for his nineteenth victory was accepted by the 7th Army[12] and by Kogenluft.[13]

However, there is no corresponding loss that day of an A.R.1, a distinctive-looking biplane with a 'negative [rearward] stagger'[14] to the long wings. It is possible that Göring shot down a Bréguet 14 B2, which somewhat resembled the A.R. series (e.g., both had long wings and a 'rhino-horn' exhaust pipe over the engine). Five Bréguets were brought down on 5 June 1918,[15] but the evidence at hand makes it difficult to match any one of them to Göring's claim. A French daily summary suggests this possibility: the French two-seater crew of Lieutenant Dijoaux and Maréchal des Logis [Sergeant] Picinbono were reported observing explosions between Soissons and Fère-en-Tardenois and failed to return.[16] The location matches Jasta 27's patrol area, but the French report does not identify the two-seater unit, which would confirm the type of aircraft lost that day. In this author's view, it is not possible to validate or discount this victory claim, as Göring may have shot down this two-seat reconnaissance aircraft.

Göring's Twentieth Victory

Jasta 27 flew patrols in the early morning, late morning and early evening on Sunday, 9 June 1918.[17] During the second mission they passed over a flight of French Spad S.VII fighters returning to their airfield.[18] Flying Fokker D.VII 324/18 (bearing his standard markings), Göring dived on one of the Spads over the most forward German lines. He reported that 'from 400 metres' altitude, [the Spad] dropped straight down like a stone and hit [the ground] at the northwest corner of Horseshoe Wood south of Corey'.[19] The French pilot, Caporal Pierre Chan, was taken prisoner.[20] Kogenluft confirmed this event as Göring's twentieth air combat triumph.[21]

A French Spad S.XIII of Escadrille Spa 94, the same unit as Göring's twentieth victory. The fuselage was black and the 'grim reaper' figure in silver or white.

Göring's Twenty-first Victory

The next Jasta 27 combat was a combination of triumph and tragedy. After the second morning patrol on Monday, 17 June, Göring reported:

> '[A]t about 8:30 a.m., I spotted five Spads … attacking our tethered balloons west of Soissons. With my Staffel [of six other fighters] I came down and attacked them. During the course of the fight, from 500 metres, I downed a 200-hp Spad that crashed at the western edge of the small woods of the Ambleny Heights. I saw, closely below me, Leutnant Brandt pass over a second Spad. At the same moment, two of my Fokkers collided and crashed. Due to our attack, the German tethered balloons remained unharmed.'[22]

He two ill-fated German pilots were twenty-four-year-old Oberleutnant Maximilian von Förster[23] and Vizefeldwebel Wilhelm Schäffer,[24] twenty-six. It is most likely that the new and relatively inexperienced pilots collided while angling for a "kill-shot" position behind one of the Spads. The two Fokkers fell to the ground and both pilots were killed.[25]

Offsetting the two German losses that day, Kogenluft confirmed that Staffelführer Hermann Göring had scored his twenty-first victory and Leutnant Rudolf Klimke attained his eighth.[26] Their victims – most likely Maréchal des Logis Francheschi and Adjudant [Warrant Officer] Breton – came down within German lines and were taken prisoner.[27]

Due to his health problems, Göring had not been able to attend the *1. Typenprüfungen* [first aircraft type tests] held at a Berlin suburban airfield in January 1918. But now – in better health, proudly wearing his Pour le Mérite and with the status of twenty-one confirmed victories to his credit – he was eager to attend the second such event, which began on 3 July at the airfield at Adlershof [literally eagles' court], home to the *Flugzeugmeisterei* [aircraft test establishment].[28] The facility enabled fighter aircraft manufacturers to compete for lucrative production contracts by having their new models test flown by successful German single-seat pilots. The legendary Manfred von Richthofen had helped establish this forum for aircraft evaluation, as his former comrade Richard Wenzl recalled:

> 'Richthofen … was of the viewpoint that not just any old home front pilot, most of all [not] one working for one of the aircraft companies, should be the man who determines what will be flown at the Front. Thus, representatives from … the Jagdstaffeln at the Front came to these tests. The individual types were test-flown, [and] then the gentlemen agreed amongst themselves on which types were best suited at the time . . .'[29]

Many attending pilots distrusted one radical new design[30] that proposed to replace the battle-proven Fokker D.VII fighter. Created by Claudius Dornier, the new Zeppelin-Lindau D.I was of an all-metal cantilever design and the first biplane fighter with duralumin stressed "skin" covering the wings and fuselage. Unperturbed by the aeroplane's innovations, Hermann Göring boldly stepped forward to fly it.[31] He put it through its paces and, later, pronounced it to be a splendid fighter. Not to be outdone,

Hauptmann Wilhelm Reinhard, Richthofen's chosen successor as commander of Jagdgeschwader I, climbed into the cockpit, applied power to the aeroplane's 185-hp BMW engine and soon had the metal fighter aeroplane at 1,000 metres' altitude. During a dive, the struts between the top wing and the fuselage broke[32] and the top wing fell away. The remainder of the aircraft plunged to the ground; Reinhard, who had no parachute, was killed in the crash.

The loss of Reinhard, just over six weeks after Richthofen's demise on 21 April, shocked the Luftstreitkräfte. The adjutant of JG I, Oberleutnant Karl Bodenschatz, was among the first to raise the question of a successor to Germany's most prestigious aviation command. He echoed his superiors' sentiments when he noted: 'The selection [pool of potential successors] was not very big. Jagdgeschwader Richthofen had to have an absolutely first-rate man. The new Jagdgeschwadern II and III were led by Hauptmann [Rudolf] Berthold and Oberleutnant [Bruno] Loerzer, who could not be called away [from their posts]. But who should get Jagdgeschwader I? [Who should] be the next heir to Richthofen?'[33]

News about Reinhard's death was circulated widely within German military aviation,[34] and given the importance of the post, his successor was chosen in five days. A number of more accomplished, higher scoring, highly decorated Staffelführers were passed over in favour of Oberleutnant Hermann Göring. The selection process was never revealed and this author can only speculate that, soon after Reinhard's death, one of Göring's sponsors, Hauptmann Helmuth Wilberg, appealed to the highest ranking Göring admirer, Crown Prince Wilhelm, to propose that the leader of Jasta 27 succeed to leadership of JG I. Even though the Crown Prince was only nominally in charge of the army group that included the 7th Army,[35] he could exert influence in this type of personnel matter. Assuming that politics at high levels were involved and, as Göring was in Berlin at the time, he surely sought help from his godfather, Dr. Hermann Ritter von Epenstein. The doctor maintained a big house in Berlin, where he enjoyed the benefits of decades of using his inherited and earned wealth to cultivate friends in high offices. Epenstein would have known who in Berlin to ask to help support his godson's career ambitions.

Hauptmann Wilhelm Reinhard succeeded Rittmeister Manfred Freiherr von Richthofen as Kommandeur of Jagdgeschwader I.

Göring in Command of JG I

Apparently the behind-the-scenes efforts succeeded. On Monday, 8 July 1918, Oberleutnant Hermann Göring was appointed the new Kommandeur [Commander] of Jagdgeschwader Freiherr von Richthofen Nr I, as the fighter wing was formally known. The following Sunday, the 14th, he arrived at the Geschwader's airfield at Beugneux, south of Soissons, where his reception at the first meeting with his officers was characterised in glowing terms by JG I Adjutant Karl Bodenschatz:

'The Geschwader breathes easier again …[Göring] is the man who meets all the qualifications that are implicitly placed by his superiors and subordinates on the Kommandeur of the first and most famous Jagdgeschwader in the army …The new Kommandeur was 'right' [for the job] …'[36]

That observation is difficult to accept at face value, however, as Bodenschatz published it in 1935, when he was a Luftwaffe Oberst [colonel], serving as 1st Adjutant on Göring's staff.[37] A more believable contemporaneous view of JG I's new leader appeared in Bodenschatz's contribution to a 1923 anthology, in which he wrote simply: 'Oberleutnant Göring, a successful Staffelführer proven on all fronts, was appointed Geschwader-Kommandeur.'[38]

And even that short statement was exaggerated, as Göring had served only on the Western Front and not 'all fronts' (i.e., not on the Eastern Front or in Italy or Palestine), as Bodenschatz hinted. In any event, Göring soon proved his worth. Right after meeting with his key officers, he sent a memorandum to the commanding general of the Luftstreitkräfte, via Kofl 7, requesting better transport and other equipment for JG I. He argued that because 'the Geschwader is deployed only to the focal points of the [war]', and, as a result, repeatedly changes army sectors', it required maximum mobility.[39] He also noted that, in order to fulfil its mission of maintaining aerial superiority over the battlefields, 'the Geschwader needs to be fully equipped with the best [i.e., newest] aeroplanes'.[40]

As its contribution to the 7th Army's opening assault in the Second Battle of the Marne, over the next three days, JG I pilots scored thirteen confirmed aerial victories.[41] But, to amplify points of his first memorandum, Göring wrote to Kogenluft in stronger terms on 17 July:

'Until now, only the French air force appeared on the 7th Army Sector. Since the beginning of the [current] attack, strong British reinforcements have arrived, especially numerous single-seater units. In the attack zone, mainly in the Marne valley between Méry and Dormans-Verneuil, the afternoon and evening hours are dominated by numerically far superior enemy flying activity.

'The British single-seaters, mostly in numerous staggered formations up to [high] altitude, strike in the tried and true manner. The French fighter pilots seldom venture over the frontlines and avoid any serious combat. In contrast to this [manner of encounter], French two-seaters always appear in strong, tight formations, [and] carry out their bombing attacks relentlessly, [and] partly at low altitudes. The two-engined Caudrons are similarly deployed. From the experience of repeated attempts, their armour has not been penetrated by our *Kerngeschosse* [armour-piercing bullets].[42] Their armament consists of six machine guns (two double machine guns in the back, two [single] machine guns in the front).[43] The enemy Caudron formations carry out their assignments oblivious to German fighter pilots. During an attack on a Caudron on 15 July 1918, I fired almost all of my ammunition into it at close range. The Caudron flew on calmly … A serious combat with these armoured and well-armed aeroplanes would demand great sacrifices. The Flak [anti-aircraft] batteries must be mobilised primarily to combat the Caudrons. They always fly … together and thereby offer a favourable target for the Flak units.

'At the outset, the Geschwader was deployed on the right flank of the [7th] Army for defence against enemy aerial forces advancing from the southwest. The superior enemy air activity over the battlefield south of the Marne [river] drew the Geschwader to the combat zone where our troops were fighting.

'For the most part, [our] individual Staffeln took off five times a day. The pilots and aircraft cannot provide these strenuous efforts indefinitely.

'Combining the Staffeln into Halbgeschwadern [units of half an air wing's strength] and deployment of the entire Geschwader [at one time] were necessary very soon. [When] the Geschwader flew to the frontlines in closed, strong formations, air supremacy was assured. The opposition, which is numerically far superior [to us], can always deploy fresh forces. Very cleverly, he takes advantage of moments when our fighter pilots are numerically fewer and unexpectedly charges over our lines in big formations. Despite immediate take-offs after [receiving] relatively fast incoming reports, only in rare cases are we able to reach the formations that have broken through in time and combat them.

'The lack of direct telephone connections between the Geschwader and the smaller Jagdgruppe makes uniform deployment [of forces] very difficult. The laying of urgently needed [telephone] lines must be completed at all costs by the [individual] army group before the attack …

'As a result of [premature] ignition of phosphorous [incendiary tracer] ammunition in recent days, various aircraft have crashed in flames. I have suspended [the use of] this ammunition. Urgent remedy [of this problem] is needed, as attacks against tethered observation balloons are impossible for the present time.'[44]

Undaunted by the scenario he described, Göring was among the members of JG I who flew from early morning until mid-afternoon on Thursday, 18 July. Consequently, the Geschwader achieved thirteen air combat triumphs, including Göring's twenty-second (and last) victory of World War I.

Göring's Twenty-second Victory

Upon his arrival at JG I, Göring received a new Fokker D.VII (serial number F 294/18). He expressed his individuality by having his aeroplane's fuselage painted yellow from the mid-point of the cockpit back to the rudder; in honour of JG I's link to Richthofen, the forward part of the fuselage was painted red. Flying that distinctive aeroplane on Thursday, 18 July, he reported that:

> '... at 8:15 a.m., I attacked some Spads. I pressed one downward and, in a *Kurvenkampf* [dogfight], shot it down. It fell into the wooded ravine near St. Bandry. Shortly thereafter I observed a second Spad shot down by Oberleutnant von Wedel. A third Spad was shot down by Leutnant Mohnicke.'[45]

A Fokker D.VII, possibly 324/18, that Göring flew when he commanded Jagdgeschwader I in the summer of 1918.

JG I also lost two pilots that day and, later that afternoon, Geschwader-Kommandeur Göring was called on to preside at the funeral of twenty-one-victory-ace Leutnant der Reserve Fritz Friedrichs. The young pilot, who had been approved for the Pour le Mérite but had not yet received the award, died after his Fokker D.VII accidentally caught fire in the air.[46] He jumped from the aeroplane with a parachute, but became entangled in the burning wreckage as it fell and was killed. As the Pour le Mérite was not awarded posthumously,[47] the fatal accident denied Friedrichs that high honour.

Even as Göring directed a Geschwader honour guard to place Friedrichs' remains into the earth near Beugneux airfield,[48] other JG I members were preparing to move to yet another farm field, Monthussart-Ferme, some fifteen kilometres away, just outside of Braisne on the Vesle river. To avoid detection by Allied aeroplanes, the men and equipment were moved throughout the night of 18-19 July.[49]

It is interesting to note that the day after Göring scored his aerial victory, his best friend, Bruno Loerzer, now the Kommandeur of JG III, shot down his twenty-eighth enemy aeroplane. While Göring's air fighting success came to a halt in July, Loerzer continued to score until late September, at which point his total stood at forty-four.[50] But a post-World War II comment of Loerzer's casts doubt on his and Göring's success as fighter aces. In a discussion with Generalleutnant Wolfgang Vorwald,[51] Loerzer admitted that 'air combat victories [were] exaggerated'. Hence, in this author's view, aerial victory lists, such as the one in Appendix I of this book, are subject to interpretation – and scepticism (See 'What was Göring's Final Tally' on page 165).

In any event, the furious pace of battle in the summer of 1918 offered no one at JG I's new airfield any relief from their labours. On the morning of 19 July, work crews set up tent hangars, while pilots of the Staffeln flew off to the frontlines.[52] Meanwhile, mechanics prepared for the airmen's return and the inevitable post-combat repair work on the aeroplanes. The result of the pilots' work was three Staffel victories for Göring to endorse and pass along to Kofl 7 for approval.

Amidst a powerful French ground attack in bad weather on Saturday, 20 July, Göring sent his pilots out to attack tanks, a captive balloon and infantry columns. They succeeded in all cases, but at the end of the day came the sad duty of three more funerals, including that of Göring's fellow Knight of the Order Pour le Mérite, Leutnant der Reserve Hans Kirschstein.[53] A twenty-seven-victory ace and leader of Jasta 6, Kirschstein accepted a ride in a two-seater that crashed on taking off from a repair depot five days earlier.

A small joy on that rain-filled day was the arrival of a two-seater, out of which jumped one of the Geschwader's most popular pilots: Leutnant Lothar Freiherr von Richthofen, a younger brother of JG I's namesake, who had been on a long convalescent leave since he was shot down and badly wounded on 13 March. All eyes were focused on 'the other' Richthofen, who was younger (and who had shot down many more aeroplanes) than Göring. Of course, Göring could take pleasure in the knowledge that he had possession of the Geschwader walking stick created from a British propeller for Manfred von Richthofen and used by only one other person, his predecessor, Wilhelm Reinhard. Göring prized that wooden shaft, which symbolised another link in his chain of successes.

Inextricably connected to his brother's legend, Lothar von Richthofen was eager to fly again. It was very fitting that he was placed in command of Jasta 11, which his brother had shaped from a nondescript unit to one of Germany's premier air fighting Staffeln. But, as events proved, the younger Richthofen had returned to combat too soon. That fact became evident during his first flight, when he became disoriented and almost lost his way back to Monthussart-Ferme airfield. As Richthofen himself later related, his vision was so blurred that he 'could scarcely tell friend from foe'.[54] He flew as often as he could and there was no way for Göring to keep Richthofen from his honour-driven quest to serve Germany.

More aerial triumphs followed and on the early evening of 25 July, he scored a milestone victory. Richthofen and his patrol attacked a formation of Airco D.H.9 bombers and their Sopwith F.1 Camel escorts over Fismes; he pursued one of the fighters and shot it down, claiming it as his thirtieth success.[55] By Kogenluft's calculations – and they may have been for purely propaganda reasons – Lothar von Richthofen's latest air combat claim was marked as JG I's 500th overall victory.[56]

But Göring would be absent when young Richthofen was once again in the spotlight. The following afternoon, only thirteen days after he arrived at JG I, Göring went on leave[57] for almost five weeks. Appropriately, in Göring's absence, Geschwader leadership was passed to Lothar von Richthofen.

The reason for the leave is not mentioned in surviving Geschwader files. Göring was no coward and would not shrink from a hard fight, but, possibly, another bad episode of rheumatoid arthritis may have caused him to seek relief from what would have been pain so severe as to interfere with his powers of concentration. According to one account:

'[Göring] departed for Munich and Mauterndorf [in Austria]. He spent more time with his godfather and Baroness Lilli von Epenstein than he did with his unofficial fiancée. It was obvious to Marianne Mauser's father that the war was coming to a close, and not in Germany's favour; and what sort of future would a young ex-pilot, no matter how heroic, have inside a defeated Germany? Better to marry off his daughter to another farmer, who could live off his land until times changed, than to a penniless charmer without prospects.'[58]

By the time Göring returned to his post, on 22 August, the Geschwader had changed airfields several times and was back under the overall command of the 2nd Army in the Somme Sector. By that time, however, the complex of the war had changed dramatically. The Allied counter-offensive that began in the early morning hours of 8 August 1918 was so effective that Generalfeldmarschall von Hindenburg's chief of staff, General Erich Ludendorff, called the event 'the black day of the German army in the history of the war'.[59]

Geschwader losses had paralleled those on the ground. On 10 August, the day after he was promoted to Oberleutnant, Erich Loewenhardt collided with another Jasta 10 Fokker D.VII and was killed.[60] Three days later, Lothar von Richthofen was shot in the thigh in a fight and invalided back to Germany, never to return to the battlefield. By the time of his last air fight, Lothar had scored forty aerial victories, the same amount as the legendary Oswald Boelcke, but half the number of his illustrious brother.

And now those days of glory were fading, as Göring, catching up on his administrative work, could see in the steady stream of JG I casualties that occurred in his absence (see Appendix II). The weight of numerically superior and better equipped adversaries compelled Göring to write in one report:

'... the enemy biplanes are very well armed and fly extremely well in large formations, even when attacked by several German single-seaters flying close together. [Enemy aircraft] are equipped with either armoured or fireproof fuel tanks ... Very often in the 7th and 2nd Army Sectors enemy tethered observation balloons were very often attacked repeatedly, without being set on fire.'[61]

Göring could only growl and glower privately, but still observed by his adjutant, who, years later, remembered: 'Oberleutnant Göring's face became sterner during these days. Should [the enemies] have their armour-plating, one after the other, we will get them. Should they make their tethered balloons impregnable, one way or the other, we will get them.'[62]

Despite Göring's grim determination, a clear sign of JG I's diminished air power was evident in its current operational status, as noted in a message from Kogenluft dated 13 August: 'Due to great casualties [suffered] in recent days, [JG I pilots and aeroplanes are] to be condensed into one Staffel. [It is to] collaborate with Jagdgeschwader III and Jagdgruppe Greim.'[63]

For the time being, the new arrangement made Göring subordinate to his friend Oberleutnant Bruno Loerzer, commander of JG III, consisting of Jastas 2, 26, 27 and 36.[64] It also placed JG I below Jagdgruppe 10 – a smaller organisation made up of Jastas 1, 39 and 59. Then known as JaGru Greim,[65] it had been established by the Bavarian ace Oberleutnant Robert Ritter von Greim.

As a footnote to history, it should be noted that, twenty-six years later, Göring was again replaced by Greim. In the final days of the Third Reich, on 25 April 1945, after Hitler sacked Göring and ordered his arrest, the newly promoted Generalfeldmarschall von Greim was appointed as last wartime commander in chief of the Luftwaffe.[66]

CHAPTER TWELVE
END OF THE BEGINNING

*'Göring, a leader of proved worth, was possibly gifted with a temperament
more offensive [-oriented] … than that of his predecessor or it may
be that the German air service, sensing that the … war was changing,
was impelled to throw its weight into the battle heedless of cost.'*[1]

H.A. JONES

Hermann Göring faced a discouraging situation. In the midst of rising casualties, Jagdgeschwader I's then highest-scoring pilot – sixty-victory ace Ernst Udet – had gone on leave the day that Göring returned from his break. Udet's most recent string of air combat triumphs – nineteen kills within twenty-two days since 1 August[2] – had been a powerful motivational force for his JG I comrades. But, in the process, Udet had become exhausted and he needed to rest.

Unlike Manfred von Richthofen, who had been so devoted to his frontline duties in 1917 and early 1918 that he had to be ordered to take leave, Udet and other later Staffel and Geschwader leaders understood the value of recuperation. Even Göring, whose biggest struggle had become badgering his superiors for more men and equipment, went on leave with some regularity.

In his 1937 biography Ernst Gritzbach wrote:

> 'Göring had to balance the use of his resources against the enemy with the greatest adroitness at every turn. Above all things, by sheer dint of his personality, he continued to motivate the inner fighting spirit of his ever more shrinking little band of flyers. Often the Geschwader's airfield was so far forward that it lay within range of enemy artillery fire. The men could hardly think of sleep, as they really gave the utmost to their mission.'[3]

Royal Air Force historian H.A. Jones saw a darker view of Göring's situation, as he observed:

> 'The Richthofen [Geschwader], which …had been the head and front of the German air fighting formations in the West, had been fought almost to destruction … Although Göring was given some young pilots and was subsequently able to get going once more with the help of his former flight commanders, it was impossible for the [Geschwader] to recover its glory in the few weeks of active life which remained … Göring, a leader of proved worth, was possibly gifted with a temperament more offensive [-oriented]…

than that of his predecessor [Wilhelm Reinhard] or it may be that the German air service, sensing that the … war was changing, was impelled to throw its weight into the battle heedless of cost.'[4]

Göring was not that foolhardy with his ever more limited resources. Rather, he sought motivational devices, such as using the power of imagery to inspire his men. Hence, at this point, Göring broke the tradition of having the Richthofen Geschwader-Kommandeur [wing commander] fly an aeroplane with a highly visible amount of red on it. He was not the Red Baron and asserted his own identity in a way that his men would recognise during the battles to come. His final aeroplane – Fokker D.VII F 5125/18 – was all white, which, as noted aircraft markings researcher Greg VanWyngarden observed, 'almost certainly … was painted this way at the [Fokker] factory especially for Göring'.[5] Between his administrative duties and, almost certainly, the effects of his continual struggle with rheumatoid arthritis, Göring did not fly much during the last three months of the war. When he did, however, he was as recognisable in his white Fokker D.VII as Manfred von Richthofen had been in his red Albatroses and Fokker Triplanes.

Göring had Fokker D.VII F 5125/18 painted entirely in white to make himself distinctive to his comrades.

In early August 1918, JG I changed airfields in an area west of St. Quentin. The Geschwader went from Ennemain, south of the old roman road, just over ten kilometres northeast to Bernes. At the end of the month they made a longer move, still to the northeast, to Busigny and Escaufort. These towns were not the sites of great battles, but merely way stations in the slow but steady retreat of the once powerful Richthofen Jagdgeschwader. Amid this activity, Göring had to devote ground and air personnel to scouting new locations and overseeing logistics in unsettled times.

Following JG I's latest relocation, on 2 September Göring was summoned to 2nd Army headquarters for a high level discussion. When he returned two days later, it was clear he had won bureaucratic victories in the struggle for resources for the Geschwader. As proof of his success, just after his return, 4 September, the JG I staff was joined by a new medical officer, Dr. Fisser, who set up first-aid stations at the airfields of the remnants of the Geschwader's four Jagdstaffeln.[6] Fisser's arrival was a small but important step in rebuilding the Geschwader.

JG I's score of aerial victories rose slowly in September, but casualties remained steady, as overwhelming numbers of British and French aircraft relentlessly attacked German aeroplanes. On the 5th of that month, for instance, Jasta 4 lost twenty-two-year-old Leutnant Joachim von Winterfeld, whose aeroplane caught fire during an evening air combat with S.E.5a fighters of 60 Squadron, RAF. The victor in three aerial combats, Winterfeld jumped out of his aeroplane in one of the new parachutes issued to fighter pilots. His chute had been badly damaged, however, and did not fully deploy; he was found in a critical condition and taken to the first-aid station at Lieu St. Amand, where he died a few hours later.[7]

Off to a New Sector

At mid-month, the Geschwader was transferred yet again, this time to an area Göring knew well from his early air combat days: Metz, east of Verdun. On 16 September, Göring climbed into his white Fokker D.VII and, with his Staffel leaders and technical officers behind him, he headed from Busigny and Escaufort eastward to an airfield at Frescaty, just outside Metz.[8] He was informed that a large American force (the U.S. First Army[9]) was leading an Allied offensive to reduce the salient at St. Mihiel. Now, the reconstituted Jagdgeschwader I was joined with JG II (Jastas 12, 13, 15 and 19) to engage American airmen, who were superior in number – but not experience – to their German opponents.

The reportedly hapless Americans were widely discussed some days later, when, on the evening of Saturday, 23 September, Göring and many of his pilots were invited to JG II's officers' mess[10] at Stenay, north of Metz. There they heard 'wonderful things about the splendid days [the JG II pilots] experienced in the skies over Metz … [and that] the American pilots had not the slightest bit of experience in aerial combat …'[11]

Göring's JG II counterpart, Oberleutnant Oskar Freiherr von Boenigk, and some of his top people raved about the combat opportunities available among the largely unseasoned American airmen. If the JG I pilots had not already read it, that evening they became familiar with an army communiqué of three days earlier that proclaimed:

'Above the battlefield between the Meuse and Moselle [rivers], in the time from 12 to 18 September, Jagdgeschwader II under the leadership of Oberleutnant Frhr. von Boenigk shot down eighty-one enemy aeroplanes and, at the same time, lost only two [of its airmen] in combat.'[12]

Sixty-eight American fighters and bombers were recorded as lost during this period[13] – the opening of the St. Mihiel offensive – which, of course, Göring had no way of knowing. He knew only that the numbers were high, which is what he wanted JG I to attain and he would do whatever was necessary to achieve that goal. He would not have to wait long to attract attention, as the Richthofen Jagdgeschwader soon became known to its adversaries. An American Expeditionary Force bulletin at this time informed U.S. air units about the illustrious newcomer to the sector and its resources:

'From latest information, [JGI] was reported to be equipped with Fokker biplanes. Losses in machines seem to be made good immediately with the best machines obtainable. This [air wing] seems to have taken part wherever the Germans or Allies started an offensive, and its transfer to the Conflans area would …indicate that this sector is now regarded as an active one by the [Germans].'[14]

Adventures with Udet

Newly promoted Oberleutnant der Reserve Ernst Udet returned from leave and rejoined JG I on Monday, 25 September. Late the following afternoon, he shot down two British Airco D.H.9 two-seat bombers southeast of Metz. They were confirmed as his sixty-first and sixty-second aerial victories.[15] And there was little likelihood that they would not be confirmed, as the Geschwader-Kommandeur participated in the flight and was among seven witnesses whose statements were appended to Udet's combat report and victory claim. Göring wrote: 'I observed at about 5:15 p.m. how the red [Fokker D.VII] of Oblt. Udet caused one D.H.9 to break up in the air and the second to go down in flames southeast of Metz.'[16]

One day after that fight, Göring took Udet with him on a short two-seater plane ride to visit the home defence Kampfeinsitzerstaffeln [single-seat combat sections] 1a and 1b, which were in the process of being combined to form Jagdstaffel 90.[17] Göring had wide latitude in selecting men for JG I and, with luck, might find some likely prospects among these flyers. Udet was familiar with this method of recruitment, as Manfred von Richthofen had 'discovered' him in charge of Jasta 37 when a new leader was needed for a more prestigious unit in the Red Baron's famous Jagdgeschwader.[18]

Oberleutnant Rudolf Nebel, Jasta 90's prospective commanding officer, was also familiar with that method – and, when he heard that Göring was coming for a visit, he enlisted one of his most trusted comrades to help ward off this 'grosse Kanone' [big gun]. Nebel had served briefly in Jasta 5 with Göring in 1916 and he knew how formidable the Kommandeur could be. As Nebel later described the situation:

'[I was] in the office of my Jagdstaffel when a message came that, shortly, Göring and the most successful [living German] fighter pilot of the First World War, Ernst Udet, would land at my airfield. I instructed my Werkmeister [senior non-commissioned officer] to keep a watchful eye, no matter what happened. Both comrades, who were Oberleutnants, as I was, had scarcely landed when Göring immediately snapped at the unshrinking Werkmeister: "Have a car brought around right away!"

'Duty bound, the terrified Werkmeister begged the [Kommandeur's] pardon, but he had to seek the approval of Oberleutnant Nebel in the office.

'Göring responded: "I order you to have a car brought around right away!"

'The Werkmeister was feeling smaller and smaller, but [he was] steadfast and stood by his instructions.

'Göring became ever more enraged: "Then I will court-martial you!"

'The Werkmeister, who was stuck in the middle, countered: "Whether you or Oberleutnant Nebel court-martials me, it is all the same."

'The car did not come and Göring and Udet marched by foot to the city six kilometres away. They made the trip back [to retrieve their aeroplane] in a car they hired in the city.

'One time later at a nice gathering in … Berlin, I asked Udet what he thought about that incident at the time and he said, grinning: "You know Hermann. If he wants to do something, he will do it, and so we simply walked."[19]

Chivalry or Chimera?

Nearly all wars have produced stories of horrible acts perpetrated by ordinary people caught up in the unholy passion of battle, but there have also been reports of individual actions so exemplary as to be considered chivalric. One such incident was recounted in the early 1930s by Niels Paulli Krause, a Dane who earned high decorations for flying with a French two-seater escadrille [squadron] during most of World War I.[20] Later, he told of a hotly-contested aerial combat in which he became the beneficiary of a grand gesture by Hermann Göring.

In his biography, Erich Gritzbach used Krause's 1930s-era account to demonstrate 'the esteem in which [Göring] was held by his enemies'.[21]

According to the Dane:

'One day I was alone on a long mission with my machine and I had taken some photographs when in the distance I could make out a German aeroplane returning from the French lines. As we had to cross paths, I was eager to know who this lone wolf might be. My opponent had also seen me and was heading toward me. We probed a little, circling each another at a great distance. I really had little desire for this circular angling while I was on the way home, but my opponent abruptly began the fight and forced me to respond. We flew around one another, coming ever closer, without finding a clear target. Then suddenly the German machine made a tight turn, almost into a loop, and in an instant its machine gun was trained on me.

'It all happened so suddenly that I was totally unable to respond. All that ran through my head was that [the pilot] must be some great opponent. Then once again the enemy aeroplane made such an incredible and for that time almost impossible manoeuvre that I knew my opponent was …Göring.

'Every great flyer has … special tactics. Thus, only Göring could fly like that. As for

Even though Sous-lieutenant Niels Paulli Krause lost an eye in a flight accident, he continued to fly throughout the war.

me, I fought like I had never fought before … And yet I clearly recognised that my opponent was better than I. This was no mere cat-and-mouse game, but a battle with a flying genius against whom it was impossible for me to prevail. I do not know how long we circled each other and strained our bracing wires. Linen tatters in my wings showed that I had been hit many times. But the decisive shot had not yet struck.

'Then, in the midst of … [my gaining the advantage], my machine gun jammed. I pounded with my fists against the red-hot gun breech, to no avail. I tugged at the ammunition belt, to no avail. My only thought was: "It is all over!" My opponent seemed perplexed that, suddenly, I was no longer shooting at him. He circled around me, noticed me hammering away at the machine gun and understood that I was no longer able to fight. Then suddenly … he flew quite close to me, put his hand to his flying helmet in a military salute, and turned toward the German lines …'[22]

In considering what Niels Paulli Krause described as his air battle with Hermann Göring, it is important to take into account Krause's exemplary combat record and his experience in various aircraft. He was a talented pilot and, even after he lost an eye, he flew two-seat single-engine Farman aircraft, as well as two-engine Caudron G.IV and Letord 5A.3 aeroplanes. In 1918 he switched over to Spad S.XI A.2 two-seaters[23], which were developed from the famed Spad S.VII and S.XIII single-seat fighters, but were disappointing; they were found to be 'tiring to fly and difficult to control'.[24] Supposedly improved Spad S.XII two-seaters later assigned to Krause's unit also had problems.[25]

Without being specific, Krause hinted that he was flying a fast and agile single-seat fighter against Göring – who was then at the controls of a swift, rugged Fokker D.VII –

This captured Spad S.XI was the type that Krause would have been flying during his claimed encounter with Göring.

and on a combat sector opposite the Dane's unit. Krause's records and his escadrille's history, however, show that he was flying slower, much less manoeuvrable two-seaters at this time; indeed, the 'long mission' during which Krause said that he 'had taken some photographs' surely would have been an extensive reconnaissance flight to gather intelligence information about German forces. (There were camera-equipped Spad S.XIII fighters, but none were used by Krause's unit.[26]) His desire to avoid combat with an enemy fighter plane was not due to a lack of courage, but motivated by his dedication to bringing home the valuable photographic negatives.

The timing of this air fight can only be estimated, as Krause did not provide a date or location for it. Likewise, he did not elaborate on the 'incredible and … almost impossible manoeuvre' Göring allegedly performed, nor did Krause indicate how he identified his opponent's aeroplane. At this time, Göring was flying his distinctive, all-white Fokker D.VII (F 5125/18), which in a fight must have looked like an unforgettable ghostly menace, but Krause did not mention the type or colour of his opponent's aeroplane. Further, Krause made no mention of being accompanied by a backseat man, who would have taken the photos and been armed with a flexible, ring-mounted machine gun that would have been a distinct advantage in combat in such close quarters.

Krause's story does not comport with what reasonably would have occurred in his unit, which in 1918 was known as Escadrille Spa 2, reflecting the use of Spad and other two-seaters.[27] And Krause's motives for allowing post-war publication of the alleged chivalric combat are not clear. He was already a prominent airman, having been decorated with Britain's Military Cross, the National Order of Denmark, and the Swedish Order of the Sword, First Class[28]. In the summer of 1918 the French news magazine *Le Guerre Aérienne Illustrée*[29] published a two-part article about his heroism and personal sacrifice. In view of those well earned accolades, one can only wonder why Niels Paulli Krause felt the need to humble himself before Hermann Göring.

Krause's story sounds quite thrilling and would have enlivened any dinner conversation, but the likelihood that an aerial combatant (and especially the aggressive Göring) would simply let an enemy fly away strains credulity. A more realistic German view of so-called chivalric aerial combat was offered by former wartime pilot Conrad Horster[30] in an article published in a popular German veterans' magazine four years before Krause's paean to Göring appeared. According to Horster:

'In order to make the expression "force down [an aeroplane]" understandable one must mention that aerial combats on the Western Front were settled with a certain *Ritterlichkeit* [chivalry]. The vanquished or wounded adversary was spared the moment he gave up all resistance and sought his salvation in an involuntary landing. Such a moment always occurred when … totally unexpected, the German pilot made a deft manoeuvre that put him right on his opponent's neck and he had the enemy aeroplane directly in his machine gun's stream of fire. In this situation the opponent knew that the German had only to press the firing button on his guns and in a few seconds his own crate would be fired on and at least his fuel tank would be set on fire or he would be hit. In this circumstance, therefore, the opponent gave up resistance and acquiesced to the victor that he would have to land, i.e., to be "forced down" to the ground at a minimum behind [the victor's] lines.'[31]

This view of a post-war all-white Fokker D.VII approximates what Niels Paulli Krause would have seen had Göring attacked him as claimed. Most likely the Dane would have remembered the Fokker's distinctive appearance.

Göring was a skilled fighter pilot who had no qualms about killing his adversaries and it is hard to imagine him letting an easy victory slip away by releasing a reconnaissance aircraft, laden with information that would surely have contributed to the destruction of German ground forces that he was defending. If circumstances allowed, Göring might have forced the French aeroplane to land within German lines, as he and his AEG bomber crew had done on 14 March 1916, which resulted in his second confirmed aerial victory. Moreover, Göring's flight logs show he adhered strictly to the doctrine of flying only in the company of other fighters and not using the 'lone wolf' approach mentioned by Krause.

In the absence of more details about Niels Paulli Krause's claimed aerial combat with Hermann Göring, this writer considers the Dane's account to be a confabulation of unknown motivation. But once the story was out, it would have been consistent with Göring's sense of self-grandeur to take credit for such a magnanimous role in this tale.

JG I Fights the Americans

Factual aerial combats continued after JG I moved from Metz to Marville, north of Verdun in the 5th Army Sector, on 7 October 1918. Three days later, five JG I Fokkers intercepted a flight of Spads from the American 147th Aero Squadron that were about to attack a German observation balloon at Dun-sur-Meuse. American Captain Edward V. Rickenbacker, commanding officer of the 94th Aero Squadron, USAS, led a second Spad flight against what he described as Fokkers bearing 'the red noses of the von Richthofen Circus',[32] a name applied to JG I due to its colourful aircraft markings and mobility to move quickly from sector to sector.

German pilots had the initial success, as Leutnants Justus Grassmann and Wilhelm Kohlbach of Jasta 10 each claimed a Spad.[33] But then Rickenbacker set fire to Kohlbach's aircraft and witnessed an amazing scene of aviation progress, as his adversary was saved from certain death by using a parachute:

> '. . . the next second …the German pilot level[led] off his blazing machine and with a sudden leap overboard into space let the Fokker slide safely away without him. Attached to his back and sides was a rope which immediately pulled a dainty parachute from the bottom of his seat. The [canopy] opened within a fifty-foot drop and lowered him gradually to earth within his own lines.'[34]

After that fight, JG I's air combat activity dropped drastically when over two weeks of rainy weather made flying more difficult. In any event, by this time 'the German government … was convinced of the hopelessness of the situation' and on 20 October accepted U.S. President Woodrow Wilson's 'Fourteen Points',[35] including the evacuation of all occupied territories.

Dinners in Berlin

Hermann Göring and Ernst Udet departed JG I together on 22 October.[36] Göring headed to Berlin, his favourite city, for a short leave and then went on to the nearby Adlershof aviation testing facility for the third and final evaluation of new fighter aircraft. He must have known the trip was futile, as no one then believed that Germany would be able to fight much longer. Indeed, at this point it was all the German army could do to withdraw its forces in as orderly a manner as possible. Udet had been transferred to Flieger-Ersatz-Abteilung 3 at Gotha in eastern Germany, from which he would proceed to Berlin[37] and join Göring in inspecting the new aeroplanes – even though neither of them nor the aircraft would ever again fly over the Western Front.

In late October 1918, less than two weeks before the end of World War I, leading German fighter pilots attended one last party hosted by the Pfalz Aeroplane Works at the Adlon Hotel on Unter den Linden in downtown Berlin. Seen here on the left side of the table are: Hermann Göring, Friedrich Mallinckrodt, Heinrich Bongartz, Hans Klein, Fritz von Falkenhayn, Josef Veltjens, unknown, Paul Bäumer, and a series of unidentifiable attendees. Seated across the table (right to left): Alfred Eversbusch, Bruno Loerzer, Ernst Udet, Eduard Ritter von Schleich, Oskar Freiherr von Boenigk, Josef Jacobs and more unidentifiable attendees.

To the uninformed observer at the fighter competition, it would have been difficult to believe that the German Luftstreitkräfte was waging a final, bloody rearguard action in eastern France. Following the daily tests of new aeroplanes at Adlershof, Göring and Udet joined a gallery of Germany's top fighter pilots at elegant dinners in the best hotels in Berlin. On one evening, Göring and the other élite airmen were hosted in fine style by Anthony Fokker and his staff at the Bristol Hotel,[38] and on another evening, Ernst and Alfred Eversbusch, founders of the Pfalz Flugzeug-Werke [aeroplane works], invited the group to dine at the luxurious Adlon Hotel.[39] Not content with offering only fine dining, the Eversbusch brothers also arranged for a famous exotic dancer to appear after dinner. Noted World War I German aviation expert Peter M. Grosz related the event, as he heard it during a visit with Alfred Eversbusch in the early 1960s:

'… Tony Fokker had a real knack for entertaining the visiting frontline pilots when they came to Berlin … [His] method of entertaining, mixing *demi-monde* damsels with flowing wine and the best culinary delicacies the Bristol Hotel could offer, was well known to his competitors, if not envied. After all, Fokker was no older than the pilots and he understood their needs. Herr Eversbusch reasoned that, to counter Fokker's persuasive largesse, an event of equal magnitude and excitement was required, something so extraordinary that it would make a lasting impression.

'During a board meeting at the Pfalz Works … it was decided to go all out. Herr Eversbusch would approach the most famous … contemporary dancer, Fräulein Lucy Kieselhausen, and inquire [whether] she would dance "totally in the nude" for a group of deserving fighter pilots, bemedalled, battle-weary, heroic and in need of some diversion … After discussing the offer with her mother, she told Herr Eversbusch: "I'll do it for 10,000 gold, not paper, Marks and under the condition there is no applause and my mother is allowed to chaperone in the wings." Herr Eversbusch [agreed and] … was delighted over his coup. But I could see that he still felt the loss of hard, gold coin-of-the-realm, judging by the sigh followed by a solid gulp of wine.'[40]

Fading Glory in France

While Hermann Göring and other air leaders enjoyed themselves in Berlin, their pilots continued to drive up their unit and personal victory scores. The Geschwader was being pressed hard by the relentless American offensive 'with its enormous masses of men, artillery [and], tanks …'[41] In response, during the first week of November, JG I fought high in the skies over the battlefield and close to the ground, accompanying low-level Schlachtstaffeln [ground attack units] in their attempt to halt the overwhelming tide of Allied troops.[42]

But it was all for naught. Jagdgeschwader I's last day of battle was Wednesday, 6 November 1918. Still operating from Marville, a prominent ace, Leutnant Ulrich Neckel, and two lower-scoring pilots shot down an American Spad S.XIII apiece near Woevre Wood.[43] Any sense of triumph did not last, however, as the Geschwader withdrew further east the next day, to Tellancourt.

On Saturday, 9 November, Kaiser Wilhelm II abdicated and went into exile in the Netherlands, thereby ending the German empire. Also on that day, the recently-returned Oberleutnant Hermann Göring received some good news: Jasta 6 pilot Ulrich Neckel, with thirty victories to his credit, had been awarded the Pour le Mérite a day earlier.[44] The twenty-year-old ace was the Geschwader's last pilot to receive the honour.

Next, Göring organised JG I's withdrawal to Germany. Several hundred men and the Geschwader's engines, spare parts, provisions and other necessary equipment were to be loaded into forty-six lorries for the final journey back to Germany. The following day, wearying and confusing orders and counter-orders came in, directing and redirecting the units.

Göring was informed that the Armistice would take effect at 11:00 a.m. on Monday, 11 November 1918. That morning, however, the airfield was covered with fog and Göring worried that, if the fog persisted, he and his men would not be allowed to fly the aeroplanes back to Germany – and be forced to leave them in France. Finally, at 10:00 a.m., the fog lifted and the aeroplanes took off for Darmstadt,[45] where they would wait for the lorries to catch up with them.

On the flight to Darmstadt, however, one Staffel inadvertently landed in Mannheim. Unbeknownst to them, that city had fallen under the influence of the uprising in Kiel, which on 29 October 1918 saw soldiers mutiny against continuing the war by rising up against their officers. The JG I pilots were quickly overpowered by the renegades, who seized their personal side-arms and aircraft and then released them.

But they had not reckoned with Hermann Göring's towering rage. When his humiliated men arrived in Darmstadt and recounted their misfortune, the Geschwader-Kommandeur roared at them and all of his other men: 'I will make those thugs pay for that [insult]. Load your machine guns.'[46] Then, exercising the type of ruthless authority for which he would become notorious some fifteen years hence, he led the Geschwader to Mannheim, where the other aeroplanes had landed previously and he presented this ultimatum: 'If the officers are not allowed to take off immediately, with their [machine guns], the airfield will be razed to the ground.'[47] Something in Göring's bearing made it clear to his new German adversaries that his threat was deadly serious. In short order, the briefly-interned warplanes were released to Göring's men.

That evening, Göring prepared his final daily report for JG I's war diary, with no mention of the incident at Mannheim: '11 November. Armistice. Geschwader flight in unfavourable weather conditions to Darmstadt. Misty …'.[48]

Geschwader pilots performed a final act of defiance against the Allied victors. After they had returned to Darmstadt, a general staff officer ordered Göring to have his men fly the aeroplanes to Strasbourg and surrender them to the French authorities. Göring said he could not carry out such an order. On their own, however, his pilots made things easier for him: during a subsequent flight, most of them had "accidents" while landing back at Darmstadt and wrecked many aeroplanes; their machine guns were "somehow" sabotaged, as well. The surviving aircraft met with a similar fate at Strasbourg.[49]

Hermann Göring, last wartime commander of Jagdgeschwader Freiherr von Richthofen Nr I, led his men and what was left of their provisions and equipment from Darmstadt to the *Buntpapierfabrik AG* [coloured paper manufactory] in Aschaffenburg for demobilisation. The factory building became a barracks for the enlisted men, while the officers were honoured guests of the factory's director, commercial privy councillor Wilhelm Schmitt-Prym.[50]

On the evening of Tuesday, 19 November, Göring convened the Geschwader's fifty-three officers and 473 non-commissioned officers and other ranks[51] for a final meeting. Gathered in the *Stiftskeller* [monastery wine cellar] in the historic city along the Main river, these men, like the contents of the casks on the walls, had been distilled to their essence, and Göring would not let them go to their homes throughout Germany without offering his heartfelt thanks and whatever inspirational words he could muster. He reminded them that JG I had accounted for 644 British, French and American aircraft at a cost of fifty-six of their own officer and enlisted pilots and six ground-crewmen killed – and another fifty-two officers and pilots and seven enlisted men wounded.[52] He told them that theirs was a record to be envied and the stuff of legend and did his best to give them hope in an uncertain future.

As for Hermann Göring, he would face years of disappointment and personal failure. But he kept going, bolstered by an innate toughness and, when needed, an ability to detach himself from reality. The latter was evidenced a short time after the war ended, when the father of his Austrian fiancée, Marianne Mauser, wrote and asked, 'What have you now to offer my daughter?' Not to be trifled with, Göring steeled himself against the disappointment he sensed coming and replied: 'Nothing'.[53] With that, the lovely Marianne was consigned to his past.

The Call of a Dark Future

Göring's future was best presaged by remarks he made after he returned to his beloved Berlin in December 1918. At a meeting of a new officers' association, held in the Berlin Philharmonic Hall, he rose, resplendent in his dress uniform with the Pour le Mérite and other medals, and responded to a speaker who counselled moderation of Germany's post-war military influence by saying:

> 'For four long years, we officers did our duty on the ground, at sea and in the air, and risked our lives for our Fatherland. Now we come home and what do some people do to us? They spit on us and want to take our honour away from us. And I will tell you this: the real [German] people are not responsible for this [conduct]. Each and every one of them was a comrade, irrespective of social standing, for four long, difficult years of war. It is not the real people who are to blame; rather, it is the ones who incited them, who stabbed our glorious army in the back and who wanted nothing more than to enrich themselves at the expense of the real people. And for that reason I urge everyone here today to [nurture] the deepest and most abiding hatred against these criminals [who are] against the German people. The day will come – that I know and I ask that you believe it – when these gentlemen are finished and driven out of our Germany. Prepare yourselves, arm yourselves and work toward that day ...'[54]

In those dark times for Germany, Hermann Göring began a whole new cycle of his usual fantasy, bundled in paranoia, lies and boundless ambition. World War I was over – but the armistice gave rise to a false sense of peace that was only the end of the beginning of another world disaster, one in which Göring would rise to become a major figure.

APPENDIX I

VICTORY LIST OF HERMANN GÖRING AND HIS SQUADRON COMRADES

Author's note: To view Hermann Göring's air combat triumphs within an organisational context, the following list of aerial victories – scored by him and his comrades when he was assigned to his four air units (prior to assuming overall command of Jagdgeschwader I) – was compiled from the official *Nachrichtenblatt der deutschen Luftstreitkräfte* weekly news and intelligence summary, various Kommandeur der Flieger bi-monthly, weekly and other reports, resources from the former Reichsarchiv and research material provided by the late Dr. Gustav Bock. Comparable British and French reports provided potentially corresponding casualty and other information. Dates are stated in the German numerical style (day, month) and times are expressed in military time, with chronological sub-headings to clarify whether the local time was an hour ahead of British/French time, or matched it. Airfields used by the air units to which Göring was assigned at the time of the victories are also noted, to indicate their proximity to the air combat sites noted. In cases of two-seater casualties, pilots are listed first, observers second. Fates of the airmen are indicated by the abbreviations: DoW = Died of Wounds; KiA = Killed in Action; PoW = Prisoner of War; WiA = Wounded in Action. Otherwise, it is assumed the airman was uninjured and returned to his own unit. Aerial victories claimed, but not confirmed are indicated by n/c, and aircraft Forced to Land (which may have been credited as victories) are identified by FtL. During most of Göring's time with Jasta 27, the overall Staffel victory numbers were recorded and listed after individual numbers – at times even when some victories were not confirmed officially.

Date	Time	Location	Aircraft Type	Victor & Aircraft	Vic. No.	Crew / Disposition
1915						
		Stenay (FFA 25 airfield)				
20.5		near Fresnoy	EA	Hptm Keck & Off.Stv Schmidt, FFA 25	1 / 1	
26.5		Vienne	EA	Hptm Keck & Off.Stv Schmidt, FFA 25	1 / 2	
3.6		Stenay	EA	Ltn Göring & Ltn Loerzer, FFA 25 Albatros B.I B.990/14	n/c	

Date	Time	Location	Aircraft Type	Victor & Aircraft	Vic. No.	Crew / Disposition
1.9	1800	Vauquois	EA	Ltn Wuthmann & Off.Stv Schmidt, FFA 25	1 3	Sgt C. Couturier & Lt L. Moisan (KiA) Esc MF 2
3.10	1100	3 km south of Tahure	EA	Ltn Bernert FFA 34 & Ltn Ehrhardt, FFA 25	1 1	
4.10	1700	Luippes	EA	Ltn Cammann, FFA 44 & Vzfw Schramm, FFA 25	1 1	
11.10	0820	Montlainville	EA	Oblt Veiel & Ltn.d.R Schülke, FFA 25	1 1	
12.10	1725	2 km east of Tahure	EA	Ltn Cammann, FFA 44 & Vzfw Schramm, FFA 25	2 2	Sol Bremond & Lt du Beauviez (PoW) Esc VB 112
12.10	1730	6 km south of Tahure	EA	Oblt Kirsch & Ltn Kaehler, FFA 25	1 1	may also have shot down Bremond & du Beauviez
16.11	1430	Tahure	Farman	Ltn Göring & Ltn Bernert, FFA 25 Albatros C.I C.486/15	1 1	no comparable French loss recorded

1916

Date	Time	Location	Aircraft Type	Victor & Aircraft	Vic. No.	Crew / Disposition
14.3	1130	southeast of Haumont Wood	Caudron G.4	Ltn Göring, Ltn von Schaesberg & Vzfw Boje, FFA 25 AEG G.I G 49/15	FtL / 2 1 1	Sgt G. Depèche & S/Lt G. Theremin (PoW) Esc C.6
1.5		German time one hour ahead of Allied time				
19.5			EA	Ltn.d.R Schülke, FFA 25	1	
20.6			EA	Oblt.d.R Schmidt, FFA 25	1	
			EA	Uffz Wellhausen, FFA 25	1	
15.7	0815	Marre Ridge	Voisin biplane	Ltn Göring, FAA 203	FtL / n/c	
30.7	1030	Mamey (s.w. Pont à Mousson), west of the Moselle river	Caudron G.4	Ltn Göring, FAA 203	3	Sgt Girard-Varet (WiA) Esc C.10
		Gonnelieu (Ja 5 airfield: 20.9.16 – 10.3.17)				
20.10	1700	southeast of Le Transloy	F.E.2b	Oblt Berr, Ja 5	5	
22.10	1100	northwest of Sailley-Saillisel	Morane Parasol	Oblt Berr, Ja 5	6	3 Sqn, RFC
	1200	Bapaume	Airco D.H.2	Vzfw H.K. Müller, Ja 5	7	
26.10	1800	Le Transloy	F.E.2b	Oblt Berr, Ja 5	7	18 Sqn, RFC
	1810	south of Maurepas	Balloon	Oblt Berr, Ja 5	8	
29.10	1745	southeast of Combles	F.E. type	Ltn.d.R Theiller, Ja 5	4	
1.11	1530	south of Le Transloy	Nieuport	Ltn.d.R Theiller, Ja 5	5	
	1615	southeast of Courcelette	Caudron	Oblt Berr, Ja 5	9	
2.11	1700	Combles	B.E.2d 5760	Ltn Göring, Ja 5	n/c	Sgt C. Bromley (DoW) & Lt G.H. Wood (WiA), 7 Sqn, RFC
3.11	1745	Courcelette	B.E.2	Oblt Berr, Ja 5	10	

Date	Time	Location	Aircraft Type	Victor & Aircraft	Vic. No.	Crew / Disposition
1917						
		Colmar Nord (Ja 26 airfield: 20.1 – 2.3.17)				
25.2		south of Lutterbach	Nieuport	Ltn Weitz, Ja 26 Albatros D.III	2	
		Habsheim (Ja 26 airfield: 2.3 – 12.4.17)				
6.3		Dammerkirch	Nieuport	Oblt B. Loerzer, Ja 26 Albatros D.III	3	
10.3	1630	Carspach	Spad	Oblt B. Loerzer, Ja 26 Albatros D.III	4	
11.3	1020	south of Ammerzweiler	Nieuport	Ltn Weitz, Ja 26 Albatros D.III	3	
16.3	1630	between Niedersulzbach and Ober-Aspach	Nieuport	Vzfw F. Loerzer, Ja 26 Albatros D.III	2	
25.3		German time synchronized with Allied time				
5.4	1806	Sennheim	Nieuport	Ltn.d.R H. Auer, Ja 26 Albatros D.III	1	
		Guise-Ost (Ja 26 airfield: 16.4 – 23.4.17)				
17.4		German time one hour ahead of Allied time				
		Bohain-Nord (Ja 26 airfield: 23.4 – 6.6.17)				
23.4	1728	northeast of Arras	F.E.2b	Ltn Göring, Ja 26 Albatros D.III 2049/16	4	2/Lt E.L. Zink (WiA) & 2/Lt G.B. Bate (WiA/DoW), 18 Sqn, RFC
	1800	southwest of Hancourt	Airco D.H.4 / Martinsyde	Off.St Weckbrodt, Ja 26 Albatros D.III	2	27 Sqn, RFC
28.4	1830	near Harly / southeast of St. Quentin	Sopwith 1½ Strutter A.993	Ltn Göring, Ja 26 Albatros D.III 2049/16	5	2/Lt C.M. Reece & 2/AM A. Moult (PoW)43 Sqn, RFC
29.4	1945	Ramicourt	Nieuport 17bis	Ltn Göring, Ja 26 Albatros D.III 2049/16	6	F/S/L A.H.V. Fletcher (WiA / PoW) 6 Sqn, RNAS
10.5	1505	northeast of Le Pavé	Airco D.H.4	Ltn Göring, Ja 26 Albatros D.III 2049/16	7	2/Lt T. Webb & 1/AM W. Bond (KiA) 55 Sqn, RFC
	1510	northeast of Gouzeaucourt	Airco D.H.4	Ltn Blume, Ja 26 Albatros D.III	1	55 Sqn, RFC
		Bersée (Ja 27 airfield: 19.4 – 18.6.17)				
3.6	1850	Bousbecque	Sopwith Triplane	Off.Stv Klein, Ja 27 Albatros D.III 2026/16	2/2	10 Sqn, RNAS
8.6	0740	Moorslede	Nieuport 23	Ltn Göring, Ja 27 Albatros D.III 2049/16	8/3	2/Lt F.D. Slee (PoW) 1 Sqn, RFC
9.6	1700	east of Roulers	B.E.	Ltn Göring, Ja 27 Albatros D.V 1027/17	n/c	
		Iseghem (Ja 27 airfield: 18.6 – 31.10.17)				
24.6	0745	near Ypres	Nieuport	Ltn Göring, Ja 27 Albatros D.III 2049/16	n/c	
7.7	1140	east of Ypres	Spad	Ltn Göring, Ja 27 Albatros D.III 2049/16	n/c	

Date	Time	Location	Aircraft Type	Victor & Aircraft	Vic. No.	Crew / Disposition
	1145	northwest of Ypres	R.E.8	Vzfw Krauss, Ja 27 Albatros D.V 1108/17	1/4	
16.7	2010	northeast of Ypres	S.E.5a	Ltn Göring, Ja 27 Albatros D.III 2049/16	9/5	2/Lt R.G. Jardine 56 Sqn, RFC
	2010	northeast of Ypres	Sopwith	Vzfw Krauss, Ja 27 Albatros D.V 1108/17	2/6	
24.7	2015	Calve	Sopwith Triplane	Ltn.d.R Dilthey, Ja 27 Albatros D.V 1109/17	1/7	F/S/L T.C. May (KiA) 10 Sqn, RNAS
	2040	south of Polygon Wood / south of Passchendaele	Martinsyde	Ltn Göring, Ja 27 Albatros D.V 2080/17	10/8	
26.7	2040	south of Roulers	Sopwith	Vzfw Muth, Ja 27 Albatros D.V 2028/17	1/9	
28.7	0745	Staden	Martinsyde	Vzfw Krauss, Ja 27 Albatros D.V 2147/17	n/c	
5.8	2015	northeast of Ypres / south of Houthulst Forest	Sopwith F.1 Camel B.3792	Ltn Göring, Ja 27 Albatros D.V 2080/17	11/10	Lt G. Budden (WiA) 70 Sqn, RFC
		northwest of Warneton	Sopwith	Vzfw Kampe Albatros D.V 2017/17	n/c	
12.8	1345	Moorslede	Nieuport 23	Vzfw Kampe, Ja 27 Albatros D.V 2017/17	1/12	1 Sqn, RFC
	1352	Brodseinde	Nieuport 23	Ltn.d.R Dilthey, Ja 27 Albatros D.V 2300/17	2/11	1 Sqn, RFC
14.8	1637	northwest of Ypres	Balloon	Ltn.d.R Luer, Ja 27 Albatros D.V 1112/17	1/13	
	1642	northwest of Ypres	Balloon	Vzfw Krauss, Ja 27 Albatros D.III (OAW) 1691/17	3/14	
20.8	1220	west of Becelaere	Airco D.H.4	Vzfw Kampe, Ja 27 Albatros D.V 2017/17	2/15	57 Sqn, RFC
	1220	Becelaere	Airco D.H.4	Fwbl Muth, Ja 27 Albatros D.V 2084/17	2/16	
25.8	2045	south of Ypres / southwest of Ypres	Sopwith F.1 Camel B.3918	Ltn Göring, Ja 27 Albatros D.V 4424/17	12/17	2/Lt O.C. Bridgeman (WiA) 70 Sqn, RFC
2.9	0950	Quesnoy / Tourcoing / west of Roubaix	Spad S.7	Ltn.d.R Dilthey, Ja 27 Albatros D.V 2300/17	3/18	19 Sqn, RFC
3.9	0900	Dixmude / north of Lampernisse	Airco D.H.4	Ltn Göring, Ja 27 Albatros D.V 4624/17	13/19	Lt G.M. Guillon (WiA) 57 Sqn, RFC
9.9	1300	Frezenberg	Balloon	Ltn.d.R Luer, Ja 27 Albatros D.V 1112/17	2/20	
15.9	1938	northwest of Wervicq	Sopwith	Ltn.d.R Berkemeyer, Ja 27 Albatros D.V 2327/17	3/21	
20.9	1815	over Polygon Wood	Sopwith	Ltn Göring, Ja 27 Albatros D.V 2159/17	n/c	
	1815	Hooge	Spad S.7	Vzfw Krauss	n/c / 39	
21.9	0700	Between Ypres and Houthulst Forest	Airco D.H.4	Vzfw Jumpelt, Ja 27 Albatros D.V 2315/17	1/25	

Date	Time	Location	Aircraft Type	Victor & Aircraft	Vic. No.	Crew / Disposition
	0715	Between Ypres and Houthulst Forest	Airco D.H.4	Ltn.d.R Rosenstein, Ja 27 Albatros D.III 1673/17	1/26	
	0905	Sleyhage, west of Roulers	Bristol F.2B A.7224	Ltn Göring, Ja 27 Albatros D.V 4424/17	14/27	2/Lt R.L.Curtis (PoW/DoW) & 2/Lt D.P. Fitzgerald-Uniacke (WiA/PoW) 48 Sqn, RFC
26.9	1145	Blankaart Lake	Sopwith F.1 Camel	Ltn,d,R Rosenstein, Ja 27 Albatros D.III 612/17	2/34	
		Pierkenhoek	Sopwith F.1 Camel	Ltn.d.R Klimke Albatros D.V 2330/17	3/22	45 Sqn, RFC
		South of Houthulst Forest	Sopwith F.1 Camel	Ltn.d.R Klimke Albatros D.V 2330/17	4/23	9 Sqn, RNAS
9.10	1115	Poelcapelle	Spad S.7	Ltn.d.R Dilthey, Ja 27 Albatros D.V	4/24	19 Sqn, RFC
18.10	0940	Clerckem	S.E.5a	Ltn.d.R Dilthey, Ja 27 Albatros D.V 2300/17	5/30	56 Sqn, RFC
	0950	Ypres	S.E.5a	Vzfw Kampe, Ja 27 Albatros D.V 2253/17	3/28	56 Sqn, RFC
	0955	west of Passchendaele	S.E.5a	Vzfw Kampe, Ja 27 Albatros D.V 2253/17	4/29	56 Sqn, RFC
21.10	1545	Bondues / Linselles	S.E.5a B.547	Ltn Göring, Ja 27 Albatros D.V 2159/17	15/32	2/Lt A.E. Hempel (PoW) 84 Sqn, RFC
	1555	south of Rumbeke	Sopwith	Ltn.d.R Berkemeyer, Ja 27 Albatros D.V 2327/17	4/31	
24.10	1010	northeast of Zonnebeke	Spad S.7	Ltn.d.R Luer, Ja 27 Albatros D.V 1112/17	3/33	
		southwest of Becelaere	Sopwith Pup	Ltn.d.R Klimke Albatros D.III (OAW) 1673/17	5/34	
		Bavichove (Ja 27 airfield: 1.11.17 – 12.2.18)				
5.11		northwest of Blankaart Lake	Sopwith F.1 Camel	Ltn.d.R Luer, Ja 27 Albatros D.V 1112/17	4/36	
7.11	0915	over Houthulst Forest / northwest of Poelcapelle	Airco D.H.5	Oblt Göring, Ja 27 Albatros D.V 2153/17	16/35	no matching RFC loss
5.12	1150	between Warneton and Konijn	Spad S.7	Vzfw Kampe, Ja 27	5/37	23 Sqn, RFC
6.12	1035	north of Becelaere / near Ghulevelt	Spad S.7	Vzfw Kampe, Ja 27	6/38	

1918

Date	Time	Location	Aircraft Type	Victor & Aircraft	Vic. No.	Crew / Disposition
3.1	1140	Rollegem-Kapelle	Sopwith	Vzfw Kampe (n/c)	7/42	
13.1	1240	southwest of Gheluwe	Spad S.7	Vzfw Krauss, Ja 27	4 / ?	
23.1	1650	Frezenberg	Sopwith F.1 Camel	Ltn Brandt, Ja 27 (n/c)	3/41	
29.1	1235	Houthulst Forest	British 2-seater	Ltn.d.R Klimke (n/c)	11/50	
5.2	1435	Keiberg / south of Passchendaele	Sopwith F.1 Camel	Ltn.d.R Dilthey, Ja 27	6/40	65 Sqn, RFC

Date	Time	Location	Aircraft Type	Victor & Aircraft	Vic. No.	Crew / Disposition
		Marckebeke (Ja 27 airfield: 13.2. – 12.3.18)				
21.2	1000	Ledeghem	S.E.5a C.5325	Oblt Göring, Ja 27	17/43	2/Lt G.B. Craig (PoW/DoW) 60 Sqn, RFC
	1000	Rolleghem-Kapelle	S.E.5a B.4860	Ltn.d.R Klimke, Ja 27	6/44	2/Lt W.M. Kent (KiA) 60 Sqn, RFC
8.3	1208	northwest of Gheluvelt / between Gheluvelt & Daimlingseck	Sopwith 5F.1 Dolphin	Vzfw Kampe, Ja 27	8/45	19 Sqn, RFC
10.3		German time synchronised with Allied time				
		Erchin (Ja 27 airfield: 12.3.17 – 15.4.18)				
23.3	0935	Hendecourt	S.E.5a	Ltn.d.R Klimke, Ja 27	7/46	
1.4	1230	northwest of Lens	S.E.5a	Vzfw Lux, Ja 27	1/47	
7.4	1250	southwest of Merville	R.E.8 B.876	Oblt Göring, Ja 27 Fokker Dr. I	18/49	2/Lt H.W. Collier & 2/Lt E.C. Musson 42 Sqn, RAF
	1250	Merville – Hazebrouck	Sopwith F.1 Camel	Ltn Brandt, Ja 27	4/48	
		Merville – Hazebrouck	R.E.8	Ltn.d.R Stoltenhoff, Ja 27	n/c 1/53	
		Halluin (Ja 27 airfield: 15.4 – 20.5.18)				
16.4		German time one hour ahead of Allied time				
		Vivaise (Ja 27 airfield: 21.5 – 2.6.18)				
31.5	1810	west of Soissons	Spad	Oblt von Förster	n/c 1/51	
1.6		Château-Thierry	French 2-seater	Ltn.d.R Roer	1 / ?	
		Mont de Soissons Ferme (Ja 27 airfield: 3.6 – 17.7.18)				
5.6	1000	northern part of woods at Villers-Cotterêts	A.R.1	Oblt Göring, Ja 27 Fokker D.VII 278/18	19/52	no A.R.1 losses, possibly a Bréguet 14 B2
9.6	0845	northwest corner of Horseshoe Wood, south of Corey	Spad S.VII	Oblt Göring, Ja 27 Fokker D.VII 324/18	20	Cpl P. Chan (PoW) Esc Spa.94
17.6	0830	western edge of small woods west of Ambleny Heights	Spad S.XIII	Oblt Göring, Ja 27 Fokker D.VII 278/18	21	Adj Breton (PoW) Esc Spa 93
	0830	Ambleny	Spad S.XIII	Ltn.d.R Klimke, Ja 27	8	MdL Franceschi (PoW) Esc Spa 93
		Beugneux (JG I airfield: 1.7 – 18.7.18)				
18.7	0815	wooded ravine near St. Bandry	Spad S.XIII	Oblt Göring, JG I Fokker D.VII 294/18	22	

What was Hermann Göring's Final Tally?

Officially, Hermann Göring was credited with shooting or forcing down twenty-two enemy aircraft. But, as pointed out in this book, some of his victory claims were questionable. Further, accounts by his contemporaries, Bruno Loerzer and Rudolf Nebel as cited in this book, challenge the overall veracity of German fighter claims. Together, these factors add weight to the question: How many aircraft did Göring truly shoot or force down?

A case by case examination shows that, given the method of awarding credit at the times of Göring's twenty-two victories, at best he accounted for eighteen or nineteen enemy aircraft between 16 November 1915 and 18 July 1918. Based on the research used in this book, the author contends that Göring's claims can be rated as follows:

No. 1   16 November 1915: Doubtful due to the lack of a corresponding French loss.

No. 2   14 March 1916: Definitely, as proven by the 'trophies' of the encounter: the aircraft and crew.

No. 3   30 July 1916: Very likely, given the circumstances of the Escadrille C. 10 loss.

No. 4   23 April 1917: Almost certainly, given the circumstances of the 18 Squadron, RFC loss.

No. 5   28 April 1917: Very likely, given the circumstances of the 43 Squadron, RFC loss.

No. 6   29 April 1917: Almost certainly, given the circumstances of the 6 Squadron, RNAS loss.

No. 7   10 May 1917: Almost certainly, given the circumstances of the 55 Squadron, RFC loss.

No. 8   8 June 1917: Almost certainly, given the circumstances of the 1 Squadron, RFC loss.

No. 9   16 July 1917: Almost certainly, given the circumstances of the 56 Squadron, RFC loss.

No. 10   24 July 1917: Doubtful due to the lack of a corresponding British loss.

No. 11   5 August 1917: Almost certainly, given the circumstances of the 70 Squadron, RFC loss.

No. 12   25 August 1917: Most likely, given the circumstances of the 70 Squadron, RFC loss.

No. 13   3 September 1917: Possibly, given the circumstances of the 57 Squadron, RFC casualty.

No.14   21 September 1917: Almost certainly, given the circumstances of the 48 Squadron, RFC loss.

No. 15 21 October 1917: Almost certainly, given the circumstances of the 84 Squadron, RFC loss.

No. 16 7 November 1917: Highly unlikely in view of weather conditions, the brief engagement noted and lack of 32 Squadron, RFC losses.

No. 17 21 February 1918: Almost certainly, given the circumstances of the 60 Squadron, RFC loss.

No. 18 7 April 1918: Almost certainly, given the circumstances of the 42 Squadron, RFC casualty.

No. 19 5 June 1918: Possible, but, due to circumstances, very difficult to confirm or deny credit.

No. 20 9 June 1918: Almost certainly, given the circumstances of the Escadrille Spa 94 loss.

No. 21 17 June 1918: Very likely, given the circumstances of the Escadrille Spa 93 loss.

No. 22 18 July 1918: Very possible, but, due to circumstances, difficult to confirm or deny credit.

In view of the evidence currently at hand, Göring's first, tenth and sixteenth victory claims seem least likely to have been graced by success and his nineteenth was tenuous at best.

A number of German fighter pilots with higher and more credible victory scores – such as Oberleutnant Harald Auffarth (twenty-nine), Leutnant Gustav Dörr (thirty-five), Leutnant Hermann Frommherz (thirty-two) and Leutnant Georg von Hantelmann (twenty-five) – did not attain the Orden Pour le Mérite or Göring's level of command success. But perhaps they also lacked the burning and amoral ambition, helpful personal contacts and just plain luck that marked Hermann Göring's early pathway through life.

APPENDIX II
CASUALTIES IN UNITS UNDER HERMANN GÖRING'S COMMAND

Author's note: The increasing ferocity of World War I air operations as the war continued and the effects of Germany's diminishing resources can be seen in the losses of men and aircraft suffered by Jagdstaffel 27 and the four Staffeln of Jagdgeschwader I when they were commanded by Hermann Göring. The following casualty list was compiled from the Jasta 27 war diary abstract, the JG I war diary in Karl Bodenschatz's book *Jagd in Fanderns Himmel* (1935), Kommandeur der Flieger bi-monthly, weekly and other reports, resources from the former Reichsarchiv, and research material provided by the late Dr. Gustav Bock. Dates are stated in the German numerical style (day, month) and times are expressed in military time. Fates of the airmen are indicated by the abbreviations: DoW = Died of Wounds; FtL = Forced to Land; IiC = Injured in Crash; KiA = Killed in Action; KiC = Killed in Crash; PoW = Prisoner of War; WiA = Wounded in Action; blank = the pilot was uninjured and returned to duty. Some (but not all) German aircraft captured or recovered for intelligence purposes were allocated 'G' identification numbers (Ref: Franks, Bailey & Duiven, *The Jasta Pilots*, pp. 335-344); they are listed when known.

Date	Time	Pilot	Status	Location	Aircraft	Victor(s) / Details
1917						
28.7		Ltn.d.R Berkemeyer, Ja 27	FtL		Albatros D.III 2069/16	
12.8		Uffz F. Wassermann, Ja 27	KiA	near Vintje	Albatros D.V 1108/17 (G 61)	Lts F.M.Green & R.M.D.Fairweather, 7 Sqn, RFC
5.9	1945	Vzw Muth, Ja 27	KiA	Moorslede	Albatros D.V 2028/17	
29.10		Ltn.d.R Berkemeyer, Ja 27	KiA	Zandvoorde	Albatros D.V	
12.12	0825	Ltn.d.R Börner, Ja 27	KiA	Boesinghe	Albatros D.V (G 98)	Lt V. Wigg, Sopwith Camel F.2416 65 Sqn, RFC

Date	Time	Pilot	Status	Location	Aircraft	Victor(s) / Details
	0825	Uffz Kählert, Ja 27	PoW	Roulers	Albatros	Lt V. Wigg

1918

Date	Time	Pilot	Status	Location	Aircraft	Victor(s) / Details
19.1	1430	Vzw Krauss, Ja 27	KiA	Blankertsee	Albatros	
8.3	1230	Off.Stv/Vzfw Kampe, Ja 27	KiA	Gheluvelt	Albatros	19 Sqn, RFC
7.5		Off.Stv von der Weppen, Ja 27	KiA	Ypres	Albatros	
8.5		Ltn Heinz Müller, Ja 27	KiA	southeast of Ypres	Albatros	
1.6		Uffz Stein, Ja 27	KiA	near Soissons	Albatros	
17.6	0830	Oblt von Förster, Ja 27	KiA	edge of small woods west of Ambleny Heights	Fokker D.VII	collided in combat
	0830	Vzw Schäffer, Ja 27	KiA	edge of small woods west of Ambleny Heights	Fokker D.VII	collided in combat
26.6		Ltn.d.R Rothe, Ja 27	KiC	Mont de Soissons Ferme	Albatros	accident in practice flight
3.7		Ltn.d.R Roer, Ja 27	KiC	Laon	Albatros	accident in practice flight
15.7	2100	Ltn.d.R Friedrichs, Ja 10	KiC	Beugneux	Fokker D.VII 309/18	accidental fire in flight
16.7	0730	Ltn.d.R Bender, Ja 10	Inj	Beugneux	Fokker D.VII 2063/18	accidental fire in flight used parachute
		Ltn.d.R Kirschstein, Ja 6	KiC	Magneaux	Hannover Cl.II	accident
		Ltn Markgraf, Ja 6	KiC	Magneaux	Hannover Cl.II	accident
18.7	0835	Ltn Bretschneider-Bodemer, Ja 6	KiA	Grand Rozoy	Fokker D.VII	Esc Br 131
		Gefr L. Möller, Ja 10	KiA	Chaudun	Fokker D.VII	
22.7		Ltn Nöldecke, Ja 6	Inj			
24.7		Vfw Schumacher, Ja 10	WiA			
25.7	1945	Ltn Graf von Hohenau, Ja 11	WiA	Cruzny, Lagery	Fokker D.VII	Lt W.S. Stephenson, Sopwith Camel C.8296 73 Sqn, RAF
26,7		Ltn Graf von Hohenau, Ja 11	DoW	Monthussart-Ferme		sent home for burial
		Ltn.d.R von Dorrien, Ja 11	WiA	Monthussart-Ferme		shot to left foot
30.7		Ltn.d.R Drekmann, Ja 4	KiA	Grand Rozoy		Esc Spa 75
1.8		Ltn.d.R Lehmann, Ja 10	PoW	Fère-en-Tardenois	Fokker D.VII	
		Ltn Wenzel, Ja 6	WiA		Fokker D.VII	
4.8		Uffz Strecker, Ja 10	IiC			
9.8		Vzw Hemer, Ja 6	WiA			
		Ltn Reinhardt, Ja 4	WiA			
10.8		Oblt Loewenhardt, Ja 10	KiC	Chaulnes	Fokker D.VII	collided with Wentz

Date	Time	Pilot	Status	Location	Aircraft	Victor(s) / Details
10.8		Ltn.d.R Wentz, Ja 10		Chaulnes	Fokker D.VII	parachuted to safety
11.8	0755	Ltn von der Wense, Ja 6	KiA	Péronne-Herbecourt	Fokker D.VII	Capt J.K. Summers, Sopwith Camel D.9637 209 Sqn, RAF
	0810	Ltn.d.R Festler, Ja 11	KiA	La Chapellette	Fokker D.VII	Lt K.M. Walker, Sopwith Camel D.9657 209 Sqn, RAF
	1215	Ltn.d.R Wenzel, Ja 6	WiA		Fokker D.VII	
13.8	1350	Ltn L. Frhr von Richthofen, Ja 11	WiA	north of Roye	Fokker D.VII	1/Lt G.V. Seibold, Sopwith Camel D.8803 148th Aero Sqn, USAS
16.8		Vzw Lechner, Ja 6	IiC	Bernes airfield	Fokker E.V	practice flight
19.8	0950	Ltn.d.R Rolff, Ja 6	KiC	Bernes airfield	Fokker E.V	wing failure in practice flight
23.8		Ltn von Barnekow, Ja 11	WiA		Fokker D.VII	remained with Ja 11
24.8		Oblt Grosch, Ja 4	WiA	Guise	Fokker D.VII	
27.8		Ltn.d.R Wolff, Ja 6	IiC	west of Nesle	Fokker D.VII	emergency landing
5.9	1820	Ltn von Winterfeld, Ja 4	WiA/DoW	Avesnes Le Sec	Fokker D.VII (G.3rd Brigade 19)	Capt G.M. Duncan, S.E.5a D.6960 60 Sqn, RAF
8.9		Gefr Blümener, Ja 6	KiA	Beaurevoir	Fokker D.VII	parachute failed
4.10		Ltn.d.R Schibilsky, Ja 10	PoW		Fokker D.VII	
10.10		Ltn Kohlbach, Ja 10	parachuted	Clery-le-Petit	Fokker D.VII	Capt E.V. Rickenbacker, Spad S.XIII 94th Aero Sqn.
18.10		Ltn.d.R Böhren, Ja 10	PoW		Fokker D.VII	
29.10		Ltn.d.R Fischer, Ja 6	WiA/DoW	Montfaucon	Fokker D.VII	
3.11		Ltn Maushake Ja 4	WiA		Fokker D.VII	
5.11		Ltn.d.R Kirst, Ja 10	KiA	Loupoy	Fokker D.VII	

APPENDIX III
GLOSSARY

Military ranks / offices / terms

Abteilung(en)	Two-seater squadron(s)
Abteilungsführer	Two-seater squadron leader
Armee-Oberkommando	Army Group Command
Fähnrich	Army Ensign
Feldwebel	Sergeant
Gefreiter	Lance Corporal
Generalfeldmarschall	Field Marshal
General der Infanterie / Kavallerie	General of the Infantry / Cavalry
Generalleutnant	Lieutenant-General
Generalmajor	Major-General
Generaloberst	Colonel-General
Hauptmann	Captain
Jagdflieger	Fighter pilot
Jagdfliegerei	Fighter aviation
Kaiser	Emperor
Kommandierende General der Luftstreitkräfte (Kogenluft)	Commanding General of the Air Force
Kommandeur der Flieger (Kofl)	Army Corps officer in charge of aviation
Leutnant	Second Lieutenant
Leutnant der Reserve	Second Lieutenant, Reserves
Oberleutnant	First Lieutenant
Oberst	Colonel
Oberstleutnant	Lieutenant-Colonel
Offizierstellvertreter	Acting Officer
Rittmeister	Cavalry Captain
Staffelführer	Fighter squadron leader
Unteroffizier	Corporal
Vizefeldwebel	Sergeant-Major

Military units

Escadrille	French word for squadron
Feld-Fliegerabteilung	Field Aviation Section (Squadron)
Flieger-Abteilung	Aviation Section (Squadron)
Flieger-Ersatz-Abteilung (FEA)	Aviation Training and Replacement Unit
Fliegertruppe	Flying Corps
Infanterie-Regiment (Inf-Reg)	Infantry Regiment
Inspektion der Fliegertruppen (Idflieg)	Inspectorate of Military Aviation
Luftstreitkräfte	Air Force
Jagdeschwader (JG)	Fighter Wing
Jagdgruppe (JaGru)	Fighter Group
Jagdstaffel (Jasta)	Fighter Squadron
Schlachtstaffel	Attack Section
Staffeln(n)	Squadron(s)

ENDNOTES

CHAPTER ONE

1   Goldensohn, *The Nuremberg Interviews*, p. 119.

2   Falls, 'Western Front, 1915-17: Stalemate', p. 90.

3   Lamberton, *Fighter Aircraft of the 1914-1918 War*, p. 134.

4   Sommerfeldt, *Hermann Göring ein Lebensbild*, p. 22.

5   Ibid., pp. 23-24.

6   Feldflieger-Abteilung 25, *Kriegstagebuch* entries for 16 November 1915 and 14 March 1916.

7   Gritzbach, *Hermann Göring, Werk und Mensch*, p. 237.

8   Kofl 1. Armee, *Wöchentliche Meldung*, 5 November 1916, p. 6.

9   Bruce, *British Aeroplanes 1914-1918*, p. 276.

10 Ibid., p. 271.

11 Ibid., p. 369.

12 As reported in Royal Flying Corps, *War Diary*, 30 September 1916, p. 652.

13 Sergeant Cecil Percy John Bromley, twenty-three, of Dover, Kent, was killed in B.E.2d 5760 of 7 Squadron, RFC; he has no known grave [Ref: Hobson, *Airmen Died in the Great War 1914-1918*, p. 27]; 2/Lt Geoffrey Hunter Wood, also twenty-three, survived the crash and the war. Born July-September 1893 in Frettenham, Norfolk, he enlisted in the army ca. January-February 1915, was promoted corporal in the 18th Battalion, Middlesex Regiment, and landed in France 17 November 1915. He qualified as an RFC observer on 9 May 1916 and was promoted temporary 2nd lieutenant, flying officer, RFC, 16 September 1916 and posted to 7 Squadron, RFC. He was promoted lieutenant, RAF on 1 April 1918 [March 1919 RAF List] and received the Silver Wound Badge on 27 April 1918 [Ref: Medal Roll Card].

14 Royal Flying Corps, *Combat Casualty List*, 2 November 1916.

15 Bruce, op.cit., pp. 361, 363.

16 Royal Flying Corps, Communiqué No. 60, 5 November 1916, p. 2.

17 Campbell, *Royal Flying Corps Casualties and Honours During the War of 1914-1917*, p. 25.

18 *London Gazette*, 14 November 1916, 29824, p. 33.

19 Goldensohn, op. cit., p. 119.

20 Manvell & Fraenkel, *Goering*, p. 25.

21 Butler & Young, *Marshal Without Glory*, p. 20.

22 Ibid.

23 Ibid.

24 Rasselsteiner Eisenwerks-Gesellschaft AG, *Familie Remy*, p. 5A.

25 Butler & Young, op.cit.

26 Göring, I. *Sterbe-Urkunde*,1872.

27 Rasselsteiner Eisenwerks-Gesellschaft AG, op.cit.

28 Göring, I. *Sterbe-Urkunde*, 1879.

29 World War I historian and physician Dr. M. Geoffrey Miller kindly responded to the author's request for a clarification of Ida Göring's condition: 'She died of puerperal fever, due to a streptococcal infection of the birth canal leading to blood poisoning. This was a very common cause of death due to transmission of the bacterium from patient to patient because of unclean hands of the midwife or obstetrician, neither of them washed their hands between cases. By its nature, puerperal fever was more common in the lying in hospitals and was less common in home births.'

30 Butler & Young, op.cit., p. 18.

31 Frischauer, *The Rise and Fall of Hermann Goering*, p. 6.

32 Paul, *Wer war Hermann Göring!*, p. 33.

33 Ibid.

34 Frischauer, op.cit., pp. 5-6.

35 Ibid., p. 7.

36 Mosley, *The Reich Marshal: A Biography of Hermann Goering*, p. 1.

37 Ibid.

38 Rosenheim *Registereintrag Nr 154* filed on 8 August 1885.

39 According to Rosenheim Einwohnermeldeamt records.

40 Butler & Young, op.cit.

41 Frischauer, op.cit., p. 8.

42 Ibid.

43 *Rosenheim Registereintrag Nr 111* filed on 17 May 1890.

44 Rosenheim Einwohnermeldeamt, op.cit.

45 Butler & Young, op.cit.

46 Rosenheim Einwohnermeldeamt, op.cit.

47 Mosley, op.cit., p. 3.

48 Paul, op.cit.

49 Frischauer, op.cit., pp. 8-9.

50 Butler & Young, op.cit., p. 22.

51 Bross, *Gespräche mit Göring*, p. 46.

52 Butler & Young, op.cit.

53 Frischauer, op.cit., p. 9.

54 Mosley, op.cit., p. 4.

55 U.S. NARA Records Group 319, Entry 134 B, IRR Personnel, Box 64, File XE 002282.

56 Mosley, op.cit., p. 6.

57 Wylie, *The Warlord and the Renegade*, p. 7.

58 Mosley, op.cit.

59 Paul, op.cit., p. 38.

60 Wylie, op.cit.

61 Gilbert, 'Hermann Goering, Amiable Psychopath,' p. 211.

62 Ibid.

63 Paul, op.cit., p. 38.

64 Manvell & Fraenkel, op.cit., p. 23.

65 Butler & Young, op.cit., p. 21

66 Paul, op.cit.

67 Frischauer, op.cit.

68 Gilbert, op.cit.

69 Ibid.

70 Ibid., pp. 211-212.

71 Manvell & Fraenkel, op.cit., p. 23.

72 Ibid.

73 Manvell & Fraenkel, op.cit.

CHAPTER TWO

1 Gritzbach, Hermann Göring, Werk und Mensch, p.232.

2 Ibid., pp. 223-224.

3 Ibid., pp. 224-225.

4 Manvell & Fraenkel, *Goering*, p. 24.

5 Gilbert, 'Hermann Goering, Amiable Psychopath,' p. 213.

6 Gritzbach, op.cit., p. 225.

7 Paul, *Wer war Hermann Göring?*, p. 39.

8 Gilbert, op.cit

9 Manvell & Fraenkel, op.cit.

10 Gritzbach, op.cit.

11 Frischauer, *The Rise and Fall of Hermann Goering*, p. 11.

12 '... for all its flagrant expansionism and sometimes illiberal undercurrents, in 1848 German nationalism gave rise to little anti-Semitism. Many German states had given Jews full civil rights several decades before (Prussia in 1812) ... Article 13 of the basic rights in the German constitution abolished religious requirements for civic rights, which essentially enfranchised the Jews.' Ref: Rapport, *1848 – Year of Revolution*, p. 170.

13 Gritzbach, op.cit.

14 Ibid.

15 Butler & Young, *Marshal Without Glory*, p. 21, which also notes that Dr. Hermann Epenstein's Jewish heritage 'was a matter of less account in Wilhelmine Germany, where Jewish industrialists and financiers who had done much to develop the Reich stood justifiably high in the Imperial order ...'

16 Frischauer, op.cit., p. 10.

17 Quoted from a letter to Wolfgang Paul in *Wer war Hermann Göring?*, p. 33; other Göring genealogical connections mentioned by Decker-Hauff were: Gertrud Freiin [Baroness] von LeFort (1876-1971), major Catholic poet and writer; the Darmstadt and Hamburg Mercks, founders of the Merck pharmaceutical company; Hermann Grimm (1828 1901), author whose concept of the German hero as a mover of history was embraced by the Nazis; Jacob Burckhardt (1818-1897), noted Renaissance cultural historian; and Carl Jacob Burckhardt (1891 1974), Swiss diplomat, historian and president of the International Red Cross.

18 Gilbert, op.cit., p. 212.

19 Frischauer, op.cit., p. 12.

20 Butler & Young, op.cit.

21 Mosley, *The Reich Marshal: A Biography of Hermann Goering*, p. 6.

22 Gritzbach, op.cit., p. 228.

23 Mosley, op.cit.

24 Gilbert, op.cit.

25 Gritzbach, op.cit., p. 229.

26 Butler & Young, op.cit., p. 22.

27 Mosley, op.cit., p. 8.

28 Ibid., pp. 8-9.

29 Gilbert, op.cit., p. 213.

30 Butler & Young, op.cit.

31 Moncure, *Forging the King's Sword*, p. 79.

32 Manvell & Fraenkel, op.cit., p. 27.

33 Moncure, op.cit., p. 80.

34 Ibid.

35 Mosley, op.cit., p. 10.

36 Deutsche Dienststelle, Göring medical summary, sent to the author dated 7 August 2009.

37 Gilbert, op.cit., p. 214.

38 Mosley, op.cit.

39 Ibid.

40 Gritzbach, op.cit., p. 232.

41 Deutsche Dienststelle, op.cit.

42 Mosley, op.cit., p.11.

43 Moncure, op.cit., p. 196.

44 Ibid., p. 6.

45 Gritzbach, op.cit., p. 230; however, Butler & Young, op.cit., p. 23 lists the gift as 2,000 Reichsmarks, the

equivalent of £100 at the time; and Frischauer, op.cit., p. 13 agrees with the higher figure, but states that it came from Dr. Hermann Ritter von Epenstein.

46 Ibid., p. 231.

47 Göring, *Lebenslauf*, p. 1.

48 Butler & Young, op.cit., p. 37.

49 Mosley, op.cit, pp. 11-13.

50 Göring, *Personal-Bogen*, p. 1.

51 Quoted in Goldensohn, *The Nuremberg Interviews*, pp. 104-105.

52 Mosley, op.cit., p, 13.

53 Goldensohn, op.cit., p. 104.

54 Göring, *Personal-Bogen*, op.cit.

55 Deutscher Offizier-Bund, *Ehren-Rangliste des ehemaligen Deutschen Heeres*, p. 291.

56 Gritzbach, op.cit., p. 233.

57 Göring, *Lebenslauf*, op.cit., p. 2.

58 Loerzer, *Kriegsranglisten-Auszug*, 1928.

59 Zuerl, *Pour-le-Mérite-Flieger*, p. 309.

60 Moncure, op.cit., p. 15.

61 Hildebrand, *Die Generale der deutschen Luftwaffe 1935-1945*, Vol. II, p. 309.

62 Viktor Stöffler received *Deutsche Luftfahrer-Verband* [German Air Travellers' Association] License No. 174 on 28 March 1912 [Ref: Supf, *Das Buch der deutschen Fluggeschichte*, Vol. I, p. 567].

63 Hildebrand, op.cit., p. 310.

64 Schiel, Das 4. *Badische Infanterie-Regiment 'Prinz Wilhelm' Nr. 112*, p. 11.

65 Ibid., pp. 11-13.

66 Göring, *Kriegsranglisten*-Auszug, p. 3.

67 Ibid.

68 O'Connor, *Aviation Awards of Imperial Germany and the Men Who Earned Them*, Vol. II, p. 11.

69 Ibid.

70 Schiel, op.cit., p. 24.

CHAPTER THREE

1 Private source.

2 Grosz, *Aviatik C.I Windsock Datafile 63*, pp. 1, 6.

3 Sommerfeldt, *Hermann Göring – Ein Lebensbild*, p. 16.

4 Loerzer, *Lebenslauf*, p. 3.

5 Supf, *Das Buch der deutschen Fluggeschichte*, Vol. II, pp. 105-106.

6 Gritzbach, *Hermann Göring, Werk und Mensch*, p. 235.

7 Gilbert, 'Hermann Goering, Amiable Psychopath,' p. 215.

8 Loerzer, op.cit.

9 Frischauer, *The Rise and Fall of Hermann Goering*, p. 17; Göring, *Kriegsranglisten-Auszug*, p. 3.

10 Schiel, Das 4. *Badische Infanterie-Regiment 'Prinz Wilhelm' Nr. 112*, p. 26.

11 Mosley, op.cit., pp. 16-17.

12 Göring, op.cit., pp. 2-3.

13 Gritzbach, op.cit., p. 236.

14 Göring, op.cit., p. 3.

15 Loerzer, *Kriegsranglisten-Auszug*, p. 3.

16 Sommerfeldt, op.cit., p. 17.

17 Hildebrand, *Die Generale der deutschen Luftwaffe 1935-1945*, Vol. III, pp. 567-568.

18 Kriegsministerium, *Teil 10 Abschnitt B, Flieger Formationen*, p. 132.

19 Cron, 'Organization of the German Luftstreitkräfte,' p. 55.

20 Hoeppner, *Deutschlands Krieg in der Luft*, p. 7; Loewenstern & Bertkau, *Mobilmachung, Aufmarsch und erster Einsatz der deutschen Luftstreitkräfte im August 1914*, p. 1 adds that wartime personnel strength of each unit was fifteen commissioned officers and 117 non-commissioned officers and lower ranking enlisted men.

21 Loewenstern & Bertkau, ibid., p. 2.

22 Ibid.

23 Blum, *Kriegsranglisten-Auszug*, p. 3.

24 Sommerfeldt, op.cit., p. 18.

25 Loerzer, *Lebenslauf*, op.cit., pp. 3-4.

26 Lamberton, *Reconnaissance and Bomber Aircraft of the 1914-1918 War*, p. 220.

27 Reichsarchiv, *Kriegstagebuch der königlich preussischen Feldflieger-Abteilung 25*, 5 November 1914.

28 Loerzer, *Kriegsranglisten-Auszug*, op.cit.

29 Neubecker, *Für Tapferkeit und Verdienst*, p. 28.

30 Göring, op.cit.

31 Blum, op.cit., he received the badge on 1 April 1915.

32 Neubecker, op.cit.

33 Reichsarchiv, op.cit., 17 November 1914.

34 Loerzer, *Lebenslauf*, op.cit., pp. 4-6.

35 Reichsarchiv, op.cit., 18 January 1915.

36 Bailey & Cony, *The French Air War Chronology*, p. 9.

37 Schmidt, *Personal-Bogen*, p. 4.

38 Ibid., 23 January-17 February 1914.

39 Private source.

40 Grosz, *Albatros B.I Windsock Datafile 87*, pp. 22, 33.

41 Sommerfeldt, op.cit., pp. 18-19.

42 Göring, op.cit.

43 Loerzer, *Kriegsranglisten-Auszug*, op.cit.

44 Wilhelm, *Meine Erinnerungen aus Deutschlands Heldenkampf*, p. 24.

45 Ibid., p. 190.

46 Reichsarchiv, op.cit., 19-20 March 1915.

47 Reichsarchiv, op.cit., 15 April 1915.

48 Ibid, 22 April 1915.

49 Loerzer, *Kriegsranglisten-Auszug*, op.cit., p. 3.

50 Neubecker, op.cit., p. 12.

51 O'Connor, *Aviation Awards of Imperial Germany and the Men Who Earned Them*, Vol. I, p. 7.

52 Neumann, *Die deutschen Luftstreitkräfte im Weltkriege*, p. 187.

53 Ibid., p. 194.

54 Reichsarchiv, op.cit., 22 April-26 May 1915.

55 Feldflieger-Abteilung 25, *Tätigkeits-Bericht*, 2 June 1916.

56 Keck, *Personal-Bogen*, p. 2.

57 Ibid., p. 3; Keck later transferred to Flieger-Abteilung (A) 210 and was killed in action over Beaumont, north of Douaumont, on 26 August 1917. Ref: Deutscher Offizier-Bund, *Ehren-Rangliste des ehemaligen Deutschen Heeres*, p. 975.

58 Ltn.Dr Kurt Wegener received Deutsche Luftfahrer Verband License No. 796 on 22 June 1914. Ref: Supf, *Das Buch der deutschen Fluggeschichte*, Vol. II, p. 667.

59 Reichsarchiv, op.cit., 30 May 1915.

60 Ibid., 3 June 1915.

61 Loerzer, *Lebenslauf*, op.cit., pp. 6-8.

CHAPTER FOUR

1 Mosley, *The Reich Marshal*, p. 18.

2 Sommerfeldt, *Hermann Göring – Ein Lebensbild*, p. 22.

3 Reichsarchiv, *Kriegstagebuch der königlich preussischen Feldflieger-Abteilung 25*, 4 June 1915.

4 Ibid., 10 June 1915.

5 Hoeppner, *Deutschlands Krieg in der Luft*, p. 39.

6 Grosz, *Fokker E.I/II Windsock Datafile 91*, pp. 3-5.

7 Göring, *Lebenslauf*, p. 3

8 Loerzer, *Kriegsranglisten-Auszug*, p. 3.

9 Reichsarchiv, op.cit., 8 July 1915.

10 O'Connor. *Aviation Awards of Imperial Germany and the Men Who Earned Them*, Vol. VI, p. 115.

11 Ibid.

12 Loerzer, op.cit.

13 Ibid.

14 Zuerl, *Pour-le-Mérite-Flieger*, pp. 305-306.

15 Leonhardy, *Mit der deutschen Luftfahrt durch dick und dünn*, pp. 47-48.

16 Feldflieger-Abteilung 25, *Tätigkeits-Bericht*, 2 June 1916.

17 Their likely opponents were Sergent Claude Couturier (pilot) and Lieutenant Louis Moisan (observer) of Escadrille MF 2, both of whom were killed in the fight. Ref: Bailey, & Cony, *The French Air War Chronology*, p. 23.

18 Göring, photo album caption.

19 Liddell Hart, *The Real War 1914-1918*, p. 188.

20 Kriegsministerium, *Teil 10 Abschnitt B, Flieger Formationen*, p. 192.

21 Stabsoffizier der Flieger der 3. Armee, *Bericht Nr Ia 5821*, 28 September 1915.

22 Göring, op.cit.

23 Zuerl, op.cit., p. 310.

24 Mosley, op.cit.

25 Gilbert, 'Hermann Goering, Amiable Psychopath', p. 213.

26 Reichsarchiv, op.cit., 17 September 1915.

27 Ibid., 23 September 1915.

28 Kriegsministerium, op.cit., pp. 158-159; established on 6 August 1915, the units were Flieger-Abteilung (A) 201, 202, 203, 204, 205 and 206.

29 Wilberg received the civilian Deutsche Luftfahrer Verband [German Air Travelers Association] License

No. 26 on 15 September 1910. Ref: Supf, *Das Buch der deutschen Fluggeschichte*, Vol. I, p. 562.

30 Loewenstern & Bertkau, *Mobilmachung, Aufmarsch und erster Einsatz der deutschen Luftstreitkräfte im August 1914*, p. 119.

31 Hildebrand, *Die Generale der deutschen Luftwaffe 1935-1945*, Vol. III, pp. 514.

32 Anonymous, 'Ein braunschweiger Ritter des Ordens Pour le Mérite – Oberleutnant Hans Berr,' pp. 482-484.

33 Leonhardy, op.cit., pp. 48-49.

34 Ibid., p. 47.

35 Göring, *Kriegsranglisten-Auszug*, p. 3.

36 Göring, *Lebenslauf*, op.cit.

37 Reichsarchiv, op.cit., 2 October-5 December 1915.

38 Loerzer, op.cit.

39 Zuerl, op.cit., p. 548.

40 Siegert, 'Heeresflugwesen Entwicklung' in *Die deutschen Luftstreitkräfte im Weltkriege*, p. 64.

41 Reichsarchiv, op.cit., 3 October 1915.

42 Ibid.

43 Feldflieger-Abteilung 25, op.cit.

44 Bailey, & Cony, op.cit., p. 26.

45 Reichsarchiv, op.cit., 4 October 1915.

46 Feldflieger-Abteilung 25, op.cit.

47 Bailey, & Cony, *The French Air War Chronology*, 11 October 1915.

48 Feldflieger-Abteilung 25, op.cit.

49 Ibid. and confirmed in Stabsoffizier der Flieger der 5. Armee, *Bericht Nr 22787*, 14 August 1916, p. 1.

50 Bailey, & Cony, op.cit., p. 27.

51 Göring, *Kriegsranglisten-Auszug*, p. 3.

52 Leonhardy, op.cit., p. 56.

53 Rittmeister Ziegler hailed from the mounted rifle unit Jäger-Regiment zu Pferde Nr. 12 and concluded his service with Bombengeschwader 4, with which he was killed in action on 20 April 1918 [Ref: Deutscher Offizier-Bund, *Ehren-Rangliste des ehemaligen Deutschen Heeres*, p. 464].

54 Reichsarchiv, op.cit., 22 October-6 November 1915.

55 Falls, 'Western Front, 1915-17: Stalemate,' p. 86.

56 Ibid., 16 November 1915.

57 Feldflieger-Abteilung 25, op.cit. and confirmed in Stabsoffizier der Flieger der 5. Armee, op.cit.

58 Stabsoffizier der Flieger der 5. Armee, Ibid.

59 Bailey, & Cony, op.cit., p. 29.

60 Despite speculation to the contrary, this officer was not the pilot who became the twenty-seven-victory fighter ace and Pour le Mérite recipient Oberleutnant Fritz Otto Bernert, who was still serving in the infantry when the 16 November 1915 event occurred. Ref: Zuerl, op.cit., p. 50.

61 Stofl 5. Armee, op.cit., *Bericht Nr Ia 6524*, 3 November 1915.

62 Falls, op.cit.

63 Leonhardy, op.cit., pp. 51-52.

CHAPTER FIVE

1   Quoted in Liddell Hart, *The Real War 1914-1918*, p. 200.

2   Ibid., p. 201.

3   Falls, 'Western Front, 1915-17: Stalemate' in *A Concise History of World War I*, p. 86.

4   No relation or connection to the major U.S. Corporation by that name.

5   Grosz, *AEG G.IV Windsock Datafile 51*, p. 1.

6   Reichsarchiv, *Kriegstagebuch der königlich preussischen Feldflieger-Abteilung 25*, 29-31 January 1916.

7   Leonhardy, *Mit der deutschen Luftfahrt durch dick und dünn*, pp. 54-55.

8   Liddell Hart, op.cit., pp. 201, 218.

9   Leonhardy, op.cit., p. 54.

10 Reichsarchiv, op.cit., 21 February 1916.

11 Liddell Hart, op.cit.

12 Reichsarchiv, op.cit., 22 February 1916.

13 Ibid., 26 February 1916.

14 Ibid., 28 February-13 March 1916.

15 Bailey, & Cony, *The French Air War Chronology*, p. 40.

16 Feldflieger-Abteilung 25, *Kampf-Bericht*, 14 March 1916 and confirmed in Stabsoffizier der Flieger der 5. Armee, *Bericht Nr 22787*, 14 August 1916, p. 1.

17 Stabsoffizier der Flieger der 5. Armee, op.cit.

18 Wills, 'Feldfliegerabteilung 25 – The Eyes of the Kronprinz' in *Cross & Cockade Journal*, p. 22.

19 Ibid., p. 23.

20 Davilla, & Soltan, *French Aircraft of the First World War*, p. 156.

21 Wills, op.cit.

22 Kulenkampff-Post, *Reiter unterm Himmel*, p. 121.

23 Ibid., p. 106.

24 Ibid., pp. 115-116.

25 Ibid., p. 117.

26 Reichsarchiv, op.cit., 4 April 1916.

27 Wills, op.cit., p. 24.

28 Kulenkampff-Post, op.cit., p. 120.

29 Lamberton, *Reconnaissance and Bomber Aircraft of the 1914-1918 War*, p. 220.

30 Reichsarchiv, op.cit., 7 April 1916.

31 Ibid., 17 April 1916.

32 Radloff, & Niemann, 'The Ehrenbechers – Where are They Now?' p. 366.

33 Werner, *Boelcke – der mensch, der Flieger, der Führer der deutschen Jagdfliegerei*, pp. 136-137.

34 Ibid., p. 136.

35 Kriegsministerium, *Teil 10 Abschnitt B, Flieger Formationen*, p. 158.

36 Stabsoffizier der Flieger der 5. Armee, op.cit., p. 3.

37 Ibid.

38 Loerzer, *Kriegsranglisten-Auszug*, p. 3.

39 Göring, *Kriegsranglisten-Auszug*, p. 3.

40 Stabsoffizier der Flieger der 5. Armee, op.cit.

41 Loerzer, op.cit.

42 Leonhardy, op.cit., p. 52.

43 Ibid.

44 Reichsarchiv, op.cit., 21 April 1916.

45 Leonhardy, op.cit., p. 53.

46 Reichsarchiv, op.cit., 30 April 1916.

47 Richthofen, M. *Ein Heldenleben*, p. 60.

48 Kulenkampff-Post, op.cit., pp. 123-124.

49 Ibid., p. 124.

50 Zuerl, *Pour le Mérite-Flieger*, p. 306.

51 Hildebrand, *Die Generale der deutschen Luftwaffe 1935-1945*, Vol. I, pp. 159-160.

52 Kulenkampff-Post, p. 125.

53 Ibid., p. 126.

54 Ibid., p. 128.

55 Reichsarchiv, op.cit., 2 May 1916.

56 Grosz, *Albatros C.III Windsock Datafile 13*, p. 2.

57 Reichsarchiv, op.cit., 17 June 1916.

58 Loerzer, op.cit.

59 Hildebrand, *Die Generale der deutschen Luftwaffe 1935 1945*, Vol. II, p. 309.

60 Kulenkampff-Post, op.cit., p. 133.

61 Leonhardy, op.cit., pp. 55-56.

62 Reichsarchiv, op.cit., 16 May-23 June 1916.

63 Ibid., 9 July 1916.

CHAPTER SIX

1   Kulenkampff-Post, *Reiter unterm Himmel*, p. 146.

2   Falls, 'Western Front, 1915-17: Stalemate' in *A Concise History of World War I*, p. 86.

3   Liddell Hart, *The Real War 1914-1918*, p. 223.

4   Oberleutnant Ernst Freiherr von Gersdorff received Deutsche Luftfahrer-Verband License No. 356 on 24 January 1913. Ref: Supf, *Das Buch der deutschen Fluggeschichte*, Vol. II, p. 663.

5   Perthes, J. *Ehrentafel der Kriegsopfer des reichsdeutschen Adels 1914-1918*, p. 75.

6   Kulenkampff-Post, op.cit., p. 137.

7   Ibid., p. 138.

8   Reichsarchiv, *Kriegstagebuch der königlich preussischen Feldflieger-Abteilung 25*, 1 July 1916.

9   Ibid., 9 July 1916.

10 Loerzer, *Militärärztliches-Zeugnis*, p. 1.

11 Lamberton, W. *Fighter Aircraft of the 1914-1918 War*, p. 134.

12 FAA 203, *Kampf-Bericht Nr. 605* by Leutnant Göring, 15 July 1916.

13 Lamberton, op.cit., pp. 218, 216.

14 FAA 203, *Kriegstagebuch* [War Diary] entry, 16 July 1916.

15 Bailey & Cony, *The French Air War Chronology*, p. 59.

16 Lamberton, op.cit., p. 92.

17 Kulenkampff-Post, op,cit., pp. 141-142.

18 FAA 203, *Kriegstagebuch*, op.cit. 22 July 1916.

19 Reichsarchiv, op.cit., 23 July 1916.

20 Feldflieger-Abteilung 71 Metz, *Tätigkleits-Bericht Nr. 334/16*, 30 September 1916.

21 Kriegsministerium, Teil 10 Abschnitt B, *Flieger Formationen*, p. 138.

22 Loewenstern & Bertkau, *Mobilmachung, Aufmarsch und erster Einsatz der deutschen Luftstreitkräfte im August 1914*, pp. 5-6.

23 Kulenkampff-Post, op,cit., p. 143.

24 FAA 203, Combat Report No. 616 by Leutnant Göring, 24 July 1916.

25 Feldflugchef Bericht Nr. 22305 to Stofl 5, 9 August 1916.

26 Metz Gouvernment, *Befehl, Ausgabe B*, 31 July 1916.

27 Bailey & Cony, op.cit. p. 62.

28 FAA 203, *Kriegstagebuch*, op.cit., addendum, 2 August 1916.

29 Feldflieger-Abteilung 71 Metz, op.cit.

30 Göring, *Kriegsranglisten-Auszug*, p. 3.

31 Reichsarchiv, op.cit., 5 August 1916.

32 Ibid., 6-8 August 1916.

33 Kulenkampff-Post, op.cit., p. 146.

34 Reichsarchiv, op.cit., 9 August 1916.

35 Ibid., 12 August 1916.

36 Falls, op.cit., p. 88.

37 Reichsarchiv, op.cit., 14 August 1916.

38 Kriegsministerium, op.cit., p. 234.

39 Kulenkampff-Post, op.cit., p. 150.

40 Feldflieger-Abteilung 71 Metz, op.cit.

41 Supf, *Das Buch der deutschen Fluggeschichte*, Vol. I, pp. 435, 498.

42 Franks, Bailey & Guest, Above the Lines, p. 143.

43 Feldflieger-Abteilung 71 Metz, op.cit.

44 Ibid.

45 Göring, op.cit.

46 Franks, Bailey & Duiven, *The Jasta Pilots*, pp. 20-21.

47 Neumann, *Die Deutschen Luftstreitkräfte im Weltkriege*, p. 5; Zuerl, Pour-le-Mérite-Flieger, p. 227 lists him as having commanded the 75th Reserve Division; Deutscher Offizier-Bund, *Ehren-Rangliste des ehemaligen Deutschen Heeres*, p. 37 lists him as holding a command in the 4th Kavallerie-Brigade.

48 Hoeppner, *Deutschlands Krieg in der Luft*, p. 82.

49 Kriegsministerium, op.cit., pp. 234-239.

50 Merrill, G. *Jagdstaffel 5 – Volume One*, p. 6.

51 Ibid.

52 Franks, Bailey & Guest, op.cit., p. 71.

53 Reichsarchiv, *Kriegstagebuch der königlich preussischen Jagdstaffel 5*, 21 October 1916.

54 Ibid., 22 October 1916.

55 Franks, Bailey & Guest, op.cit.

56 Ibid., p. 169.

57 Jones, *The War in the Air*, Vol. II, p. 309.

58 Reichsarchiv, *KTB Jasta 5*, op.cit., 23 October 1916.

59 Jones, op.cit., pp. 310-311.

60 Kommandeur der Flieger der 1. Armee, *Wochenbericht*, 28 October 1916.

61 Zuerl, op.cit., p. 59.

62 Royal Flying Corps, *War Diary*, 2 November 1916, p. 762.

63 Sommerfeldt, *Hermann Göring ein Lebensbild*, p. 23.

64 RFC, *War Diary*, op.cit.

65 Deutsche Dienststelle, Göring medical summary, sent to the author dated 7 August 2009.

66 Göring, op.cit.

67 Gritzbach, *Hermann Göring Werk und Mensch*, p. 238.

68 Göring, op.cit.

69 Loerzer, *Lebenslauf*, p. 9.

70 Franks, Bailey & Guest, op.cit., p. 143.

71 Ref: Deutscher Offizier-Bund, *Ehren-Rangliste des ehemaligen Deutschen Heeres*, p. 601.

72 Theilhaber, *Jüdische Flieger im Weltkrieg*, p. 66.

73 Zuerl, *Pour-le-Mérite-Flieger*, p. 310.

CHAPTER SEVEN

1   Quoted in Mosley, *The Reich Marshal: A Biography of Hermann Goering*, p. 31.

2   Göring, *Kriegsranglisten-Auszug*, p. 2.

3   Mosley, op.cit., p. 24

4   Ibid.

5   Ibid., p. 25.

6   Ibid., pp. 25-26.

7   Ibid., p. 25

8   Butler & Young, *Marshal Without Glory*, p. 33.

9   Mosley, op.cit., p. 25

10 Quoted in ibid., p. 26.

11 Kriegsministerium, *Teil 10 Abschnitt B, Flieger Formationen*, pp. 238-239.

12 Göring, op.cit., p. 3.

13 Quoted in Mosley, op.cit., p. 31.

14 Grosz, *Albatros D.III – A Windsock Datafile Special*, p. 1.

15 Franks, Bailey & Guest, *Above the Lines*, p. 156.

16 Ibid., p. 157.

17 Kogenluft, *Nachrichtenblatt der Luftstreitkräfte*, Nr. 7, 12 April 1917, p. 11.

18 Jasta 26, *Flieger-Bericht* by Leutnant Göring, 16 March 1917.

19 Grosz, op.cit., pp. 4-5.

20 Jasta 26, *Flieger-Bericht* Nr. 93 by Leutnant Göring, 18 March 1917.

21 Jagdstaffel 26, *Kriegstagebuch I*, 11 April 1917.

22 Morris, *Bloody April*, p. 15.

23 Kilduff, *Red Baron – The Life and Death of an Ace*, pp. 242-245.

24 Jones, *The War in the Air*, Vol III, p. 323.

25 Royal Flying Corps, *War Diary*, daily weather reports, April 1917, pp. 110-197.

26 Jones, op.cit., p. 359.

27 Royal Flying Corps, *War Diary*, 23 April 1917, pp. 164-169.

28 Jasta 26, KTB I, 23 April 1917.

29 Kogenluft, *Nachrichtenblatt*, Nr. 12, 17 May 1917, p. 11.

30 Jasta 26, *Flieger-Bericht* Nr. 132 by Leutnant Göring, 23 April 1917.

31 Royal Flying Corps, *Combat Casualty List*, 23 April 1917.

32 12/Lt Edmund Leonard Zink, born 21 February 1899 in London, enlisted under-age, giving his year of birth as 1897, commissioned T/2Lt. In 10 (Res.) Bn., Suffolk Regt., 7 October 1915; transferred to RFC on 12 April 1916 and posted to 12 Reserve Squadron, RFC; assigned to 64 Reserve Squadron. RFC on 20 August 1916; received Royal Aero Club flying certificate on 27 September 1916; assigned to British Expeditionary Force on 13 November 1916, then to 18 Squadron. RFC on 14 November 1916; wounded in action / gunshot wound on 23 April 1917; assigned to light duties on 5 June 1917; Instructor, 18 Squadron. RFC, No. 2 Auxiliary School of Gunnery, BEF on 26 June 1917; declared fit for general service, 29 June 1917; No. 35 Training School, BEF, 3 December 1917; No.1 School of Aerial Fighting, Turnberry, 15 January 1918; promoted 1/Lt. 1 April 1918; to BEF, 18 August 1918 and promoted T/Capt; appointed A Flight Commander, 32 Squadron, 12 August 1918 [Ref: National Archives file WO 76/567].

33 George Beaumont Bate, twenty-two, of Bersham, near Wrexham, Denbighshire, died as a result of wounds received in F.E.2b A.823 of 18 Squadron, RFC; he was educated at Downside School, Somerset, 1909-1911; accepted as Private 6754 in 19 Bn. (Public Schools) Royal Fusiliers, April 1915; to BEF 14 November 1915; commissioned T2/Lt., 9 Bn. Loyal North Lancs., 25 September 1916; to No.1 School of Aeronautics 12 March 1917; appointed Observer 13 March 1917; to School of Aerial Gunnery, Hythe, 20 March 1917; to BEF as aviation observer 5 April 1917; died of wounds 29 April 1917 [Ref: National Archives file WO 76/567, BMD, Army List; Air Force List; CWGC].

34 Hobson, *Airmen Died in the Great War 1914-1918*, p. 22.

35 Graham, *Downside and the War 1914-1919*, p. 173.

36 Royal Flying Corps, *War Diary*, op.cit.

37 Jasta 26, KTB I, op.cit.

38 Jones, op.cit., p. 366.

39 Jasta 26, Flieger-Bericht Nr. 149 by Leutnant Göring, 28 April 1917.

40 Kogenluft, op.cit., p. 12.

41 Clifford Mansel Reece, born 17 November 1894, educated at Rossall School, Fylde, Lancs. to 1913; Magdalene College, 1913; commissioned Lt., 1/4 Bn. Cheshire Regiment, 10 October 1914; posted to Oxford, 25 September 1916; 8 Reserve Squadron, RFC on 8 November 1916; to 55 Squadron, 11 December 1916; WIA 13 January 1917; School of Aerial Gunnery, Hythe 13.2.17; flight officer, 43 Reserve Squadron, 9 March 1917; 28 Reserve Squadron, 25 March 1917; to 43 Squadron. RFC, 31 March 1917; reported missing in action 28 April 1917; reported unwounded and prisoner of war at Gustren, Schweidnitz (Silesia), 28 April 1917; promoted Lt., 1 July 1917; repatriated 14 January 1919 Ref: BMD; Rossall School Register; *London Gazette*; War List of the University of Cambridge 1914-1919; TNA WO 76/567; Army List; Air Force List].

42 William E. Moult, born in 1888 in Nottinghamshire; enlisted as Private, No. 12375, 9 Bn. Notts. & Derbyshire Regt., 12 August 1914; posted to Gallipoli, 1 July 1915; wounded in action / gunshot wound / arm in Gallipoli, 9 August 1915; hospitalized in Malta; admitted No.6 General Hospital at Rouen, 12 October 1916; discharged to No.2 Convalescent Depot, Rouen, 15 October 1916; discharged to base depot, Calais, 6 November 1916; posted to France, 19 March 1917; enlisted RFC, 19 March 1917; 2/AM No. 77562, 19 March 1917; aerial gunner; reported missing in action 28 April 1917; repatriated from Germany, arrived POW Reception Camp, Ripon, 17 December 1918 [Ref: National Archives file AIR 79/704; Medal Roll].

43 Jasta 26, *Flieger-Bericht* Nr. 155 by Leutnant Göring, 29 April 1917.

44 Albert Henry ('Harry') Victor Fletcher, born 24 May 1893 in Durban, South Africa; entered Royal Naval Air Service on 11 February 1916 and commissioned temporary flight sub-lieutenant (probationary); assigned for flight instruction at Chingford, 18 February 1916; as flight sub-Lt. RN received Aviator's Certificate 2853 on a Grahame-White biplane at RNAS Chingford, 11 May 1916; assigned as aeroplane pilot at Cranwell, 16 June 1916; Eastchurch Gunnery School, 18 June 1916; Dover, 3 July 1916; Eastchurch Observer School cancelled due to sickness; classified as fit for active service, 1 September 1916; Dover 9 March 1917; posted to 6 Squadron. RNAS, Dunkirk, reported to be 'an efficient and reliable officer, has flown at night', [ten hours flight time] 1 April 1917; Dunkirk 'capable and zealous officer', [hours flown: 22 hours 20 minutes], 1 July 1917; declared missing after offensive patrol (in Clerget-powered Nieuport, N.3192): wounded/POW in Germany, 9 July 1917; promoted flight-lieutenant, 31 December 1917; WO Report: Arrived at Hague for repatriation to England, 14 January 1918; arrived London, 20 January 1918; left leg amputated at Queen Alexandra's Military Hospital, 21 January 1918 [Ref: National Archives ADM 273/8, p.177].

45 Robertson, B. *British Military Aircraft Serials 1911 1971*, pp. 27-72.

46 Kogenluft, op.cit.

47 Göring, 'Aus dem Tagebuch eines Jagdfliegers,' pp. 209-211.

48 RFC, *War Diary*, 10 May 1917, p. 235.

49 Franks, Bailey & Duiven, *Casualties of the German Air Service 1914-1920*, p. 211.

50 Hobson, op.cit., pp. 83, 57.

51 RFC, *Combat Casualty List*, 10 May 1917.

52 Hobson, op.cit., pp. 57, 58.

53 RFC, *Combat Casualty List*, op.cit.

54 Ibid., pp. 105, 25.

55 RFC, Combat Casualty List, op.cit.

56 Kogenluft, op.cit., p. 13.

57 Kogenluft, *Nachrichtenblatt*, Nr. 16, 14 June 1917, p. 28.

58 Zuerl, *Pour-le-Mérite-Flieger*, pp. 71-75.

59 Kriegsministerium, op.cit.

60 Tornuss, *Jagdstaffel 27 Kriegstagebuch* abstract, p. 1.

61 Kommandeur der Flieger der 4. Armee, *Wöchentliche Meldung B-Nr 12690/19*, 18 February 1917, p. 1.

62 Ibid., p. 7.

63 Wieland, *Personal-Bogen*, pp. 2-4

64 Jasta 27 last reported in the 4th Army Sector in Kofl 4, *Meldung B-Nr 14790/197*, 25 March 1917, p. 1.

65 Kommandeur der Flieger der 6. Armee, *Wöchentliche Tätigkeitsbericht Nr 25000*, 30 March 1917, p. 1a.

66 Ibid., *Verzeichnis Nr. 25940*, 14 April 1917, pp. 1-2.

67 Ibid., Schutzstaffeln 17, 19 and 27.

68 Ibid., Flieger-Abteilung 48b and Artillerie-Flieger Abteilungen 211, 224 and 235.

69 Lamberton, *Fighter Aircraft of the 1914-1918 War*, p. 112.

70 Helmuth Dilthey was born on 9 February 1894 in the Rhineland city of Rheydt. In November 1914, aged twenty, he enlisted in the Fliegertruppe and began training at the school run by the Rumpler Luftfahrzeugbau Johannisthal, near Berlin. Upon completion of his pilot's qualifications, Dilthey was transferred to the German 10th Army's Air Park on the Eastern Front. Assigned to Flieger-Abteilung 50, he flew many bombing missions against Russian troops. In view of his aggressive nature, Leutnant der Reserve Dilthey was transferred to Jagdstaffelschule I in Valenciennes in March 1917. He was assigned to Jasta 27 a month later. After attaining his sixth confirmed victory, on 5 February 1918, Dilthey was appointed to lead Jasta 40. He was killed in combat on 9 July 1918. [Ref: von Langsdorff, *Flieger am Feind* pp. 214, 340].

71 Dilthey, 'In der Staffel Göring,' p. 214.

CHAPTER EIGHT

1 Göring, 'Aus dem Tagebuch eines Jagdfliegers,' p. 214.

2 Liddell Hart, *The Real War 1914-1918*, p. 329.

3 Jones, *The War in the Air*, Vol. IV, p. 112.

4 Liddell Hart, op.cit., p. 331.

5 Göring, 'Luftkämpfe,' pp. 287-288.

6 Hildebrand, *Die Generale der deutschen Luftwaffe*, vol. I, p. 370.

7 Gritzbach, *Hermann Göring, Werk und Mensch*, 1937.

8 According to Royal Flying Corps, *War Diary*, 2 June 1917, p. 307.

9 Jagdstaffel 27, *Kriegstagebuch III*, op.cit., 2 June 1917.

10 Ibid. and Kofl 6. Armee, *Wöchentlichler Tätigkeits Bericht Nr. 469 I*, 8 June 1917, p. 1.

11 Tornuss, *Jagdstaffel 27 Kriegstagebuch* abstract, p. 2; Kofl 6. Armee, op.cit., p. 6; and Kogenluft, *Nachrichtenblatt der Luftstreitkräfte*, Nr. 20, 12 July 1917, p. 80.

12 Jasta 27, KTB III, op.cit., 5 June 1917.

13 Jasta 27, *Flieger-Bericht* by Leutnant Göring, 5 June 1917.

14 Kogenluft, op.cit.

15 Ibid., and Jasta 27, *Flieger-Bericht* by Leutnant Göring, 8 June 1917.

16 Jasta 27, *Flieger-Bericht* by Leutnant Göring, 9 June 1917.

17 Ibid., 16 June 1917.

18 Kommandeur der Flieger der 4. Armee, *Meldung B-Nr 22090*, 22 June 1917, p. 1.

19 Jasta 27, *KTB III*, op.cit., 24 June 1917.

20 RFC, *War Diary*, op.cit., p. 375.

21 Frank Dilloway Slee, born 20 August 1893 in Fremantle, Western Australia, educated at Perth High School; enlisted in the Australian Imperial Force (AIF), 30 June 1915; accepted as private No.3077, 16th Inf. Bn., Depot, 7-15 1915; promoted Sergeant, 16th Inf. Bn., 10 August 1915; sent overseas 13 October 1915; reported sick, sent to Abbassia Hospital in Cairo, Egyptian Expeditionary Force, 9 November 1915; 16 Inf. Bn., Tel el Kebir, 1 December 1915; 48th Inf. Bn., reverted to private, 8 March 1916; promoted sergeant 9 March 1916; CSM (WO Class 2), 20 March 1916; HMT *Caledonia*, departed Alexandria, 2 August 1916, arrived Marseilles, 9 August 1916; discharged AIF to No. 3 School of Instruction, RFC, Oxford (Exeter College), 10 November 1916; commissioned T/2Lt, RFC,16 March 1917; 8 Reserve Squadron, RFC at Netheravon, 20 March 1917; 55 Reserve Squadron, RFC at Yatesbury (Wilts.), 17 May 1917; posted to 1 Squadron. RFC at Bailleul, 2 June 1917; MIA/POW, 8 June 1917; POW at Freiburg, Karlsruhe; repatriated to UK, 5 December 1918 [Ref: Australian National Archives: http://naa12.naa.gov.au/scripts/ Imagine.asp, *London Gazette*, TNA WO 76/567, Army List, Air Force List].

22 Kofl 4, *Meldung B-Nr 20652/17*, 9 June 1917, p. 6.

23 Göring, 'Aus dem Tagebuch', op.cit. pp. 212-214.

24 RFC, *1 Squadron Record Book*, 8 June 1918.

25 Franks, Bailey, & Duiven, *Casualties of the German Air Service 1914-1920*, p. 215.

26 Slee, 'The Day Goering Nearly Copped It.' p. 2.

27 Ibid.

28 Jasta 27, *KTB III*, op.cit., 8 June 1917.

29 Göring, photo album caption.

30 Bronnenkant, *The Imperial Eagles in World War I – Their Postcards and Pictures*, p. 301.

CHAPTER NINE

1 Göring, "Luftkämpfe," pp. 291.

2 Liddell Hart, *The Real War 1914-1918*, p, 339.

3 Jagdstaffel 27, *Kriegstagebuch III*, 16 July 1917.

4 Kogenluft, *Nachrichtenblatt der Luftstreitkräfte*, Nr. 25, 16 August 1917, p. 157.

5 Jasta 27, *Flieger-Bericht* by Leutnant Göring, 16 August 1917.

6 Robert Gordon Jardine, born in Toronto, Ontario, Canada on 20 July 1888; educated at Ridley College, Ontario [Ref: CWGC Arras Memorial; *Flight* magazine; ADM 340/314].

7 Dilthey, 'In der Staffel Göring,' pp. 211-212.

8 Lamberton, *Fighter Aircraft of the 1914-1918 War*, p. 74.

9 Collishaw, *Air Command – A Fighter Pilot's Story*, p. 125.

10 Royal Flying Corps, *Combat Casualty List*, 24 July 1917.

11 Kogenluft, op.cit.

12 Zuerl, *Pour-le-Mérite-Flieger*, p. 547.

13 Ascheberg was one of the first nine air observers, trained by Wilhelm Grade, brother of German aviation pioneer Hans Grade [Ref: Supf, *Das Buch der deutschen Fluggeschichte*, Vol. 1, p. 504]; later Ascheberg received Deutsche Luftfahrer-Verband License No. 383 on 22 April 1913 [Ref: Supf, *Das Buch der deutschen Fluggeschichte*, Vol. 2, p. 663].

14 On 19 April 1917 [Ref: Kriegsministerium, *Teil 10 Abschnitt B, Flieger-Formationen*, p. 122].

15 Gruppenführer der Flieger 15, *Ordens-Vorschlag 124/9*, 28 July 1917.

16 Hauptquartier der 4. Armee, *Communiqué B.Nr. 27358/2 Ia*, 13 August 1917.

17 Reichsarchiv, *Kriegstagebuch der königlich preussischen Jagdstaffel 27*, p. 2.

18 Ibid.

19 Kommandeur der Flieger der 4. Armee, *Wochenbericht B-Nr 27466/17*, 9 August 1917, p. 8.

20 Jasta 27, *Flieger-Bericht* by Leutnant Göring, 5 August 1917.

21 Gilbert Budden, born October/December 1890 in Leamington, Warwickshire; educated at Manchester University, B.Sc (Engineering) 1909-1912; accepted into officers training corps; commissioned T2/Lt., No.12 Company, Royal Engineers, 24 April 1915; promoted T/Lt., 29 June 1916; appointed flying officer, Royal Flying Corps, 6 February 1917; WIA, 5 August 1917; listed as lieutenant, Royal Air Force, 1 April 1918; declared unfit due to a gunshot wound, 5 April 1918; dispersed, 14 September 1919. [Ref: BMD; Army List; Air Force List; AIR file 76/65].

22 Royal Flying Corps, *Combat Casualty List*, 5 August 1917.

23 Hauptquartier der 4. Armee, *Täglicher Bericht der Gruppe Jeperen*, 15 August 1917.

24 Kommandeur der Flieger der 4. Armee, *Meldung B Nr 23592/19*, 6 July 1917, p. 1.

25 Kofl 4, *Wochenbericht B-Nr 116 op*, 30 August 1917, p. 2.

26 Ibid., p. 11.

27 Orlando Clive Bridgeman, born 29 November 1898 in Donington, Shifnal, Shropshire; educated at Harrow School; entered OCB, Denham, 8 October 1916; 2 School of Aeronautics, 26 January 1917; posted to 23 Reserve Squadron, 14 March 1917; commissioned T/2Lt (on probation), Royal Flying Corps, 17 March 1917; posted to B Squadron. Central Flying School, 10 April 1917; assigned as flying officer to 70 Squadron, 19 June 1917; WIA, 5 August 1917; declared unfit for general service by medical board, 4 October 1917; assigned light duties by medical board, 5 November 1917; HQ NTB, 7 December 1917; declared fit for general service after one month's high flying, medical board, 29 December 1917; assigned as instructor, 80 Squadron, RFC, 27 January 1918; appointed B Flight commander, 80 Squadron, 28 March 1918; promoted acting captain, 6 April 1918; awarded Military Cross [for action against Jasta 11 on 10 May 1918]; admitted, No.14 General Hospital Wimereaux, 27 August 1918; Southeast Area for dispersal, 29 September 1918; assigned to 204 Training Depot Squadron, Eastchurch, September 1918; Royal Navy Hospital, Chatham, 28 February

1919 [Ref: *London Gazette*; TNA, AIR 76/54; Army List; Air Force List].

28 RFC, *Combat Casualty List*, 25 August 1917.

29 Kogenluft, *Korrespondenz Nr. 889 A I*, 1 September 1917.

30 O'Connor, *Aviation Awards of Imperial Germany and the Men Who Earned Them*, Vol. II, p. 62.

31 Ibid., p. 219.

32 Royal Flying Corps, *Periodical Summary of Aeronautical Information No. 12*, 8 August 1917, p. 7.

33 RFC, *Summary No. 14*, 23 August 1917, p. 7.

34 RFC, *Summary No. 15*, 31 August 1917, p. 6.

35 Kofl 4, *Wochenbericht B-Nr 192 op*, 13 September 1917, p. 9.

36 Georges Marie Guillon, born 2 May 1890 in Brussels, Belgium; educated at the Institute of St Louis in Brussels, 1898-1911, then University of Alberta in Edmonton, Alberta, Canada, 1914-1915; enlisted in 4th University Company, 19th Alberta Dragoons; commissioned Lt., 57 Bn. Militia, 22 March 1916; eventually assigned as Lt/ flight officer (observer), 25 August 1917; while with 57 Squadron, WIA 3 September 1917; declared unfit for general service, 21 September 1917; declared fit as pilot for training in Egypt, 5 December 1917; assigned as pilot instructor in Egypt, 1 December 1917; army observer, Hythe, 1 April 1918; School of Aerial Gunnery; posted to 96 Squadron, 7 May 1918; 3 School of Aeronautics, 22 July 1918; attached to HQ, 32 Wing, 7 August 1918; 18 TDS, 22 August 1918; 18 Training Depot Squadron, 25 September 1918; 3 School of Navigation and Bomb Dropping Middle East, 17 March 1919 [Ref: National Archives of Canada, CEF Attestation List; Army List, Air Force List; TNA AIR 76/199].

37 Kogenluft, *Nachrichtenblatt*, Nr. 33, 11 October 1917, p. 306.

38 Tornuss, *Jagdstaffel 27 Kriegstagebuch* abstract, p. 3

39 Jasta 27, *Flieger-Bericht B.Nr. 1960/17* by Leutnant Göring, 21 September 1917.

40 Ibid.

41 2/Lt Ralph Luxmore Curtis, age nineteen, died of his wounds and was buried at Harlebeke, Belgium [Ref: Hobson, *Airmen Died in the Great War 1914-1918*, p. 38].

42 RFC, *Combat Casualty List*, 21 September 1917.

43 Kogenluft, *Nachrichtenblatt*, Nr. 34, 18 October 1917, p. 328.

44 Nebel qualified for Kgl. Bayer. *Inspektion des Luft- und Kraftfahrwesens* [Royal Bavarian air and land transport] License No. 178 on 15 August 1912 [Ref: Supf, *Das Buch der deutschen Fluggeschichte*, Vol. II, p. 481; Nebel, *Die Narren von Tegel*, pp. 30-31].

45 Nebel, ibid., p. 40.

46 Reichsarchiv, *Jagdstaffel 27*, 26 September-18 October 1917.

47 Kogenluft, *Ordens-Vorschlag Nr. 109/10.17*, 8 October 1917.

48 O'Connor, op.cit., p. 132.

49 Göring, *Kriegsranglisten-Auszug*, p. 10.

50 Liddell Hart, op.cit., p. 342.

51 Göring, *"Luftkämpfe,"* pp. 289-292.

52 Jagdstaffel 27, *Kriegstagebuch V*, 21 October 1917.

53 84 Squadron, RFC, Combat Report by Capt Leask, 21 October 1917.

54 Bodenschatz, *Jagd in Flanderns Himmel*, p. 161.

55 Kogenluft, *Nachrichtenblatt*, Nr. 38, 15 November 1917, p. 414.

56 Arthur Ernest Hempel, born 3 April 1892 (possibly 1895) in St. Kilda, Victoria, Australia; enlisted in Melbourne on 14 September 1914 as Private 1025, 7 Bn. Australian Imperial Force; promoted corporal, 28 September 1914; eventually sent to 3 School of Military Aeronautics, Oxford, 5 March 1917; discharged from AIF / enlisted RFC, 16 March 1916; commissioned 2/Lt (on probation), Central Flying School, RFC Upavon, 17 March 1917; appointed flying officer, RFC, Sleaford, Lincs., 3 July 1917; posted to 84 Squadron. RFC, 14 August to 21 October 1917; POW, 21 October 1917 to 17 December 1918; sent to Australia, n.d [Ref: Air Force List; AIF Embarkation Lists (AWM); AIR 76/220; AIF Record of Service, http://naa12.naa.gov.au/scripts/Imagine.asp].

CHAPTER TEN

1 Jagdstaffel 27, *Bericht B-Nr 2259/17*, 1 November 1917.

2 Jasta 27, *Kriegstagebuch V*, 30 October 1917.

3 Liddell Hart, *The Real War 1914-1918*, pp. 342-343.

4 Jones, *The War in the Air*, Vol. IV, p. 228.

5 Bodenschatz, *Jagd in Flanderns Himmel*, p. 163.

6 Weather report in Royal Flying Corps, *Communiqué No. 112*, 7 November 1917, p. 2.

7 Jasta 27, *Bericht* op.cit.

8 Hildebrand, K. *Die Generale der deutschen Luftwaffe 1935-1945*, Vol. I, p. 370.

9 Franks, Bailey & Guest, *Above the Lines*, pp. 117, 156.

10 Franks, Bailey & Duiven, *The Jasta Pilots*, pp. 294, 291.

11 Jagdstaffel 27, *Kriegstagebuch*, 7 November 1917.

12 Royal Flying Corps, 32 Squadron Record Book, 7 November 1917.

13 Ibid.

14 Kogenluft, *Nachrichtenblatt der Luftstreitkräfte*, Nr. 41, 6 December 1917, p. 455.

15 RFC, op.cit.; Viscount Glentworth's later demise, while flying as a captain with 32 Squadron on 18 May 1918, had no connection with Hermann Göring [Ref: Hobson, C. *Airmen Died in the Great War 1914-1918*, p. 144].

16 Jasta 27, *KTB VI*, 19 November – 5 December 1917.

17 Weather report in RFC, *Communiqué No. 115*, 29 November 1917, p. 3.

18 Kommandeur der Flieger der 4. Armee, *Tagesbefehl Nr. 132*, 12 November 1917, p. 2.

19 Willy Rosenstein was born on 28 January 1892 in Stuttgart, capital of the Kingdom of Württemberg. On 15 August 1911, he began flight training at flight pioneer Edmund Rumpler's flying school at Johannisthal, near Berlin. Rosenstein became associated with early military aviation and, after qualifying for Deutsche Luftfahrer Verband (DLV) private pilot's licence No. 170 on 14 March 1912, he was hired by Dr. Rumpler to teach small groups of military officers how to fly and he joined them in such prestigious events as the national competition in Berlin in 1912. He was decorated by early aviation supporter Carl Eduard, Duke of Saxe Coburg-Gotha, on 7 August 1913 and a year later, repaid the duke's generosity by enlisting in the 6. Thüringisches Infanterie-Regiment Nr. 95 in Gotha. On 24 August 1914, to gain his military indoctrination, Rosenstein was posted to the Militär Fliegerschule in Gotha. Rosenstein completed his military aviation requirements at Flieger-Ersatz Abteilung 5 at Hannover, where he was promoted to Unteroffizier on 18 October and received his military pilot's badge on 22 October. He was promoted to Vizefeldwebel and appointed Offizierstellvertreter on 24 November. Rosenstein was posted to the German 5th Army's air park at Montmédy on 11 January 1915 and then to Flieger Abteilung 19, where he flew combat missions in Fokker and Pfalz Eindeckers. Commissioned Leutnant der Reserve on 17 February 1916, he was wounded in aerial combat in April and then posted to training duties at FEA 10 at Böblingen on 31 May 1916. He was returned to combat flying on 17 September and posted to the German 5th Army's air park. Rosenstein was posted to Jagdstaffel 9 on 7 October 1916 and remained there until 13 February 1917, when he was transferred to Jasta 27, where he scored his first two aerial victories. Assigned to an aviation observer school on 10 December 1917, he was reassigned to the home defence command on 5 January 1918. He flew against enemy aircraft attacking the German homeland, first with Kampfeinsitzerstaffel 1a based in Mannheim and then Kest 1b out of Freiburg. During the latter assignment, on 31 May, he shot down an Airco D.H.4 attacking Karlsruhe, for which he was later awarded Grand Duchy of Baden's Knight's Cross Second Class of the Order of the Zähringer Lion. He was posted to Jasta 40 on 2 July 1918 and served with that unit for the remainder of the war [Ref: Gill, 'The Albums of Willy Rosenstein,' pp. 289-334; Supf, *Das Buch der deutschen Fluggeschichte*, Vol. I, pp. 499, 566; Theilhaber, *Jüdische Flieger im Weltkrieg*, pp. 76-78; Rosenstein, Personal Bogen].

20 This victory, over an Airco D.H.4, is not listed in Kogenluft, *Nachrichtenblatt*, Vol. I, Nr. 34, 18 October 1917, p. 328. However, Rosenstein's *Personal-Bogen* [service record] lists the Kogenluft confirmation number Fl.IIIc 113092, which indicates the victory was, indeed, credited to him.

21 Quoted in O'Connor, *Aviation Awards of Imperial Germany and the Men Who Earned Them*, Vol. IV, p. 181.

22 Gill, op.cit., p. 311.

23 Kofl 4. Armee, *Tagesbefehl Nr. 159*, 9 December 1917, p. 1.

24 Göring, Letter of, 1 January 1918 (in USAMHI Göring papers).

25 Kofl 4. Armee, *Tagesbefehl Nr. 168*, 19 December 1917, p. 1.

26 Kofl 4. Armee, *Tagesbefehl Nr. 198*, 18 January 1918, p. 2.

27 Göring, photo album.

28 Kofl 4. Armee, *Tagesbefehl Nr. 199*, 19 January 1918.

29 O'Connor, *Aviation Awards of Imperial Germany and the Men Who Earned Them*, Vol. VI, pp. 17-19.

30 Kofl 4. Armee, *Tagesbefehl Nr. 231*, 20 February 1918, p. 1.

31 Zuerl, *Pour-le-Mérite-Flieger*, p. 311.

32 Bodenschatz, *Jagd in Flanderns Himmel*, p. 16.

33 Göring, 'A Gallant British Airman', p. 193.

34 Ibid.

35 Ibid.

36 Ibid.

37 2/Lt George Barton Craig, born 1895 in Vancouver, British Columbia; enlisted in RFC, Toronto, April 1917; training at Camp Borden; commissioned T/2Lt (probationary), General List, 23 July 1917; Training Battalion to Central Flying School, 5 August 1917; 28 TD(S?), 16 August 1917; designated flight officer, 3 September 1917; assigned to 45 Squadron, RFC, 16 September 1917; posted to France; transferred to 60 Squadron and appointed acting flight commander, C Flight, February 1917, reported MIA/killed, 21 February 1918; buried in Common-wealth War Graves Commission Cemetery, Moorsele, Belgium, 18 March 1918 [Ref: S.K. Taylor files; Air Force List; *London Gazette*; TNA WO 76/567; CWGC].

38 2/Lt William Morley Kent was a native of Bathurst, New Brunswick; he is buried at Moorsele [Ref: Hobson, *Airmen Died in the Great War 1914-1918*, p. 62].

39 RFC, *Combat Casualty List*, 21 February 1918.

40 Kofl 4. Armee, *Wochenbericht Abt. Ia Nr. 1104 op.*, 7 March 1918; Kogenluft, Nachrichtenblatt, Vol. II, Nr. 12, 16 May 1918, p. 180.

41 Taylor, letter to the author, 2 October 2009.

42 Deutsche Dienststelle, Göring medical summary, sent to the author dated 7 August 2009.

43 Kofl 4. Armee, *Tagesbefehl Nr. 240*, 1 March 1918.

44 Esposito, *A Concise History of World War I*, p. 104.

45 Jasta 27, *KTB VI*, 21 March 1918.

46 Bodenschatz, op.cit., p. 172.

47 Jones, op.cit., p. 264ff.

48 Jasta 27, *KTB VI*, 21 March 1918.

49 Ibid., 22-30 March 1918.

50 Jones, op.cit., p. 346ff.

51 Jasta 27, *KTB VI*, 1 April 1918.

52 Ibid., 7 April 1918.

53 Kogenluft, *Nachrichtenblatt der Luftstreitkräfte*, Vol. II, Nr. 19, 4 July 1918, p. 280.

54 Franks & Giblin, *Under the Guns of the German Aces*, p. 60.

55 Ibid.

56 Harry Waldo Collier, born 31 October 1893 in Wanganui, New Zealand; took flight instruction at his own expense, earned Royal Aero Club Certificate No. 3863, 20 November 1916; commissioned RFC, 19 January 1917; appointed flying officer, 18 August 1917; posted to 42 Squadron, RFC, 2 September 1917; WIA, 13 April 1918, sent to London Hospital; awarded Military Cross (*London Gazette*, 26 July 1918); assigned to School of Artillery Co-Operation;

57 Eric Campbell Musson, born 27 April 1894 in Teignmount, South Devon; commissioned into East Essex Regiment; posted to France, 10 November 1915; home convalescence; returned to France, 9 November 1916; application to Royal Flying Corps accepted, summer 1917; after training, posted as observer (probationary) to 42 Squadron, RFC, 2 October 1917; WIA, 7 April 1918; returned to U.K. for treatment, 20 April 1918; appointed instructor, 9 December 1918 [Ref: Ibid., pp. 60-61]

58 Jones, op.cit., p. 370.

59 VanWyngarden, *Fokker Dr.I Jagdstaffeln*, p. 74.

60 Dilthey, 'In der Staffel Göring' pp. 215-216.

61 Kogenluft, *Nachrichtenblatt*, Vol. II, Nr. 9, 25 April 1918, p. 128a.

62 Jasta 27, *KTB VI*, 22 April 1918.

63 Kogenluft, *Nachrichtenblatt*, Vol. II, Nr. 10, 2 May 1918, pp. 125-136.

64 Kofl 4. *Armee, Wochenbericht B.Nr. 1559 op.*, 31 May 1918, p. 4.

65 Jasta 27, *KTB VI*, 23-29 April 1918.

66 Likely an Airco D.H.4 from 25 Squadron, which bombed Tournai railway station that day [Ref: Royal

67 Air Force, Communiqué No. 5, 8 May 1918, p. 4].

68 Jasta 27, *KTB VI*, 3 May 1918.

69 Ibid., 7 May 1918.

70 Tornuss, *Jagdstaffel 27 Kriegstagebuch* abstract, p. 5.

CHAPTER ELEVEN

1 Bodenschatz, *Jagd in Flanderns Himmel*, p.119.

2 Kilduff, *The Red Baron Combat Wing*, pp. 265-266.

3 Tornuss, *Jagdstaffel 27 Kriegstagebuch* abstract, p. 5.

4 Kommandierende General der Luftstreitkräfte, *Ordensvorschlag Kr. II 773*, 15 May 1918.

5 O'Connor, *Aviation Awards of Imperial Germany and the Men Who Earned Them*, Vol. II, p. 64.

6 Hildebrand, *Die Generale der deutschen Luftwaffe 1935-1945*, Vol. I, p. 179.

7 Manvell & Fraenkel, *Goering*, p. 404, ff 4.

8 Ibid.

9 Wynne, 'Project Aerodromes', p. 52.

10 Jasta 27, *Kampf-Bericht* by Leutnant Göring, 5 June 1918.

11 Ibid.

12 Kommandeur der Flieger der 7. Armee, *Übersicht Nr. 112*, 16 June 1918, p. 9.

13 Kogenluft, *Nachrichtenblatt der Luftstreitkräfte*, Vol. II, Nr. 24, 8 August 1918, p. 363.

14 Davila and Soltan, *French Aircraft of the First World War*, p. 37.

15 Bailey & Cony, *The French Air War Chronology*, p. 218.

16 Grand Quartier Général, *Résumé des Opérations Aériennes No, 6032*, 6 June 1918.

17 Jasta 27, *Kriegstagebuch VI*, 5 June 1918.

18 Bailey & Clausen, 'The Grim Reapers of Spa 94', p. 116.

19 Jasta 27, KTB VI, 10 June 1918 (dated a day after the combat).

20 Bailey & Cony, op.cit., p. 241.

21 Kogenluft, op.cit., p. 364.

22 Jasta 27, *Kampf-Bericht* by Leutnant Göring, 17 June 1918.

23 Deutscher Offizier-Bund, *Ehren-Rangliste des ehemaligen Deutschen Heeres*, p. 430; Perthes, *Ehrentafel der Kriegsopfer des reichsdeutschen Adels 1914-1918*, p. 66]

24 Franks, Bailey & Duiven, *Casualties of the German Air Service 1914-1920*, p. 280.

25 Tornuss, op.cit.

26 Kogenluft, op.cit., p. 365.

27 Chamberlain & Bailey, 'History of Escadrille Spa 93,' p. 70.

28 Cron, 'Organization of the German Luftstreitkräfte,' p. 55.

29 Wenzl, *Richthofen-Flieger*, pp. 46-47.

30 Lamberton, *Fighter Aircraft of the 1914-1918 War*, p. 118.

31 Bodenschatz, *op.cit.*, p. 112.

32 Ibid.

33 Ibid., p. 113.

34 Kogenluft, *Nachrichtenblatt*, Vol. II, Nr. 20, 11 July 1918, p. 293; ibid., *Nachrichtenblatt*, Vol. II, Nr. 23, 1 August 1918, p. 338.

35 Cron, *Imperial German Army 1914-1918*, p. 71.

36 Bodenschatz, *Jagd*, op.cit., p. 113.

37 Hildebrand, op.cit., p. 90.

38 Bodenschatz, 'Das Jagdgeschwader Frhr. v. Richthofen Nr. 1 im Verbande der 2. Armee,' p. 235.

39 Jagdgeschwader I, *an den Kogenluft Tgb. Nr. I/1300*, 14 July 1918, p. 1.

40 Ibid., p. 2.

41 Bodenschatz, *Jagd*, op.cit., p. 191.

42 Woodman, *Early Aircraft Armament*, p. 163.

43 Göring almost certainly described the Caudron R.11, a 'three-seat long-range escort fighter … [which carried] light-weight armor … [and] was well-armed with twin 7.7-mm Lewis guns in the nose and rear fuselage …' [Ref: Davilla & Soltan, op.cit., p. 167].

44 Quoted in Bodenschatz, op.cit., pp. 119-120.

45 JG I, *Kampf-Bericht B. Nr. 1366/I/18* by Leutnant Göring, 18 July 1918.

46 Zuerl, *Pour-le-Mérite-Flieger*, pp. 507-508.

47 O'Connor, *Aviation Awards of Imperial Germany and the Men Who Earned Them*, Vol. II, p. 61.

48 Haehnelt, *Ehrentafel der im Flugdienst während des Weltkrieges gefallenen Offiziere der Deutschen Fliegerverbände*, p. 22.

49 Bodenschatz, *Jagd*, op.cit., p. 192.

50 Franks, Bailey & Guest, *Above the Lines*, p. 157.

51 Noted in U.S. National Archives Record Group 238, which references the Loerzer-von Vorwald conversation as being 'reported in [GFM Erhard] Milch diary, April 5, 1947.'

52 Bodenschatz, *Jagd*, op.cit., p. 193.

53 Ibid.

54 Richthofen, 'Das letzte Mal an der Front' in *Im Felde unbesiegt*, p. 279.

55 Kogenluft, *Nachrichtenblatt*, Vol. II, Nr. 29, 12 September 1918, p. 453

56 Kofl 7. Armee, *Fliegertagsmeldung Nr. 211*, 27 July 1918.

57 Bodenschatz, *Jagd*, op.cit., p. 194.

58 Mosley, *The Reich Marshal*, p. 42.

59 Quoted in Bodenschatz, *Jagd*, op.cit., p. 123.

60 Ibid., p. 125.

61 Quoted in ibid., p. 134.

62 Ibid., pp. 134-135.

63 Quoted in ibid., p. 130.

64 7. Armee-Oberkommando, *Befehl über die Rückverlegung und Aufklärung der Fliegerverbände bei der Einnahme der Vesle-Stellung*, 29 July 1918, p. 7.

65 Franks, Bailey & Duiven, *The Jasta Pilots*, p. 322.

66 Hildebrand, op.cit., pp. 387-389.

CHAPTER TWELVE

1 Jones, *The War in the Air*, Vol. VI, p. 443.

2 Franks, Bailey & Guest, *Above the Lines*, pp. 220-221.

3 Gritzbach, *Hermann Göring, Werk und Mensch*, pp. 244-245.

4 Jones, op.cit.

5 VanWyngarden, 'The Aircraft of Hermann Göring,' p. 235.

6 Bodenschatz, *Jagd in Flanderns Himmel*, p. 202.

7 Perthes, *Ehrentafel der Kriegsopfer des reichsdeutschen Adels 1914-1919*, p. 274; according to the Winterfeld family chronicle, the pilot's body was brought back to his ancestral home in Saxony for burial. Later, the family estate was expropriated by the post-World War II communist government and the family cemetery, including Winterfeld's grave, was paved over and used as a tractor repair station.

8 Bodenschatz, op.cit., p. 203.

9 Esposito, 'Western Front, 1918: The Year of Decision,' p. 121.

10 Möller, *Kampf und Sieg eines Jagdgeschwaders*, p. 88.

11 Bodenschatz, op.cit., pp. 135-136.

12 Quoted in Möller, op.cit., p. 87.

13 Henshaw, *The Sky Their Battlefield*, pp. 464-466.

14 National Archives and Records Administration (U.S.). *Air Service Bulletin No. 58*, 28 September 1918, p. 175.

15 Bodenschatz, op.cit., p. 204.

16 Jagdstaffel 4, *Luftkampfbericht*, Oberleutnant Udet, 29 September 1918 [reproduced in Udet, *Mein Fliegerleben*, pp. 104b-104c].

17 Kriegsministerium, *Teil 10 Abschnitt B, Flieger Formationen*, p. 244.

18 Udet, op.cit., p. 66.

19 Nebel, *Die Narren von Tegel*, pp. 40-41.

20 Niels Paulli Krause was qualified to comment on his adversary's flying and combat skills. He was born on 19 May 1894 in the Danish east coast town of Skødstrup and left his homeland to enlist in the

French *Aviation Militaire* in February 1914. By the outbreak of war just over five months later, his newly-acquired love for France made him eager to defend it as a frontline pilot. And he was well motivated to fight Germans, as he knew from his country's history that Prussia had humiliated Denmark by seizing Schleswig-Holstein in 1864 [Ref: Guttman, "France's Foreign Legion of the Air, Part 14," p. 16]. Krause was assigned to fly two-seat reconnaissance and bomber aircraft in Escadrille MF.2 and by mid-1915 he was promoted to sergent and awarded the *Medaille Militaire* [Military Medal] for bravery in combat. The following June, while learning to fly single-seat fighters, a crash cost him his right eye. Undaunted, he returned to his unit some weeks later, wearing a glass eye and eager to resume combat flying. Krause's determination paid off when, on 13 April 1917, he and his observer, Sous-lieutenant Henri Clave, shot down an Albatros fighter and fought off its two companions. Wounded again five months later, Krause convalesced and, once more, returned to combat. On 7 October, he was awarded the *Légion d'Honneur* and two weeks later received a rare distinction for a non-French native by being promoted to the commissioned rank of Sous lieutenant [Ref: Anonymous, '*Un Volontaire Danois: Pauli Krause*,' pp. 598-600, 615-616].

21   Gritzbach, op.cit., p. 239

22   Krause in ibid., pp. 239-240

23   Ibid., p. 18

24   Davilla and Soltan, *French Aircraft of the First World War*, p. 497

25   Ibid., p. 516

26   Ibid., p. 503.

27   Ibid., p. 497.

28   Guttman, op.cit.

29   Anonymous, op.cit.

30   Ref: Historisches Archiv der Stadt Köln, Sig.Bestand 1417.

31   Horster, '*Von Richthofen bis Göring*,' p. 130.

32   Rickenbacker, *Fighting the Flying Circus*, p. 282.

33   The 147th Aero Squadron lost two Spads and pilots that day: 2/Lt William E. Brotherton (KiA) and the other flown by 2/Lt Wilbur W. White, Jr., both KiA. White collided with a Fokker D.VII of Jasta 60 [Ref: Parks, 'No Greater Love, the Story of Lt Wilbur W. White,' p. 46].

34   Rickenbacker, op.cit., p. 285. Rickenbacker shot down two Fokker D.VIIs that day, recorded as the nineteenth and twentieth of his twenty-six-victory total; his adversary, Leutnant Wilhelm Kohlbach, left a grenadier regiment to become an observer with Flieger-Abteilung (A) 255 before becoming a pilot and being posted to JG I. In 1935, Kohlbach was reactivated in the Luftwaffe, where he rose to the rank of Generalmajor and died aged fifty as a PoW in Britain on 11 February 1947 [Ref: Hildebrand, *Die Generale der deutschen Luftwaffe 1935-1945*, Vol. II, pp. 207-208].

35   Esposito, op.cit., p. 131.

36   Bodenschatz, op.cit., 207.

37   Van Ishoven, *The Fall of an Eagle*, p. 72.

38   Van Ishoven, op.cit.

39   O'Connor, *Aviation Awards of Imperial Germany and the Men Who Earned Them*, Vol. VI, p. 358.

40   Grosz, 'Archiv,' p. 78.

41   Bodenschatz, op.cit., p. 137.

42   Ibid., pp. 208-209.

43   Ibid., pp. 139, 209; JG I's last aerial combat was with aircraft of the 28th Aero Squadron, USAS, which lost two pilots, both PoW [Ref: Anonymous, *A History of the 28th Aero Squadron*, pp. 344-345].

44   Zuerl, *Pour le Mérite-Flieger*, p. 343.

45   Bodenschatz, op.cit., p. 141.

46   Gritzbach, op.cit., p. 246

47   Bodenschatz, op.cit.

48   Ibid., p. 209.

49   Ibid., p. 142.

50   Ripphausen, '*Göring musterte 1918 in Aschaffenburg ab.*'

51   Ibid.

52   Ibid.

53   Mosley, *The Reich Marshal*, p. 42.

54   Gritzbach, op.cit., p. 249.

BIBLIOGRAPHY AND SOURCES

BOOKS

Bailey, F. & Cony, C. *The French Air War Chronology*, London, 2001

Bodenschatz, K. *Jagd in Flanderns Himmel*, Munich, 1935

Bronnenkant, L. *The Imperial Eagles in World War I – Their Postcards and Pictures*, Altglen, Pennsylvania, 2006

----. *The Imperial Eagles in World War I – Their Postcards and Pictures*, Vol. II, Altglen, Pennsylvania, 2008

Bross, W. *Gespräche mit Göring: Nürnberg 1946*, Kiel, 2003

Bruce, J. *British Aeroplanes 1914-1918*, London, 1969

Bücking, M. (ed.). *Die Braunschweiger im Weltkriege 1914-1918*, Braunschweig, 1920

Butler, W. & Young G. *Marshal Without Glory*, London, 1951

Collishaw, R. *Air Command – A Fighter Pilot's Story*, London, 1973

Cron, H. (Translated by C. Colton). *Imperial German Army 1914-1918*, London, 2006

Cross & Cockade International. *Nieuports in RNAS, RFC and RAF Service*, London, 2007

Davilla, J. & Soltan, A. *French Aircraft of the First World War*, Stratford, Connecticut, 1997

Deutscher Offizier-Bund, *Ehren-Rangliste des ehemaligen Deutschen Heeres*, Berlin, 1926

Dickhuth-Harrach, G. von (ed.). *Im Felde unbesiegt*, Vol. I, Munich, 1921

Douglas, W.S. *Years of Combat*, London, 1963

Eberhardt, W. von (ed.). *Unsere Luftstreitkräfte 1914-1918*, Berlin, 1930

Esposito, V. (ed). *A Concise History of World War I*, New York, 1965

Franks, N., Bailey, F. & Guest, R. *Above the Lines*, London, 1993

Franks, N., Bailey, F. & Duiven, R. *Casualties of the German Air Service 1914-1920*, London, 1999

----. *The Jasta Pilots*, London, 1996

Franks, N. & Giblin, H. *Under the Guns of the German Aces*, London, 1997

Franks, N. & VanWyngarden, G. *Fokker Dr.I Aces of World War I*, Oxford, 2001

----. *Fokker D.VII Aces of World War I – Part 2*, Oxford, 2003

Frischauer, W. *The Rise and Fall of Hermann Goering*, Boston, 1951

Goldensohn, L. (ed. R. Gellateley) *The Nuremberg Interviews*, New York, 2004

Graham, D. *Downside and the War 1914-1919*, London, 1925

Gritzbach, E. *Hermann Göring Werk und Mensch*, 39th ed., Munich, 1941

Haehnelt, W. *Ehrentafel der im Flugdienst während des Weltkrieges gefallenen Offiziere der Deutschen Fliegerverbände*, Berlin, 1920

Henshaw, T. *The Sky Their Battlefield*, London, 1995

Hildebrand, K. *Die Generale der deutschen Luftwaffe 1935-1945*, Vol. I, Osnabrück, 1990

----. *Die Generale der deutschen Luftwaffe 1935-1945*, Vol. II, Osnabrück, 1990

----. *Die Generale der deutschen Luftwaffe 1935-1945*, Vol. III, Osnabrück, 1992

Hobson, C. *Airmen Died in the Great War 1914-1918*, London, 1995

Hoeppner, W. von. *Deutschlands Krieg in der Luft*, Leipzig, 1921

Immelmann, F. *Immelmann – Der Adler von Lille*, Leipzig, 1934

Jones, H. *The War in the Air*, Vol. II, Oxford, 1928

----. *The War in the Air*, Vol. VI, Oxford, 1937

Kilduff, P. *Red Baron – The Life and Death of an Ace*, Devon, 2007

----. *The Red Baron Combat Wing*, London, 1997

Kulenkampff-Post, C. *Reiter unterm Himmel*, Stuttgart, 1939

Lamberton, W. *Fighter Aircraft of the 1914-1918 War*, Letchworth, 1960

----. *Reconnaissance and Bomber Aircraft of the 1914-1918 War*, Letchworth, 1962

Langsdorff, W. von (ed.). *Flieger am Feind*, Gütersloh, 1934

Liddell Hart, B. *The Real War 1914-1918*, Boston, 1964

Leonhardy, L. *Mit der deutschen Luftfahrt durch dick und dünn*, Berlin, 1926

Lewis, P. *Squadron Histories RFC, RNAS & RAF Since 1911*, London, 1968

Loewenstern, E. von & Bertkau, M. *Mobilmachung, Aufmarsch und erster Einsatz der deutschen Luftstreitkräfte im August 1914*, Berlin, 1939

Manvell, R. & Fraenkel, H. *Goering*, London, 2005

Moncure, J. *Forging the King's Sword*, New York, 1993

Möller, H. *Kampf und Sieg eines Jagdgeschwaders*, Berlin, 1939

Morris, A. *Bloody April*, London, 1967

Morris, R. *Untold Valor*, Washington, DC, 2006

Mosley, L. *The Reich Marshal: A Biography of Hermann Goering*, New York, 1974

Nebel, R. *Die Narren von Tegel*, Düsseldorf, 1972

Neubecker, Dr. O. *Für Tapferkeit und Verdienst*, Munich, 1956

Neumann, G. (ed.). *Die deutschen Luftstreitkräfte im Weltkriege*, Berlin, 1920

----. (ed.). *In der Luft unbesiegt*, Munich, 1923

O'Connor, N. *Aviation Awards of Imperial Germany and the Men Who Earned Them*, Vol. II, Princeton, 1990

----. *Aviation Awards of Imperial Germany and the Men Who Earned Them*, Vol. IV, Princeton, 1995

----. *Aviation Awards of Imperial Germany and the Men Who Earned Them*, Vol. VI, Princeton, 1999

----. *Aviation Awards of Imperial Germany and the Men Who Earned Them*, Vol. VII, Princeton, 2002

Paul, W. *Wer war Hermann Göring?*, Esslingen, 1983

Perthes, J. *Ehrentafel der Kriegsopfer des reichsdeutschen Adels 1914-1918*, Gotha, 1921

Rapport, M. *1848 – Year of Revolution*, New York, 2009

Rasselsteiner Eisenwerks-Gesellschaft AG, *Familie Remy*, Rasselstein, 1935

Richthofen, M. *Ein Heldenleben*, Berlin 1920

Rickenbacker, E. *Fighting the Flying Circus*, New York, repr. 1967

Robertson, B. *British Military Aircraft Serials 1911-1971*, London, 1971

Ronningstam, E. *Identifying and Understanding the Narcissistic Personality*, New York, 2005

Schiel, O. *Das 4. Badische Infanterie-Regiment 'Prinz Wilhelm' Nr. 112*, Berlin, 1927

Sholto Douglas, W. *Years of Combat*, London, 1963

Shores, C., Franks, N. & Guest, R. *Above the Trenches*, London, 1990

Sommerfeldt, M. *Hermann Göring – Ein Lebensbild*, 8th ed., Berlin, 1933

Sturtivant, R. & Page, G. *The S.E.5 File*, Essex, 1996

----. *The D.H.4/D.H.9 File*, Essex, 1999

Supf, P. *Das Buch der deutschen Fluggeschichte*, Vol. I, Stuttgart, 1956

----. *Das Buch der deutschen Fluggeschichte*, Vol. II, Stuttgart, 1956

Theilhaber, F. *Jüdische Flieger im Weltkrieg*, Berlin, 1924

Udet, E. *Mein Fliegerleben*, Berlin, 1935.

Ursinus, O. (ed.). *Flugsport*, Vol. X, Frankfurt am Main, 1918

Van Ishoven, A. (ed. C. Bowyer) *The Fall of an Eagle*, London, 1979

VanWyngarden, G. *Albatros Aces of World War I – Part 2*, Oxford, 2007

----. *Fokker Dr.I Jagdstaffeln*, Berkhamsted, 2007

Wenzl, R. *Richthofen-Flieger*, Freiburg im Breisgau, ca. 1930

Werner, J. *Boelcke – der mensch, der Flieger, der Führer der deutschen Jagdfliegerei*, Leipzig, 1932

Wilhelm, Kronprinz. *Meine Erinnerungen aus Deutschlands Heldenkampf*, Berlin, 1923

Woodman, H. *Early Aircraft Armament*, London, 1989

Wylie, J. *The Warlord and the Renegade: The Story of Hermann and Albert Goering*, Stroud, Gloucestershire, 2006

Zuerl, W. *Pour-le-Mérite-Flieger*, Munich, 1938

DOCUMENTS

Armée de l'Air. *Etat Nominatif des militaires du Personnel Navigant de l'Aéronautique Tués, Blesses ou Disparus aux Armées*, in the field, 1916, 1917, 1918.

General Headquarters American Expeditionary Force. *Summary of Air Information*, in the field, 1918.

Grand Quartier Général, *Résumé des Opérations Aériennes*, Paris, 1918

Kommandeur der Flieger der 1. Armee (Kofl 1). *Wöchentliche Meldungen*, in the field, 1916

Kommandeur der Flieger der 4. Armee (Kofl 4). *Tagesbefehle*, in the field, 1917

----. *Wöchentliche Meldungen*, in the field, 1917

----. *Wochenberichte*, in the field, 1918

Kommandeur der Flieger der 6. Armee (Kofl 6). *Flieger-Wochenberichte*, in the field, 1918

Kommandeur der Flieger der 7. Armee (Kofl 7). *Wochenberichte*, in the field, 1918

----. [Daily] *Fliegertagesmeldungen*, in the field, 1918

Kriegsministerium (organisational manual), *Teil 10 Abschnitt B, Flieger-Formationen*, Berlin, 1918

Kommandierende General der Luftstreitkräfte (Kogenluft). *Nachrichtenblatt der Luftstreitkräfte*, Vol. I, in the field, 1917

----. *Nachrichtenblatt der Luftstreitkräfte*, Vol. II, in the field, 1918

Kriegswissenschaftliche Abteilung der Luftwaffe (RLM). *Jagdstaffel 26 Kriegstagebuch I 1917*, Potsdam, n.d. via U.S. Army Military History Institute

----. *Jagdstaffel 27 Kriegstagebuch II 1917*, Potsdam, n.d. via U.S. Army Military History Institute

----. *Jagdstaffel 27 Kriegstagebuch III 1917*, Potsdam, n.d. via U.S. Army Military History Institute

----. *Jagdstaffel 27 Kriegstagebuch IV 1917*, Potsdam, n.d. via U.S. Army Military History Institute

----. *Jagdstaffel 27 Kriegstagebuch V 1917*, Potsdam, n.d. via U.S. Army Military History Institute

----. *Jagdstaffel 27 Kriegstagebuch VI 1918*, Potsdam, n.d. via U.S. Army Military History Institute

National Archives (U.K.). 1 Squadron, RFC, *Squadron Record Book*, in the field, 1917 (PRO File Air 1/1333/204/17/61)

----. 32 Squadron, RFC, *Squadron Record Book*, in the field, 1917 (PRO File Air 1/1222/204/5/2634/32 Sqdn)

----. 84 Squadron, RFC, *Combat Reports*, in the field, 1917 (PRO File Air 1/1227/206/5/2634/84 Sqdn)

National Archives and Records Administration (U.S.). *Air Service Bulletin*, 1918 (RG 120 – Records of the American Expeditionary Forces, 1917-1923), Washington, 1959

----. *Gorrell's History of the Air Service, Individual Combat Reports of Americans Serving with the RAF*, Vol. B-13 (RG 120), Washington, 1959

Reichsarchiv. *Kriegstagebuch der königlich preussischen Feldflieger-Abteilung 25*, Potsdam, n.d. via U.S. Army Military History Institute

----. *Kriegstagebuch der königlich preussischen Jagdstaffel 26*, Potsdam, n.d. via U.S. Army Military History Institute

Stabsoffizier der Flieger der 1. Armee (Stofl 1). *Wochenberichte*, in the field, 1916

Stabsoffizier der Flieger der 3. Armee (Stofl 3). *Wochenberichte*, in the field, 1915

Stabsoffizier der Flieger der 5. Armee (Stofl 5). *Wochenberichte*, in the field, 1916

Royal Flying Corps. *Periodical Summary of Aeronautical Information Nos. 1-30*, in the field, 22 May 1917-11 February 1918

Royal Flying Corps / Royal Air Force. *Combat Casualty List*, in the field, 1916 (PRO File Air 1/434/15/273/2----.)

----. *Communiqués*, in the field, 1916, 1917, 1918 (PRO File Air 1/2097/207/14/1)

----. *Summaries of Air Intelligence Nos.1 - 263*. In the field, 12 February-11 November 1918

----. *War Diary*, in the field, 1916 (PRO File Air 1/1184)

ARTICLES, MONOGRAPHS, PERIODICALS AND TEXTS

Anonymous. 'A History of the 28th Aero Squadron' in *Cross & Cockade Journal*, Vol. XI, No. 4, Whittier (California), 1971

----. *'Ein braunschweiger Ritter des Ordens Pour le Mérite – Oberleutnant Hans Berr'* in *Die Braunschweiger im Weltkriege 1914 1918*, Vol. XIII, Braunschweig, 1917

----. *'Un Volontaire Danois: Pauli Krause'* in *La Guerre Aérienne Illustrée*, Vol. IV, Nos. 89 and 90, Paris, 1918

Bailey, F. & Clausen, A. 'The Grim Reapers of Spa 94' in *Cross & Cockade Great Britain Journal*, Vol. IX, No. 3, Farnborough, 1978

Bodenschatz, K. *'Das Jagdgeschwader Frhr. v. Richthofen Nr. 1 im Verbande der 2. Armee'* in *In der Luft unbesiegt*

Chamberlain, P. & Bailey, F. 'History of Escadrille Spa 93' in *Cross & Cockade Great Britain Journal*, Vol. IX, No. 2, Farnborough, 1978

Cron, H. (Translated by P. Grosz) 'Organization of the German Luftstreitkräfte' in *Cross & Cockade Journal*, Vol. VII, No. 1, Whittier (California), 1966

Dilthey, H. *'In der Staffel Göring'* in *Flieger am Feind*

Esposito, V. 'Western Front, 1918: The Year of Decision' in *A Concise History of World War I*

Falls, C. 'Western Front, 1915-17: Stalemate' in *A Concise History of World War I*

Ferko, E. 'Jagdflieger Friedrich Noltenius' in *Cross & Cockade Journal*, Vol. VII, No. 4, Whittier (California), 1966

Franks, N. & Bailey, F. 'Top Scorers – The Record of 20 Squadron, RFC/RAF' in *Cross & Cockade Great Britain Journal*, Vol. IV, No.12, Farnborough, 1973

Gilbert, G. 'Hermann Goering, Amiable Psychopath' in *Journal of Abnormal and Social Psychology*, Vol. XLIII, Washington, DC, 1948

Gill, R. 'The Albums of Willy Rosenstein' in *Cross & Cockade Journal*, Vol. XXV, No. 4, Whittier (California), 1984

Göring, H. *'Aus dem Tagebuch eines Jagdfliegers'* in *In der Luft unbesiegt*

----. 'A Gallant British Airman' in *Popular Flying*, London, 1933

----. *'Luftkämpfe'* in *Unsere Luftstreitkräfte 1914-1918*

Grosz, P. *AEG G.IV Windsock Datafile 51*, Berkhamsted, 1995

----. *Albatros B.I Windsock Datafile 87*, Berkhamsted, 2001

----. *Albatros C.III Windsock Datafile 13*, Berkhamsted, 1989

----. *Albatros D.III – A Windsock Datafile Special*, Berkhamsted, 2003

----. 'Archiv' in *World War One Aeroplanes*, No. 125, Poughkeepsie (New York), August 1989

----. *Aviatik C.I Windsock Datafile 63*, Berkhamsted, 1997

----. *Fokker E.I/II Windsock Datafile 91*, Berkhamsted, 2002

----. *Gotha G.I Windsock Datafile 83*, Berkhamsted, 2000

Guttman, J. 'France's Foreign Legion of the Air Part 14, Two Great Danes' in *Windsock International*, Vol. 8 No. 2, Berkhamsted, 1992

Horster, C. *'Von Richthofen bis Göring'* in *Der Frontsoldat erzählt*, Vol. III, No. 5, Kiel, 1933

Merrill, G. *Jagdstaffel 5 – Volume One*, Berkhamsted, 2004

Olynyk, F. 'The Combat Records of Hermann Göring' in *Over the Front*, Vol. X, No. 3, Dallas (Texas), 1995

Richthofen, L. von. *'Das letzte Mal an der Front'* in *Im Felde unbesiegt*, 1921

Slee, F. 'The Day Goering Nearly Copped It' in Australian Broadcasting Corporation Lateline transcript, http://www.abc.net.au/lateline/content/2003/hc14.htm, 2003

Radloff, B. & Niemann, R. 'The Ehrenbechers – Where are They Now?' in *Cross & Cockade Journal*, Vol. X, No. 4, Whittier (California), 1969

Ripphausen, J. 'Göring *musterte 1918 in Aschaffenburg ab*' in *Aschaffenburger Volksblatt Nr 273*, 26 November 1988

Siegert, W. *'Heeresflugwesen Entwicklung'* in *Die deutschen Luftstreitkräfte im Weltkriege*

Tornuss, E. *Jagdstaffel 27 Kriegstagebuch* abstract, Germany, ca. 1938

VanWyngarden, G. 'The Aircraft of Hermann Göring' in *Over the Front*, Vol. X, No. 3, Dallas (Texas), 1995

Wills, Jr., K. 'Feldfliegerabteilung 25 – The Eyes of the Kronprinz' in *Cross & Cockade Journal*, Vol. IX, No. 1, Whittier (California), 1968

Wynne, H. 'Project Aerodromes' in *Over the Front*, Vol. VI, No. 1, Dallas (Texas), 1991

Zickerick, W. *'Verlustliste der deutschen Luftstreitkräfte im Weltkriege'* in *Unsere Luftstreitkräfte 1914-1918*

Zuerl, H. *'Hermann Göring, Deutschlands erste Luftfahrtminister'* in *Der Frontsoldat erzählt*, Vol. IV, No. 11, Kiel, 1935

OTHER SOURCES

Blum, E. *Kriegsranglisten-Auszug,* 1920

Göring, A. *Interrogation,* 1945

Göring, C. *Geburts-Urkunde,* 1879

Göring, H. *Geburts-Urkunde,* 1893

----. *Dienstlaufbahnzeugnis,* 1920

----. *Kriegsranglisten-Auszug,* 1918

----. *Lebenslauf,* 1917

 ----. *Personal-Bogen,* 1918

Göring, I. (daughter) *Sterbe-Urkunde,* 1872

Göring, I. (mother) *Sterbe-Urkunde,* 1879

Göring, K. *Geburts-Urkunde,* 1885

Göring, P. *Geburts-Urkunde,* 1890

Keck, K. *Personal-Bogen,* 1917

Loerzer, B. *Kriegsranglisten-Auszug,* 1928

----. *Lebenslauf,* ca. 1946

----. *Militärärztliches-Zeugnis,* 1919

----. *Personal-Bogen,* 1918

Nebel, R. *Personal-Bogen,* 1920

Rosenstein, W. *Personal-Bogen,* 1918; miscellaneous correspondence, 1946-1949

Schmidt, W. *Personal-Bogen,* 1919

Wieland, P. *Personal-Bogen,* 1919

INDEX

FURTHER INFORMATION

Readers interested in obtaining additional information about military aviation of the First World War may wish to contact websites of research-oriented, non-profit organizations, including:

The Aerodrome
URL: http://www.theaerodrome.com/

Australian Society of World War I Aero Historians
URL: http://asww1ah.0catch.com

Cross & Cockade International (UK)
URL: http://www.crossandcockade.com

League of World War I Aviation Historians (USA)
URL: http://www.overthefront.com

Das Propellerblatt (Germany)
URL: www.Propellerblatt.de

World War One Aeroplanes (USA)
URL: http://www.avation-history.com/ww1aero.htm